# My Journey &
## Sovereign United Bengal

# My Journey &
## Sovereign United Bengal

HP Roychoudhury

PARTRIDGE
A Penguin Random House Company

**To order additional copies of this book, contact**
Partridge India
000 800 10062 62
www. partridgepublishing. com/india
orders. india@partridgepublishing. com

# CONTENTS

The Book is dedicated to those souls who sacrificed their lives for the cause of Independence of India.

# SYNOPSIS

The main features of the book are outlined as (i) A little of Author's life under political situation of India, (ii) Function of Democracy in India (iii) What was the status of Hindus in Bengal and where is the future? (iv)Why the economic growth of India does went down while the economic growth of Japan went up? (v) What was the function of religion in India? (vi) The ancient India & the wonder Taj Mohal. (vii) How does the life prevail in India and in the neighbor country of India?

It is also being remembered here by the two genius of the last century Prof. S. W. Sudmerson, a British fellow, who dedicated his life in the service of teaching in a College of extreme North East of India in the beginning of the 20th century and Swami Vivekananda who had not only enlighten the world by his glorious speech on the religion of Hindu philosophy in Chicago but also who had thought of the formation of the present existing India hundred years before of Independence. Is it one nation one India of Vivekananda? Is it the Bengal wanted by the Stalwarts of the then Bengal-who initiated the independence movement in India or something else? Are they really wanted the economic growth of India or the power of chair?

# ACKNOWLEDGEMENTS

I am most grateful to Advocates of Advocate Associations of Guwahati and Professors of Cotton College (Retired) and all other friends for encouraging me to write this book. I am also thankful to my daughter Dr B S Roychoudhury for her help time to time in writing the book

Thanks to all the other persons of the publishing company under whose untiring efforts the book has taken the shape to come out in public for marketing. Any suggestion made or mistake pointed out will be thankfully received, incorporated or corrected in the next edition.

# [1]

## Life in UK

I passed a part of my life in the United Kingdom, a country full of high intellectuals who ruled almost the whole world once by virtue of their efficiency in the art of administration, sincerity in duty and faithfulness in the character of morality, although the Island of UK is a small region in the Earth consisting of insignificant number of individuals in compare to Greek, Rome, French, German, Russia or USA. But the great people of this Island had made UK, the center of power of the Globe once in the earlier times of history.

**UMIST (University of Manchester Institute of Science and Technology), Manchester, my working place, the place where the principle of first Rail way Engine was designed**

**Photo From:** http://commons. wikimedia. org/wiki/File:UMIST_main_ building_Whitworth_Street._jpg by Lmno on 24 September 2004

Well, it is as simple as that I had the opportunity to do research in UMIST of Manchester under a benevolent professor of versatile knowledge Mr. Hazeldine, published something new in the International Journal and got the degree Ph. D. Simultaneously, my work was continued in the 'O' floor of the adjacent Research tower, where a good number of Research workers were always remained busy in their work in order to find a new clue of their objective in the search of either to discover a new approach of science or a new technique of a manufacturing process to enhance the industrial out put in the field of efficiency of production and purity of the product under the guidance of learned doctorate genius.

No doubt, it was a unique place of pleasure to live in the land of UK, where the climate was smooth, the streets and roads were neat and clean, the weekend was enjoyable, where one can roam freely day and night without fear and foe. There was easy communication everywhere with luxury and comfort under the decorum of civilized society. In view of my financial constraint I prefer to live in a Terrace house (shown below), a low cost residential shelter but that too was not devoid of any kind of modern facility of living.

Again financial constraint compelled me to work in a bar for the sake of work only but I never took part in the club because, my early traditional life never allowed me mentally to take part in club life for refreshment although it was really a busy period of my life in the foreign land. Thus the weekend was ended in the club in the business of work with a sense of visual love from distance without participating in the dense stage. I must thought of the early years of our marriage with all my sincerity and liking for her (Sulekha), I left her alone in India as at that time I was the person, utterly a different person, giving everything to the cause of myself, living in a dream world of my own and looking to the real goal of my achievement in the field of research work and had little time left for her to write to her in the absence of any other low cost communication existed at that time. But I was very much close to her again when she arrived there on her own after a gap of one year. Miraculously she adjusted there very quickly and she began to earn for me and there she stood like a rock behind me. While my satisfaction of love starts at home during the week days with family and with my little daughter. It was the greatest charm we enjoyed when we heard the sweet Lancashire-English from the mouth of our little daughter.

[The Terrace House of Manchester, where the family was living]

In UK, our financial condition of constraint vanished with the appointment of my service in UMIST, while she was in the stream of happiness in the working of the Firm as because her expertise made her the champion in the tailoring work to earn the highest emolument.

Once we went to see London, people call a place of Heaven and roamed with travelling Bus to West minister area to see the Houses of Parliament and Downing Street and also West Minister Abbey, the historic venue for coronations, and royal wedding of British Land. We went to Piccadilly Circus, the centre of the entertainment district, leading to Trafalgar Square. We also took a glimpse of the Westminster Abbey where the royal ceremonial functions were held. The Royal stricture of Westminster Abbey is gorgeous to see. My mind and body was not ready to absorb so much happiness and comfort of the place of Heaven. My mind was dipped into the sea of tragedies of Hindus of East Bengal from where I hailed. It was a small village named 'Derai' of the District of Sylhet where my father was a graduate in British period who was a School Teacher and who devoted his life in teaching in the village School in the service of giving the learning knowledge of English to the children of villagers so that they could at least one day read and understand the message of Telegraph written in English what he realized in his life time when everyday he used to meet with a number of villagers to make them understand the meaning of Telegraph.

His desire was to see his children are living in mental peace and happiness in any part of India as he could not get happiness in the struggle of Independence of India at the juncture of the partition of Bengal and even after the partition of Bengal when he was bewildered to see the holocaust of human killings in the rioting and loss of innocent lives. He was helpless to see he could not give his children the right of Land, having being the right of birth as they belonging to a faith of religion by birth called Hinduism where the Land of birth being transformed into a Land of Islam, a separate home land for the Muslims of India but his faith and conscious did not dictate him to say his children to transform their faith of religion to the faith of Islam at that time but now in the later period it is going to happen if not in direct but in the indirect path of slow transformation.

To fulfill the desire of my father I returned to India. I enjoyed the life in India although living in the atmosphere of chaotic situation as every one used to do and under poor economic condition. I left the comfort and physical happiness of UK but here I was mentally forced to acclimatize with the age old Indian traditions and Indian varied culture and above all by the over all land, river, sea, hills and natural beauty of the Land of Himalayan Kingdom. I will definitely write my feelings with the beauty of the Land and the people. I might be mistaken in writing somewhere the administration and politics of India at different time and its effect over the people of India as because I also belong to one of the victims of them. But again how the pleasure of Unity is reflected in the cultural activity could be seen in their joyful mood when they forget all sorts of strain of life. Once India was ruled under many Kings but after Independence India was transformed into a country of one Union and a country of 'Democracy'.

**Very often my little girl speaks Lancashire-English with her mother when they move out in the nearby garden, to get the pleasure of sweet breeze of cold wind in the site of resident of Manchester.** We spent more than 6 years in Manchester, She was happy there in all account and never she feel that she had been treated differently as she was not a native. She was reluctant to return. I forcefully convinced her to return to India to have a better life along with relatives and other Indians. At last she agreed and returned. But after returning to India, the life started a fresh in strain and turmoil. Finally she could not consume so much of strain and suffering and succumb to her injury for the last. She is no more of to-day but she is always with me.

**The history of Indian subcontinent is summarized as such:**

| | |
|---|---|
| Stone age | : [7000-3000 BC ] |
| Bronage age | : [3000-1300 BC ] |
| Iron age | : [1200-26 BC ] |
| Classical period | : [1-1279 AD ] |
| Late Medieval age | : [ 1206-1596 AD ] |
| Early Modern period | : [ 1526-1858 AD ] |
| Colonial Period | : [ 1505-1961 AD] |

The Indus valley civilization which spread and flourished in the north western part of Indian subcontinent in the period of 3300-1300 BCE, was the first major civilization in South Asia. It also includes the present Pakistan and the North West India. The Maurya Empire existed in the 4th and 3rd century BCE, The Gupta Empire existed in the 2nd century BCE. It was the period in which Hindu religious and intellectual resurgence occurred. This period is also known as the "Golden Age of India". It extended to Southern India under the rule of Chalukyas, Cholas, and Pallavas. It was the period of Hinduism and Buddhism. During this period, aspects of Indian Civilization, administration, culture and religion spread to different regions of Asia. In the 4th Century, a large part of India was united under the King Ashoka. Islam came in India in the 8th century and by the time of 11th century it established itself a political force. It was the North Indian dynasties of Lodhis, Tughlaqs and later Mughals. European occupation began to grow in the 16th century.

# [2]

## India as a Nation of Union

The Second World War had changed the concept of Rulers of powerful countries. The motto of territorial expansion has vanished. A country is said to be powerful not by the military might but by the strength of its economy. The economy of UK government went down after the 2nd world war. In 1946 the Labour government of Britain had decided to hand over the administration of India to the people of India after the end of World War II, the war being culminated by the fall of Atom Bomb at Nagasaki and Hiroshima in demolishing the mighty power of Japan Empire. The intellectuals of British government realized the ground situation. With heavy hearts Government of Britain came to the conclusion to give up India to Indians. Finally, the government of Britain had realized that it had neither the mandate at home, nor the faithful native force at India who could help the government to fight to control an increasing restless in India. Understanding the ground situation, on February 1947, Prime Minister Clement Attlee had announced that the British government would grant full self-governance to British India by June 1948 at the latest. There was continuous tussle between the congress and the Muslim League. Fearing the tussle might lead to a collapse of the interim government, the new viceroy, Louis Mountbatten, advanced the date for the transfer of power. He had chosen 15th August, the date of transfer of power as it was the date of second anniversary of Japan's surrender in World War II. Accordingly British Mission came forward with a plan for the transfer of power to India. Independence to India was happy news. This had brought a moment of joy to all Indians. But the details of actual proposed plan brought a sigh of despair. The plan of 16th May 1946 was a proposal for the partition of India on religious line, with over 600 princely states free to choose between Independence and accession to either dominion. There was considerable opposition within the congress to the proposed plan. Gandhi was against the partition of India but there are other congress leaders particularly Sardar Petal thought otherwise. Sardar Vallabhbhai.

Jhaverbhai Petal was an Indian barrister and statesman. He was one the important leaders of the Indian National Congress who played an unparallel role in the country's struggle for independence and who guided its integration into a united, independent nation. As he had been outraged by Jinnah's Direct Action campaign, that had being provoked communal violence across India, he thought of no other alternative but to sitting with Nehru and others and finally agreed to the proposal of partition to get independence of India without further delay. But simultaneously he chalked out a plan to integrate all the princely states to join India to form the Republic of Indian Union. On the one hand he was the person to divide India but again he was the person to integrate all the princely state to India. He persuaded the princess of all the states by giving favorable terms for the merger creating the system of privy purses for the descendants of the rulers. 565 States joined the Indian Union except the three Jammu & Kashmir, Junagar and Hyderabad. Hyderabad was the largest of the princely states as it included present Andhra Pradesh, Karnataka and Maharashtra states. It's Ruler Nizam Osman Ali Khan being a Muslim wanted to join Pakistan although 80% Hindus were being living in the state. Petal was successful to keep Hyderabad along with India. In addition to the division of India the two states Punjab and Bengal were also divided. In Punjab lots of killing continued immediately after the declaration of division of Punjab. Muslims were killed in East Punjab and Hindus were killed in West Punjab particularly in Lahore. Similarly migration of huge Hindu people began from East Pakistan to India and Muslims from West Bengal to East Pakistan. Human tragedy with loss of property, and loss of life continued for years together. The joy of independence is submerged with the agony of loss of belongings and human slaughter.

When Lord Louis Mountbatten formally proposed the plan on 3 June 1947, Patel gave his approval and lobbied Nehru and other Congress leaders to accept the proposal. A meeting of All India Congress Committee was held to vote on the proposal where Patel said:

"I fully appreciate the fears of our brothers from the Muslim-majority areas. Nobody likes the division of India and my heart is heavy. But the choice is between one division and many divisions. We must face facts. We cannot give way to emotionalism and sentimentality. The working Committee has not acted out of fear. But I am afraid of one thing, that all our toil and hard work of these many years might go waste or prove unfruitful. My nine months in office has completely disillusioned me regarding the supposed merits of the Cabinet Mission Plan. Except for a few honourable exceptions, Muslim officials from the top down to the chaprasis (peon or servants) are working for the League. The right of veto given to the League in the Mission Plan would have blocked India's progress at every stage whether we like it or not, de facto Pakistan already exists in the Punjab and Bengal. Under the circumstances I would prefer a de jure Pakistan, which may make the League more responsible. Freedom is coming. We have 75 to 80 percent of India, which we can make strong with our own genius. The League can develop the rest of the country". With the consent of Gandhi's and congress' approval, Patel represented India on the Partition Council. Country was divided. However, neither he nor any other Indian leader had foreseen the intense violence and population transfer that take place with partition. Death toll continued to rise from five hundred thousand to a million people. The number of refugees exceeded 15 million in both sides.

Patel addressed a massive crowd of approximately 200,000 refugees.

"Here, in this same city, the blood of Hindus, Sikhs and Muslims mingled in the bloodbath of Jallianwala Bagh. I am grieved to think that things have come to such a pass that no Muslim can go about in Amritsar and no Hindu or Sikh can even think of living in Lahore. The butchery of innocent and defense less men, women and children does not behave brave men . . . I am quite certain that India's interest lies in getting all her men and women across the border and sending out all Muslims from East Punjab. I have come to you with a specific appeal. Pledge the safety of Muslim refugee crossing the city. Any obstacles or hindrances will only worsen the plight of our refugees who are already performing prodigious feats of endurance. If we have to fight, we must fight clean. Such a fight must wait on appropriate time and conditions and you must be watchful in choosing your ground. To fight against the refugees is no fight at all. No laws of humanity or war among honorable men permit the murder of people who have sought shelter and protection. Let there be truce for three months in which both sides can exchange their refugees. This sort of truce is permitted even by laws of war. Let us take the initiative in breaking this vicious circle of attacks and counter-attacks. Hold your hands for a week and see what happens. Make way for the refugees with your own force of volunteers and let them deliver the refugees safely at our frontier".

**Winston Churchill:** He was a legendary orator, a prolific writer, an artist and a long-term British statesman. Yet Churchill, who twice served the nation as the Prime Minister of United Kingdom, is best remembered as the tenacious and forthright war leader that led his country against the seemingly undefeatable Nazi during World War II. Churchill was the most successful leader of the United Kingdom during the World War of the 20th century. He opposed Gandhi's peaceful disobedience revolt and the movement of 1930. The later report indicated that Churchill would be happy to see Gandhi die if he went on hunger strike. He was an outspoken person in the opposition in granting devaluation of power to India. He was very critical towards India. "The truth is," he declared in 1930, "that Gandhi-ism and everything it stands for will have to be grappled with and crushed." In view of widespread unemployment in Britain and civil strife in India, the then Viceroy Lord Irwin thought of granting Dominion Status to India but Churchill was dead against of it. Not only that he said, "It is alarming and also nauseating to see Mr. Gandhi, a seditious Middle Temple Lawyer, now posing as a FAKIR of a type well-known in the East, striding half-naked up the steps of the Vice-regal palace . . . to parley on equal terms with the representative of the King-Emperor. "But at last he had to made a comment on February 1931, as

"The loss of India would be final and fatal to us. It could not fail to be part of a process that would reduce us to the scab of a minor power."

WINSTON CHURCHILL:
London, February, 1931:

# [3]

India achieved Independence (1947). Jawaharlal Nehru made an emotional comment on 14ᵗʰ August, 1947, it goes as:

"Long years ago we made a tryst with destiny, now the time comes when we shall redeem our pledge . . . At the stroke of the midnight hour, while the world sleeps, India will awake to life and freedom. A moment comes, which comes but rarely in history, when we step out from the old to the new, when an age ends, and when the soul of a nation, long suppressed, finds utterance . . ."

## JAWAHARLAL NEHRU:
### New Delhi, August 14, 1947

The historical record shows that the first British outpost in India was established in 1619 and gradually led to the establishment of the British East India Company. Gradually after stabilizing its footing in the coastal area, British spread their control to a greater part of India by the time of 1850, and nearly all of present day India, Pakistan and Bangladesh. At the outset British faced with the problem of language communication in administration because of illiteracy of the Indian people. However the British made it their principle to rule India according to English culture. Keeping the principle in mind, the British set up institutions for learning English and English was made the official language making outlawed the several traditional Hindu customs and other local customs. By the time the strength of English was increased by their efficient ruling. They were successful to create

British Force not with only made of British people but of mostly of Indian people very obedient to British administration. In spite of intelligent management of administration, there built up ant-British feeling due to various factors that finally led to Indian rebellion. Sepoy Mutiny took place in 1857. Facing the bloody rebellion, the British thought it wise to strengthen the power of faithful British Army as well as the power of administration. Finally political power was transferred from the East India Company directly to the British Crown and the company dissolved. Why British do came to India, to do business, to increase the growth of economy of the country because economic strength is mightier than military strength.

In the earlier history it is found that in 1617 the British East India Company was given permission by Mughal Emperor Jahangir to trade in India. In course of time because of their increasing influence the Mughal emperor Farrukh Siyar granted them permits for duty free trade in Bengal in 1717. However, the Nawab of Bengal Siraj Ud Daulah, opposed British to trade with trade permit. British as well as French were equally interested to set up trade centers in India. In the result of colonial competition between them, the two countries met with war, the first Carnatic War in 1746-1748. The French troops attacked and captured the British city of Madras located in the east coast of India on 21 September 1746. There were British prisoners, who were captured at Madras and Robert Clive was one among them. Although the War was ended by a treaty in 1748 but again in 1749, the Second Carnatic War broke out for the cause of taking up the throne of Hyderabad. Robert Clive was restless, he again in 1751, led British armed forces and captured Arcot to reinstate the incumbent Nawab and finally the War came to an end in 1754 with the treaty of Pondicherry. In 1756, War once again broke out between the two great powers of Europe, which was called the Third Carnatic War. In the Eastern sector, the armed forces of French captured the British base of Calcutta in north-eastern India. However, armed forces under Robert Clive later recaptured Calcutta and extended their force to capture the French settlement of Chandannagar in 1757. This led to the Battle of Plassey on 23rd June 1757 in which the Bengal Army of East India Company, led by Robert Clive proceeded ahead making a secret pact with Mir Zaffer, the commander in Chief of Nawab, who supported

Clive to win the battle. This was the first real political foothold that British acquired in India. The success of British victory was due to the credit of Robert Clive and as such he was appointed by the Company as its first 'Governor of Bengal' in 1757.

The success of British victory made the British the exclusive controller of the Carnatic regions of India and that had reduced intensely the control of French in Madrass and Pondicherry. The British East India Company on the eastern sector extended its control over the whole of Bengal. In 1764, the success of British in the Battle of Buxar defeating the Mughal Emperor Shah Alam II, the company then acquired the rights of administration in the whole of Bengal. This had marked the beginning of its formal rule, and within the next century British engulfed most of India and finally established the British Rule and later the Queen Empire in the whole of India. They designed their system of administration and simultaneously planned how to collect state revenue. The British introduced a land taxation system in the set up of Zamindars. By 1850, the East India Company controlled most of the Indian sub-continent, which included the present-day Pakistan and Bangladesh. The British continued its rule by the policy of "Divide and Rule" fostering the principle of policy between various princely states and social and religious groups. The Hindu Ahom Kingdom of North-east India became a victim first under Burmese invasion and then under British in 1826. The Indian rebellion took place in 1857 by the Indian soldiers employed by the British East India in northern and central India against the Company's rule. It was brutally suppressed and the British government took full control of the Company. The government also took the control of administration as such so that no rebellion of such size would ever happen again. It favoured the princely states as the kings helped to suppress the rebellion. It also fovoured the Muslims as the Muslims were less rebellious compare to Hindus who dominated the rebellion. Finally, all power was transferred from East India Company to the British Crown.

British concentrated on the development of the communication for better control and better administration and began to help the people to get rid of the poor state of living and the social prejudices. British rule helped in the development of small industry in certain limited sector and in agriculture too but other views were different. According to them agriculture was developed by the natural activity of the people for the fact of maintaining the rule of law under British administration. But however communication net work was set up by the British. As there was no communication system in India, the British set up the railway network from east to west and north to south. The improved communication system helped in the increase of trade. There was social unrest under British Rule as the ancient Indian traditional customs faced with the challenge of western custom in many respect. The Indians were disturbed by the treatment of the British as the Indians and the British differ in cultural activity in many respect. The clever British always attempted to shift the blame onto the Indian Muslim for any eventuality and thereby helped in stimulating the fire of age-old hostility between the Hindus and the Muslims. However the learning of English helped the Indian leaders of different regions to come together and that had led to the formation of Indian National Congress in 1885, which was primarily a Hindu body fighting for power back in Indian hands. Initially British ignored the voice of the Indian National Congress but very soon British realized its power and quickly set up its strategy how to deal with the people of congress because of its popularity among the Indian population. On seeing the importance of Hindu Congress, the Leaders of Muslim population thought for a separate political identity and in the year 1906, they established a political body naming it as All India Muslim League. To get the favour of mighty British they made it a principle to support the Crown unlike Congress in most of the cases of convenience. Soon after, by the act of principle of the 1909 India Councils Act, Muslims won the right for separate elections. That had actually encouraged the Muslims of India to raise the voice for a separate Muslim state in India. A cry for a separate Muslim States since then was there in the air. It was true India was an ancient country ruled by Hindu Kings with the religious culture of Hinduism. But in the course of time Hindus were defeated to Sultan in Delhi and to Mughal in other places. The Mughals having being migrated from other places settled in India permanently and loved the country very much. They did their best for the development of India of course their policy was to convert the Hindus to Muslims as they believe in the faith of Islam and influenced by the rich and prosperous culture of Persia. It was their belief that these people were following a wrong path to reach to almighty. Their conversion to Islam would lead them to heaven. These Mughals and the Muslims living in India were insignificant in number. But they have shown their ability like British to rule India for more than three hundred years. But unlike British they never think to take off the wealth of India to outside of India. Indian National Congress was formed in 1885 but after twenty years in 1906, All India Muslim League was formed. The record of history shows, the Muslims of India were not happy with the activity of Congress. Considering their future progress, the Muslim Leaders thought it wise to form a separate organization. The congress could not win their heart by involving them in the Indian National Congress. Their lies the failure of our national leadership. The leadership failed to win the heart of the Indian people who believe in the faith of another religion. Since then the sense of religion has increased the distance of people to people in India. The British had utilized their administrative efficiency by bringing the act of principle of the 1909 India Councils Act, whereby Muslims were granted the right for separate electorate. That had increased the distance between people to people of Indians a step further. Mughals had shown their efficiency in administration to keep India united including the Kings. Did our national leaders showed their efficiency to keep India United? British ruled India by the policy of 'Divide and Rule'. The government of India was also following the same principle, even after partition of India. Assam was divided into seven states because that suits Delhi government. The formation of ULFA (United Liberation Force of Assam) was the out come of the frustration of Indians Youths against the policy of the government of India. The policy of division is still in existence and if these continue, India would lose its holding to its territory in the course to come. India never thinks to learn to administer in integration, be it state, territory, and language or culture. Unity of India is vitiated by the sectarian policy of the government. British Ruler knows it very well, that the cry of Muslim state would help to control the Indian Congress smoothly but British did not gave much importance for the demand of separate state although the Muslim League supported the Crown. The British knows the Muslim's religious fight, the crusade after crusade in the last few centuries at the border of Europe in the spread of Muslim religion. In the territory of Europe, the religious war had continued between Muslims and Christians for a long period of time. Even in the 20th Century to control the spread of Muslim influence, European attacks on Islamic countries continued. The vicious dormant religious Muslim fanaticism being existed in the minds of British for long had undermined the Muslim allegiance to the British Crown.

# [4]

**Sir Surendranath Banerjee (1848-1925)** better known as "Surrender not Banerjee" who was one of the earliest top political leaders of India during the rule of British Period had founded the Indian National Association. He was recognized as Rashtraguru, the teacher of the nation. In regards to his early life, the record shows that he hails from a Bengali Brahmin family. After the completion of graduation from the University of Calcutta, he traveled to England in 1868 to compete in the Indian Civil Service examination.

Although he was successful in the competitive examination in 1869, he was barred owing to a dispute over his exact age. However, after getting it cleared he appeared again in 1871 to qualify again and finally he was posted as assistant magistrate in Sylhet. Here again he was dismissed soon from his job owing to the allegation of racial discrimination. Banerjee went to England to protest against the decision. But his entire attempt was unsuccessful. Finding no other alternative he returned to India in discontent mind and became an English professor at Ripon College leaving all hope to be an employee of powerful British Government. Since then he became a man of anti-British in mind and spirit. In order to win over public support he began delivering public speeches on nationalist and liberal political subjects. Finding sympathetic response from the public, he thought it wise to form an Indian National Association to fight against the British. He publicly condemned the issue of discrimination of age-limit for Indian students in compare to British students in the ICS examination system. But it did not affect the British Officials to carry out the racial discrimination in the ICS examination. As he was restless to bring charge against the British in public, in 1879, he founded a Bengali newspaper and there he published all the issues of grievances. In 1883, Banerjee was arrested in a contempt of court for publishing a remark against the British Government. However, in support of him there was protest and hartel in whole of Bengal as well as in the cities such as Agra, Faizabad, Amritsar, Lahore and Pune. The incident of arrest made him popular through out India. After release in the annual general meeting he proposed for the formation of Indian National Congress. The proposal got the support of the majority and thus Indian National Congress came into being. After being founding of the Indian National Congress in 1885 in Bombay, Banerjee merged his organization with the National congress. He was elected congress president twice in 1895 at Poona and in 1902 at Ahmadabad.

Sri Banerjee had actually initiated the process to fight against the British for self Rule. His eloquent speech had aroused the nationalist sentiment everywhere and that formed the sentiment to form an organization for fighting against British and finally that led to the formation of the Indian National Congress. Day by day the protest against British became very much in the city of Calcutta making it more difficult for the British to govern the Empire staying at Calcutta. In order to reduce the strength of Bengali people, the British government divided the Bengal as East and West Bengal in 1905. But the protest against the division of Bengal was vigorous and that protest was not remained in Bengal alone and even spread to other parts of India. The Muslim leaders also raised their voice against the bifurcation of Bengal. The record of history shows, that was the last phase of unity between Hindus and Muslims in Bengal. British government could not resist the impact that had been started against the united resistance. Finally government withdrew the order of bifurcation of Bengal in 1912 under compulsion but at the time of convenience. The British people have the greatest knowledge in the field of administration be it in England or outside anywhere. Therefore after getting failure in their first attempt they went for a second plan to reduce the strength of Bengal and Bengali people by the transfer of capital from Bengal to Delhi where they were successful. In their first attempt they probably did not wanted to do the maximum harm to Bengal, after all it was the British who made Calcutta, the second city after London of British Empire. The British did not wanted to destroy Calcutta at the outset, because Calcutta was the place where the British established their footings and the Capital Calcutta was built up by British as the second city of British Empire but the violent agitation striking with Bomb against the British Officials in disguise compelled them to shift Capital to somewhere convenience to them. The place of Delhi was being nearer to London, become the most choice-able place for the British and the work for the formation of Capital at Delhi had continued during the agitation against the division of Bengal in disguise.

A planning committee was formed in that period of Bengal agitation to study the transfer of the capital of British India from Calcutta (now Kolkata) to Delhi. A site 3 miles (5 km) south of the existing city of Delhi, around Raisina Hill, was chosen for the new administrative centre, a well-drained, healthy area between the Delhi Ridge and the Yamuna River. It provided ample room for expansion. Though settlements after settlements have been taking place in Delhi for millennia, though there had been no record to stand by that claim but the fact was there. There was new settlement under new environment. Delhi is generally considered a close to 5000-year old city, as per Ancient Indian text The Mahabharata, since the first ever mention of the city is found in the religious scripture. Therefore, except the scripture, archaeological evidences to book the city's Ancient history are as good as nothing. As a result, Delhi's Ancient history finds no records and this period might be regarded as the lost period of its history. Extensive coverage of Delhi's history begins with the onset of the Delhi Sultanate in the 12th century. Since then, Delhi had been the seat of Islamic and British rulers until India's independence in 1947. The core of Delhi's tangible heritage is Islamic, spanning over seven centuries of Islamic rule over the city, with some British-styled architectures and zones in Lutyens' Delhi dating to the British rule in India. Whatever records exist of Delhi, in the form of scriptures or archaeological evidences, they crown Delhi as the Capital city of some empire or the other all through, with minor random breaks in between, making Delhi one of the longest serving Capitals and one of the oldest inhabited cities in the world. It is considered to be a city built, destroyed and rebuilt several times, as outsiders who successfully invaded the Indian Subcontinent would ransack the existing capital city in Delhi, and those who came to conquer and stay would be so impressed by the city's strategic location as to make it their capital and rebuild it in their own way.

At last the British declared Delhi is the Capital of India in 1911 and subsequently withdrawn the declaration of the division of Bengal after seven years. By the transfer of Capital to Delhi, the importance of Calcutta went down to down further down and that had initiated the downfall of Bengal. Sir Banerjee's impressive speech was so emotional that in every corner of Bengal so many Bengali youths became ready to sacrifice their life for the cause of nation. Of course that spirit of sacrifice was not in Bengal alone but it spread to other places too, although it remained most volatile in Bengal and particular to the place of Calcutta, the Capital city of British Empire in British India. To day the question arises what was the point of profit for Bengal? It was nothing but the loss of importance of Calcutta. It was nothing but the division Bengal which they did not wanted in the British period. It is Calcutta, the place of etiquette what had been transformed into a place of destitute and daily earners, had transformed every aristocrat streets into hawker's shop to earn to survive. Where are you now Mr. Banerjee, where is your eloquent speech to excite the young to die? Will you say British your enemy? You lost the opportunity to learn the art of administration; you lost the opportunity to earn the skill of science, like those of Japanese youth, to apply to industry. In the dearth of administration, you have nothing but to hide money behind the power of administration. The result was no development and life was in poverty and days were in despair.

# [5]

**Chittaranjan Das (1870-1925),** Born on November 5, 1870 in Calcutta, belonging to an upper middle class Vaidya family, endearingly called 'Deshbandhu' (Friend of the country), whose life is a landmark in the history of India's struggle for freedom, who came in forefront after the successful acquittal of Arobindu Ghosh in the Alipore Bomb blast Case. His father, Bhuban Mohan Das, was a reputed solicitor of the Calcutta High Court. His patriotic ideas were greatly influenced by the ideas of his father. After graduation from the Presidency College in 1890, he proceeded to England to compete for the ICS. He was successful to qualify but he was the last person for that year. It discouraged him to join any government assignment and he preferred to join the Inner Temple and was called to the Bar in India after enrolling himself as a Barrister of the Calcutta High Court in 1894. He did not get the backing badly needed to make a good start in the profession in a new place. However, the character of leadership was prevailing with him since his student life. While he was in Presidency College he was a leading figure of the Student's Association. And in later life he took his first lesson in Public service and elocution from Surendranath Banerjee. In 1907, his advocacy evoked general admiration, in the case of Brahma (bhadhav) Upedhyaya and Bhupendranath who were prosecuted for sedition where he appeared as the defense lawyer with forceful argument though he did not succeed in baffling the prosecution. The turning point of his career came when he was called upon to appear on behalf of Aurobindu Ghosh in the Alipore Bomb Case in 1908. It was due to his brilliant advocacy that resulted in the acquittal of Aurobindu. This case brought Das to the forefront professionally and politically.

It was only in 1917 he engaged himself entirely with the nationalist politics. In the period of 1917-1925, a course of eight years, he rose to all-India fame by virtue of his ardent patriotism, sterling sincerity and oratorical power. His advent into politics in 1917 took place at a crucial moment. He played a significant role in the controversy over the election of Mrs. Annie Besant as President of the Indian National Congress for its Calcutta Session. During this period (1917-18) he also took part in the agitation against the Government policy of internment and deportation under the Defense of India Act. On the eve of the Calcutta Session (1917) of the Congress, he had been on a lecturing tour on Eastern Bengal, addressing large gatherings on Self-Government. Unlike S. N. Banerjee, Das opposed the scheme of Montagu-Chelmsford Reforms as he said it was wholly inadequate and disappointing. He was a believer of non-violence and again he believed the constitutional methods were the right path for the realization of national independence. He was above religion and advocated strongly for Hindu-Muslim unity, and cooperation. According to him humanity is above all and advocated for communal harmony and national education. His legacy was carried forward by his disciples, and notably by Subhas Chandra Bose. In 1925, Das's health began to fail and in May he withdrew to a mountain home in Darjeeling, where Mahatma Gandhi visited him and he died on 16 June 1925. He gifted his house and the adjoining lands to the nation where we find to day the Chittaranjan Seva Sadan and Chittaranjan National Cancer Institute.

# [6]

Looking to the political unrest In India, in the year 1919, the British Government passed an act called Rowlatt Act, by dint of which the Government had the authority and power to arrest people and keep them in prisons without any trial for the charge of terrorism if suspected. Restrictions can also be imposed over newspaper and printing press. The law was came into being after the recommendation made in the previous year to the Imperial Legislative Council by the Rowlatt Commission, the Commission being appointed to investigate the seditious conspiracy of the Indian people. A nationwide protest was raised throughout India by Hindus and Muslims alike, by Mahatma Gandhi and other leaders by calling Hartal subjecting cessation of work. The Act had brought a severe outrage of political leaders and the common public but Government adapted more repressive measure to dominate the Native people. By the call of "Hartal" Indians suspended all the official business and showed their hatred towards the British administration. There was success of Hartal in Delhi, Punjab and other places but it resulted in the continuation of riot in Punjab and other provinces. Gandhi was in favour of protest in the path of 'Ahimsa' (non-violence) but he found it was going to take the path of violence. Indians were not ready yet to take the path of protest through the process of violence. Gandhi immediately suspended the agitation. The agitation reached the pinnacle Amritsar of Punjab. Renowned leaders were arrested. A public meeting was held on 13th April at Jallianwala Baugh in a small park encircled by buildings on all sides to protest against the arrest of their leaders. A large number of women and children attended the meeting in peaceful atmosphere. All on a sudden Brigadier General Reginald Dyer entered the Park with his British troops, closed the entrance of the park and commanded his army to fire on the gathering without any warning. Not only that, the firing continued for ten minutes exhausting sixteen hundred rounds, killing about a thousand people and more than two thousand people wounded. This massacre of Jaliwanwalabagh was the worst incidence of British Rule and that sat the final journey for the British army to return to the British Island. The fact that British rule would withdraw from India became clear and certain to the best of it lingering in the matter of time. The good will of the British government with the Indian leaders was totally destroyed. Mahatma Gandhi and other nationalist leaders had broken all dealings with the British, boycotting goods, courts, schools, and elections. But among all these unity of Hindus and Muslims, the question of separate state came in the surface and the demarcation of area was going on in secret meeting of account. The reality was that the British government lost control to rule over India. In 1945 India were over 400 million people-250 million Hindus, 90 million Muslims, 6 million Sikhs, besides few other millions of Buddhists, Christians and others speaking in 23 main languages, 200 dialects, under a community binding of 3000 castes with 60 million untouchables. The question of division of India and the formation of Pakistan had created unrest in the country. The movement of people in the secured place already had begun compelling British to quite.

In 1918, both at the Congress special session in Bombay and at the Annual Session in Delhi, Das opposed the scheme of Montagu-Chelmsford Reforms as wholly inadequate and disappointing. The demand for Provincial Autonomy was successfully propounded in the teeth of vehement opposition from Mrs. Besant and others. In 1919 Chittaranjan went to Punjab as a member of the non-official Jallianwala Bagh Enquiry Committee. At the Amritsar Congress (1919) he made the first advocacy of obstruction while opposing the idea of co-operation with the Government in the implementation of the 1919 Reforms.

In 1920 at a special session of the Congress held at Calcutta under the presidency of Lajpat Rai, Gandhi announced his famous programme of Non-Cooperation. Das sought some changes in it but in vain. He however, had the support of Pal, Malaviya, Jinnah and Mrs. Besant. Three months later the Congress met at Nagpur where he, however, accepted Gandhiji's lead and came back to Calcutta to renounce his large practice at the Bar. The whole nation was deeply impressed to see this supreme act of self-sacrifice. Besides the Non-Cooperation Movement, the large-scale exodus of the Coolies from the Assam tea garden and the strike of the Assam-Bengal railway employees engaged his attention in 1921.

In its repressive measures the Government declared as illegal the Congress Volunteers' organization which took a leading part in the boycott of the visit of the Prince of Wales (1921). Deshbandhu decided to defy the arbitrary government order. Deshbandhu himself was arrested and sentenced to six months' imprisonment. After his release in 1922, he was elected President for the Congress Session at Gaya.

With the suspension of the Non-Cooperation Movement Deshbandhu endeavored to give a new orientation to Indian politics through his Council-Entry programme, i. e. "Non-Cooperation from within the Councils". He however met with vehement opposition from the Mahatma and the "No-changer". At the Gaya Congress C. Rajagopalachari led the Council-Entry opposition. His motion being lost, Deshbandu resigned the president-ship. Thereafter he organized the Swarajya Party within the Congress in collaboration with Motilal Nehru, the Ali brothers, Ajmal Khan, V. J. Patel, Pratap Guha Roy and others. It was initially known as the Congress-Swaraj-Khilafat Party. In spite of the bitter criticism launched by the "No-changers" like Shyam, Sundar Chakraborty and J. L. Banerjee, the Jalpaiguri Conference was organized by the Swarajists in 1923. Through the efforts of the Swarajists, Maulana Azad was elected President of the Congress Special Session at Delhi, where the programme of Council-Entry was approved. The programme was later confirmed at the Cocanada Session.

Deshbandhu wanted "Swaraj for the masses, not for the classes. "He believed in non-violent and constitutional methods for the realization of national independence. In the economic field, Das stressed the need of constructive work in villages. A champion of national education and vernacular medium, he felt that the masses should be properly educated to participate in the nationalist movement. Chittaranjan also made his mark as a poet and an essayist. His religious and social outlook was liberal. A believer in women's emancipation, he supported the spread of female education and widow re-marriage. Having being an advocate of inter caste marriage, he gave his own daughters in marriage with Brahmm and Kayastha families.

Chittaranjan passed away on June 16, 1925 at Darjeeling at the age of 55. Great as a jurist, Chittaranjan was the greatest and most dynamic leader of the then Bengal. Above all, he was an apostle of Indian nationalism.

# [7]

Banerjee became the patron of rising Indian leaders like Gopal Krishna Gokhale (1866-1915) and Sarojini Naidu (1879-1949). Revolutionary sentiment created in many regional centers of India. Bal Gangadhar Tilak (1856-1920) of Moharastra began to advocate for revolution and political independence. Thus Banerjee became an important figure in the Swadeshi movement advocating goods to be manufactured in India against foreign products. His popularity reached to such an extent that his admirers recognized him as the uncrowned King of Bengal. Mohandas Gandhi entered into Indian politics in 1912, coming from South Africa who proposed to start the movement of civil disobedience. The clever British thought it right time to talk with Banerjee. Getting the opportunity first time in his life to serve under powerful British government, Banerjee accepted the portfolio of the minister in the Bengal government and in return he opposed the movement of civil disobedience advocated by Mohandas Gandhi. He lost the public support but in return got award from the British Queen. He was knighted for his political support of the British Empire. He is remembered and widely respected today as a pioneer leader of Indian politics. In the later years British also respected him and referred him the honor of "Surrender Not Banerjee". Although at the end of his life he was successful to get the British favour, but mentally he could not reconcile himself as he could accept neither the extremist view of political action nor the noncooperation of Gandhi. In 1919, the British came forward with Montague-Chelmsford to pacify the Indian leaders to stop agitation. Banerjee did not prefer to go against the government after assigning the new portfolio of the ministry; he thought it wise to support the reforms as it substantially fulfilling Congress's demands. His decision in favor of the government further isolated him from the Indian public. He raised to the peak of fame once but he again reached to the bottom after being defeated at the polls in 1923 and died at Barrackpore on August 6, 1925.

The British knows the declaration of independence for India had already been announced much earlier. At the Lahore session of 1929, the Indian National Congress, already had made the declaration of Purna Swaraj or 'Declaration of the Independence of India' and 26 January as Independence Day. The Congress asked the people to pledge themselves to civil disobedience and continued with the civil disobedience to force the British government to consider granting independence. The Parliament of the United Kingdom had transferred the complete power to the constituent Assembly of India with effect from 15th August.

The formation of Indian National Congress in 1985, the rousing of national sentiment, pushing the youth for anti-government activity, all this activity was for self Rule. So at last it came into being in 1947, 15th August. It is now more than 60 years. Did the Indians succeeded to achieve for the Nation what our earlier leaders Sir Banerjee in particular had wanted? Certainly, the answer would be no. Now we are in the thresh hold of regionalism demanding more security for our State and in future it would be more autonomy for our State, who knows the Indians might see fall out of disintegration of India as is now what is visible that look out of security on the basis of religion and on the point of political advantage. The Independence of India might bring some benefits to few states but not the slightest benefit to the State of Bengal. It was divided into two at the time of Independence of India, which the British wanted to do in 1905 but failed. Now in 1947, the British succeeded to do so to teach a lesson to the Bengali reminding them that they gave everything to Bengal, they built up the Calcutta, they favored the Hindu elite, they down graded the Muslim force but in return they faced violent agitation in Bengal in particular, in particular from the Hindu youth, they were scared of bomb, they were compelled to shift the Capital to Delhi, now they have brought forward the formula of demolishing the backbone of Hindu elite of Bengal which was made straight, strong and sound by the British, to go back to a state of no existence in near future. Is it the fore slightness of the Hindu elite of Bengal? Is it the result that what Bengals think today India thinks to morrow? Now if the Bengal things let the Hindu elite get terminated following the policy of British to have a better economic life if not a religious life under compulsion, would the rest of India think likewise? In our Indian tradition as a family is run by the father, similarly the country would be run by the guidance of Rastraguru. Where is the vision of our Rastraguru? Our Rastraguru, Sir Surendranath Banerjee, the pioneer of nationalist movement, the pioneer of Indian National Congress (1885), when he was denied the right, he became anti-British, but he became a pro-British leader as soon as he was offered the Ministry in Bengal, he accepted it. He left for heaven in 1925, but what he had left for the later generation. The British came with the formula of division of the country with prior agreement with Jinnah, now the leaders of Congress either to accept or reject. There was no distinguished leader of Bengal in the congress meeting during the time of accepting the British proposal of the division of the country for independence of India. Ballavbhai Petal took the initiative to get it pass to accept it to get the independence without further delay because he was more than 73. There was little time for him to rule over India. No body thought of what would happen to those people with opposite religion who were in other regions. Who was responsible for the senseless rioting and holocaust of human beings? The Punjabis were warrior by birth. They settled the matter once for all. But Bengalese particularly the Hindus were religious, never learn violence in their religion but learn to bear the sufferings what ever way it comes to their fate, till the last breath of life. It is still continuing in East Bengal (now Bangladesh) and in west Bengal too.

# [8]

Many of our Bengali leaders prefer to go to England to compete ICS and try to get a government post. But did they try to understand the vision of British people. United Kingdom is a small place and the number of people who were living there were also limited in number compare to any other small country of Europe not to speak of French or Rome. And it is beyond question to compare with India. But there outlook was to get settle in South Africa, Australia, New Zealand and Canada. They targeted India as their trading center. Since 1650 onwards they were trying to set their foothill in few trade centers of India. In Bengal they were refused many times but they never went away leaving the hope of settlement in Bengal. They were hopeful and they were waiting for the opportunity to come. Truly it came once, a dear one of Sultan Jahangir was sick, a British Doctor came, cured the person and in return Sultan gave the permission for British trade center in Bengal, the trade permission being sought by the British. They properly utilized the moment of opportunity for their rightful purpose. That was the beginning. When the few people of England could thing of settlement in outside world, why did not the Indian leaders think of outside settlement in the extent of the growth of huge population? Well, India was a poor country; undeveloped, uneducated, such thinking was nothing but a dream. Right, Indians should thing at least to learn how to administer a country? A student goes to teacher for learning. Here in Bengal, the Bengalese got their teacher at home. They should learn how to administer a country. To rule a vast country like India it requires a huge number of experienced persons with administrative efficiency. What was the result what we were facing since independence? It was only with few experienced officials of India when India jumps into the governance of India just after independence. Result was measurable. Unaccountable, corruption initiated in every sector, which could not be known to the public so long because of the non availability of TV and other news covering media and other advance news challenge. Once corruption was beyond control and till to day it is beyond control because of political coverage, as in most cases our political leaders have forgotten the value of politics in the service of mankind. No government can make the things right unless the right person, the experienced persons were posted in right place. Laws after laws will come forward but nothing would be implemented. This is nothing but tragedy. The account of Swiss Bank will never close unless the morality of the people had improved, unless the love for the country and love for the people aroused from within.

# [9]

Calcutta was made the second city by the British in British Empire, the first being the London. The Bengalese could learn the administration from the British, they might not be able to convert Calcutta to number one but they could easily occupy the major activity of the office by becoming a faithful and reliable citizen. Indians may not have wealth, but they have man power. The knowledge of science had revolutionized the industrial out put of United Kingdom to get the economic prosperity. The European counties borrowed the scientific knowledge from UK to improve their economy, even the Asian country like Japan never remained behind to acquire the scientific knowledge to advance the economy. But in India we never see any such initiative had taken by our leaders, rather many of our leaders went to London to qualify for administrative Examination to become an administrator in India. It seams now in consideration of the economy of other countries, had Indians devote their energy in the economic front in stead of administrative initiative in the process of taking over of power, the people of India and the Indian sub continent would be in a better position in the World of history. Japan is the example.

French in the days of economic crisis never stopped to help the American independence movement. USA achieved her independence; French took their settlement in America as well as in Canada. If Indian leaders could thing like wise, they could help British to sustain their holding in USA, when Indians could make their settlement in USA as well as in Canada. Not only that it was also easy for Indians to settle in Australia and Newzeland as the two places were nearer to India than UK. Why there was hurry to get self Rule? There was better future prospect to remain with British. Had the India be with British, USA might not be the super power. It would be Indo-British, the Super power. Our leaders always thought of negative, and with regional outlook. Our thinking in regional outlook will go on increasing unless we learn to think wide. To day we have the largest number of regional parties. We failed to keep Tibet. We are in political turmoil in Nepal. The future of Bhutan, Sikim and Arunachal are also in tribunal's question. All the neighbor countries are in hidden transitional state of hostility. Unless improvement of life with economic prosperity is achieved, the hidden hostility would never go as is the virtue of ethics of Hindu doctrine. Be happy make others happy.

The formation of Indian Union bears many similarities with the formation of United States. The economic root of the United States lies in European colonization in the 16th, 17th and 18th centuries. The growth of economy had created 13 small independent units or states with independent self sufficient farming set up, which lined together in 1776 to form the United States of America similar to the formation of the Union of India by the merger of the independent princely states. It was the year 1492, Christopher Columbus, who was sailing under Spanish Flag, set out to find Asia but happened out with "New World". Next 100 years it was a regular feature of Portuguese, Dutch, English and French Explorers to sail from Europe to 'New World'. Their look out was 'Gold'. Many of them returned and again few of them settled in the new place. The process of going and returning continued for years together unless new states were originated. In the last 230 years the United States grew into a huge, integrated, industrialized country of economy making the country a center of transaction of nearly a quarter of the World economy. India on the other hand dipped into economic disaster, misery and corruption rupturing the administrative machinery and discipline in the period of last 60 years after being independent. The major factors in the growth of the economy of the United States included a large unified market supported by a disciplined political-legal system under the command of efficient administrator, planner and faithful workers. Unlike US, few Indians took the administration under the banner of Victorious

Congress engaging the unskilled workers in all fronts in the process of Nation building. The result was miserable. People gradually lost all hopes. Unrest crippled the every state. In the backdrop of economy, the public attention was diverted towards other sector like language and regional language (i). The seed of regionalism began to grown up because of the aimless policy of the government. The US get flooded with economic growth; GDP had rises all time high, the government extended their outlook towards nation to national unlike the outlook of the government of India towards nation to regional unit. The cry for the establishment of a public sector industry in a particular State, or special economic grant for a particular State, or the economic grant for the State based on development or under-development, are the day to day increasing demand of the States being prevalent, the question of suspicion had arisen against center in the question of the distribution of Nation's wealth. Are these not threatening the functioning of Indian Union and degrading the values of the Nation? (ii) Where is our National spirit hidden now? In the process of development United States had devoted their energy and wealth for the invention of new technology, new technique for rapid industrial growth and set up the new avenues through out the world to recruit the brainy guys with high salary to engage them in the process of research to find out the new opportunity for further growth of the Nation. To-day US is a country of Super-power and India, a country reputed as poorest to poor till 1990, and now a developing country. It is still far away to reach to the foot hills of United States although a section of its citizens bears a lofty thought. United State is a very big country bigger than India by at least more than 5 times which has vast natural resources like timber, coal, and iron above all the much needed oil. Every natural material were properly utilized and still utilizing with efficient handling with a zeal of an entrepreneurial spirit and commitment to investing in material and human capital unlike India where the public fund is always a scam of corruption. Where was the national spirit of pre-independence? Throwing of bomb against British was easy, rising of national sentiment to carry out protest against the Ruler was easy but running a state with efficiency was not easy.

The miraculous discovery of 'New World' and later US and rising to the peak of super power in a span of three hundred years is undoubtly an upgrading astonishing fact while country like Egypt, India or China, the oldest in the birth of human civilization by passing thousands and thousands of years without of much progress was not a down grading fact of wonder? Civil War was there even the poor whites joined the slaves in the civil war. The impact of Civil war (1861-1865) was decreased to some extent when the North became victorious over the South. There was a boost in business after the discovery of Rail Road during the period of 1850-1873. At that time cheaper and faster river traffic was discovered in the form of 'Steam Boat' to enhance the business. 1890 was the period of beginning of rapid development, what is termed the $2^{nd}$ Second Revolution in the United States. Coal was discovered in Appalachian Mountains of Pennsylvania, south of Kentucky, and large iron was found in Lake Superior region of the upper Midwest and the skill of New found state produced a new product steel out of the two putting together. After steel, electricity came into being with new incentive for further inventions. The period 1900-1930 started to discover new tools and machines for the set up of industry. In 1913, Henry Ford brought a revolution in transport by the production of automobiles. At the out set, Americans in the Thirteen Colonies demanded their rights as Englishmen; they demanded to select their own representatives to govern and to tax them. But the British refused their demand. The Americans took the initiative to boycotts British manufactured items. But on the contrary the British became aggressive and responded with the rejection of American rights all through. In the result the Americans launched the American Revolution and finally leading to an all-out war against the British. The aim was to achieve independence for the United States of America which lasted all most seven years 1775-1783 to declare independent United States. Thus right to life, liberty and the pursuit of happiness prevailed.

The post World War II period starting from 1945 to the period up to early 1970 was a golden era of American capitalism. The middle class swelled, as did GDP and productivity. It was the period of best economic growth. Of course in 1981, the country again went back to recession when unemployment rose to a peak of 10. 8% in December 1982. In the period 1994-2000, the out come of US economy began to increase, inflation brought under control, unemployment decreased below 5% resulting a soaring stock market. The black day appeared again in the sky of NY by the thunder of lightening storm demolishing the World Trade Center by the speedy Flight used as rocket, killing and injuring hundreds and thousands and made the day a historic one, the unforgettable day "September 11 attacks" (2001). The sentiment rose high, Taliban government in Afghanistan was attacked and shattered like burning paper to bring down the culprit in front to punish, suspecting danger the government of Iraq was crush down in no time thundering the World what the might of superpower could do.

American soldiers, NATO Forces reluctantly continued their attack out of revenge. Days went by; year ends with the beginning of New Year without being the sign of appearance of ending war since the long last 12 years. Soldiers now lose faith in life having being suffocated by the War of atmosphere and losing interest in the quest of long absence from the native house and also from being long away from the dear one. Continuation of long War had already threatened the economy of the Super power. The new President Barrack Obama is now under immense pressure to pull out of war. It is always better to stop war but will US be in peace in distant America in the days of Rocket Missiles and that too with nuclear over head IBMS character. It is now a war in disguise from distance and supposed to be more dangerous than the War of Atom Bomb in front. India is next door neighbor of Afghanistan, how India could sleep in peace. India a country of tolerance never wanted to send troops to Afghanistan to kill the terrorists rather India would prefer to sacrifice few lakhs of its citizen in the event of Talaban or al-Qaida or in their combined attack like 26th Mumbai attack.

# [10]

Barrack Obama was a worried man in the event of Great Recession. Recession was also in the States of Europe. It would comprise all the different States about 48 in number and the people totaling 71 million in number where the economy or the wealth of Europe's states would vary, although the poorest are well above the richest states of other continents in terms of GDP and living standards. Europe in 2010 had a nominal GDP of $19. 920 trillion (30. 2% of the world). Europe's largest national economy was that of Germany, which ranks fourth globally in terms of GDP, followed by French, ranking fifth globally in terms of GDP. After that it is UK, ranking sixth globally in terms of GDP, followed by Italy, which ranks seventh globally in terms of GDP. Russia is ranking tenth in terms of global GDP. These 5 countries all are in parallel ranking in the world's top 10. As such it accounts for half of the 10 wealthiest ones. The leaders of European countries are very intelligent in administration and in the management of the economy of the country right from the beginning. During the time of territorial expansion, the European leaders never remained confined in the small region of their States. They went out to explore new avenues extending their journey from Europe to Asia for the growth of new economic center. Christopher Columbus went out to reach to India of Asia and accidently discovered "New World" the land of America unlike the leaders of India and the Asia. The Asians and Indian in particular remained busy in search of the source of creator flourishing the religious activity without giving importance to the economy and the well fare of the people. It was only in the later stage few religious leaders like Vivekananda realized that the service to God is nothing but the service to mankind. In the earlier times in the absence of any kind of development, the Normandy life developed in the best regions where life could survive in the presence of water and cultivable land. It appears Egypt, India and China were the best places where the growth of life flourished at ease. It was not Europe or America, it was Asia where life originated and sustained on the bank of river. It was also surprising to thing that all religions were originated in Asia be it Hinduism (oldest), Buddhism (before 400 BC), Jewesism, Christianity (7BC), and Islam (500-600 BC). The land of India and Middle East were the centers of all religions in particular. To day we find Christianity is prevailing in the Western world centering Rome but its origin was in Jerusalem of Middle East that belongs to Asia as we find in the record of human history. Religion is the study of mind and sacrificing the self to the soul of God be it Jesus, Allah, Krishna or any other. The search for territorial expansion and search for the growth of economic centers was definitely for the sake of their country and the people with whom the leaders have grown up, the place with whom thinkers have born and brought up and not for their self. Our Indian religious leaders from time immortals have sacrificed their lives in prayers, pujas, whorishings and motivated its citizens in the path of the service of Temples and regular prayers for the purification of self and to be excused for the sins performed knowingly or unknowingly so that they could escaped the sin of rebirth as is the saying in the holy Book of Religion. Thus the teachings of Religious leaders were a teaching by dint of which every one will be free from sin and would never come back to this sinful earth. Thus everyone is concentrated on self and not on the others or the country as is found among the leaders, thinkers or explorers of the Western countries.

It would not wrong to see that the continent Asia was a God gifted continent because it has everything of every States except the Middle East(which has something different and special, the oil), and India is particularly in exception to get everything as the gifts of God. It was the reason why and how life explores first in these regions, the regions of the country of river sides where life begins by the water of river and oxygen of air as a life does not exist without water. Where there is river, there is fresh water and there is life. Existence of early life found in river bank such as life was present in the river side of Punjab (Harappa Civilization), concentration of population on the bank of river Ganga and the presence of Normandy life on the river side of Nile where the early civilization of Egypt had grown up, were the testimony of the existence of life in river water (fresh water). In the Western country there were no such big rivers where life could grow at ease. The river Tames of London is equivalent to any canal of India. It is insufficient to supply drinking water to the small population of London compare to any city of India. The river Rhine of Germany is a small river to supply drinking water. By the time it is highly contaminated by the fall out of industrial nuisance. India is definitely fortunate enough in this respect. It is pity to see India was a country left of care since thousands and thousands of years, India being gifted with river, hills and planes full of huge treasures of coal, minerals and oils (if not plenty) remained undeveloped while the European countries surrounded by the sea of saline water adverse for smooth living and being left of big rivers, grows to the peak of development by the beautiful infrastructures of road networks, by the increasing day by day development of industries, by the sky rocking buildings, by the creation of health resorts, by the creation of amusement centers to attract foreign tourists and above all by the creation of facilities for smooth passing of daily life with comfort and pleasure. Who is to blame for the misery of India-political leaders, religious leaders or the citizens of India? Our political leaders not only fight for independence of India even many of them sacrificed their lives before the Bullets of British. Did they want to see the present independent India? The India where a section of people are having their life in luxury, a section of people would enjoy the privileges of MP, no matter who may be under the court notices of criminal charges, who would never be denied the tickets to contest election, who is certain to win the election by the power of muscle and by the power of money. The India where the peasants every year are dying for want of food, where the disparity of rich and poor are so much that the poor prefers to take shelter to a far distance corner of a village out of fear, where no official work, be it minor or major could not be completed without paying bribe. India where the security in Open Street is in danger, a girl in night is in super danger. Don't we find these in any where of western country? Yes, we find but very cases are in rare instances.

The discipline of duty has made the person mentally strong and sound, and morally conscious forgetting to hear anything adverse to duty.

However, the strength of the mind is further enriched by the financial status of the individuals. Prior to World War II, Europe's major financial states were UK, French, and Germany. The better financial status was due to the huge production in industries. It was the credit for the people of British to learn the technique of setting the industry in full growth of production. The people of other states of Europe never miss the opportunity to come to United Kingdom to learn the skills of industry. Very soon they became familiar with the industry and finally set industry all over Europe. Thus an Industrial Revolution occurred. The growth of economy had made the whole Europe wealthy and rich increasing the standard of living hundred times in compare to any cities of the continent of Asia except Japan. United Kingdom was the pioneer to find the ways and means of industry, which was borrowed by the European countries and made them rich. India and UK was the same country but the Indian people failed to take the opportunity of learning the techniques of Industry like the people of other states of Europe and remained backward for hundreds of year and still in turmoil. True, British would never want to set up Industry in India and British would not allow Indians to learn the all about industry. But determination never gets back tracked. The Mughal never wanted the British to set up business center at any coastal side of India. The British were waiting for an opportune moment and never get dishearten. That opportune moment came once when a British Doctor well treated a female member of the Mughal family. The satisfied Mughal gave the permission to set up business center at the coastal side of Kolkata. If the British could fulfill their objective why did not the Indians. Did the Americans want the Indian IT companies flourish in Bangalore or USA or anywhere else? Now it is under compulsion in the sphere of competitive market for the sake of economic growth, an American company has to support the Indian IT companies. Are the Indians not missed the track and made the British enemy? Indians concentrated on the politics of ruling the country by hook or cook and thought of less in terms of economic progress. It is everywhere without economic progress a country can not survive, progressed and stabilized. Japan is the brightest example. The most devastated Japan being destroyed by the burnt of Atom Bomb, have again raised its face high, high in wealth and high in superb technology bypassing the world in many respect. A nation deserves respect and command.

# [11]

**Economy of Japan:** The economy of Japan is the 3rd largest in the world in terms of nominal GDP. According to the International Monetary Fund, the country's per capita GDP (PPP) was at $34,739 or the 25th highest in 2011. Japan is a member of Group of Eight. It has now focused primarily on high-tech and precision goods such as optical equipment, hybrid cars, and robotics. Japan is the world's largest creditor nation as the nation is being generally running with an annual trade surplus. Its financial position in 2011 internationally could be assed by the presence of companies in the country. As of 2011, 68 of the Fortune 500 companies are based in Japan. In the course of three decades following 1960, Japan being involved in World War II, US military protection either denied or ignores Japan in defense spending. This favoured Japan to concentrate on electronic spending bringing a rapid economic growth referred to as the Japanese post-war economic miracle. By the efficient guidance of the Ministry of Economy, Trade and Industry, Japan could show an average growth rate of 10% in the 1960. The political leaders of Japan did not start any movement to root out American's interference in the affairs of Japan particularly in the defense sector unlike the Indian leaders. Rather the Japanese people were encouraged to maintain a good relation with US by their leaders to build up the economy of the devastated country. Japan regained its economy and was successful to establish and maintain its dignified position in the international market as the world's second largest economy from 1978 to 2010, the country was the first Asian country to surpass the per capita income of many most countries of the west although a temporary set back happened in 1990 due to many factors including the Tokyo Stock Exchange crash. Nonetheless, GDP per capita growth from 2001-2010 has still managed to outpace Europe and the United States. Japan is now thinking ahead to rule the world in the growth of electronic sector. The ICT industry and Music industry are also in the path of progress. Now Japan is the second largest music market in the world. Japan is a mountainous, volcanic island country. It has inadequate natural resources that could hardly support its growing economy and large population. Therefore it maintains its policy to exports goods in which it has a comparative advantage such as engineering-oriented, Research and Development—led industrial products etc. In exchange Japan prefers to import raw materials and petroleum. In agricultural sector also Japan is not lacking behind. It is among the top-three importers for agricultural products in the world next to the European Union and United States. Japan is the world's largest single national importer of fish and fishery products. The minerals such as gold, magnesium and silver are sufficient to meet the industrial demand but the minerals like iron ore, copper, bauxite or alumina must be imported from out side to keep the industry running. India, on the other hand, a country of the deposits of huge minerals of all most of all kinds, that does not required to be imported but yet India lacking in the generation of industrial output as because our political leaders are more concerned with power politics and less with industry and industrial goods. The progress of the country lies in the back drop of the discussion of the economic history of Japan. Its spectacular growth can be accounted by summarizing it under the strain of three different periods. These are, First period—the foundation of Edo (1603), 2nd period—Meiji Restoration (1868), and the 3rd period—after the defeat of World War II (1945). It gives us an idea about the planning, thinking and executing of the ideas of Japanese people to raise the island nation to the second largest economy of the world. The development of a country depended more on the progress of the economy and less on the political power. In the Edo period Japan learn and developed the art of ship building in the midst of interaction with European powers. During this period Japan built her first ocean-going Western-style warships, such as the "San Juan Bautista", a 500-ton galleon-type ship that transported a Japanese embassy to the Americas, under Europe. Later many more ships were built such as armed trade ships, Yamada Nagamasa etc. European power was in favour of spreading the religion Christianity there. In order to eradicate the influence of Christianization, Japan kept the European away and entered in a period of isolation called "Sakoku", during which its economy enjoyed stability and progress to a little extent. This was the progress of Edo period. The significant sight was to see the concentration of population in big city like Osaka and Kyoto each had more than 400,000 inhabitants. Many more castle towns grew as well. Osaka and Kyoto became bust trading and handicraft production centers. Edo was the center for the supply of food. Rice was the base of the economy. In spite of bitterness in spreading the religion Christianity among the common country people, the Japanese intelligentsia never remained away in the study of Western science and techniques (called rangaku, literally, Dutch studies) with emphasis on physical sciences such as the study of electrical phenomena and mechanical science, the studies of which formed the base of expanding the Japanese knowledge in the field of electronic and car manufacture, the knowledge of which kept the Japanese goods and Japanese car in Europe as well as in US at the highest demand in the market as we find to day. While in India the Indian intelligentsia never thought of such education rather Indians were habituated to go to London to compete in the ICS examination to become a civil servant under British government.

# [12]

**Meiji restoration period (1868-1912):** This period was remarkable for the fact that the Leaders of Japan realized that knowledge of science was fast developing in Europe and United States. To acquire the knowledge of science the leaders inaugurated a new Western-based education system for all young people of Japan. Thousands and thousands of students were sent to United States and Europe to learn the knowledge of science and also hired more than 3000 Westerners to teach modern science, mathematics, technology, and foreign languages in Japan. Government brought further development by building railroads, improving roads and carrying a land reform program. This was a period that sets the blue print for industrialization when factories and shipyards were built and these were sold to entrepreneurs at a fraction of their value. Many of this business grew rapidly into the larger conglomerates. Government emerged as chief promoter of private enterprise, enacting a series of pro-business policies. The Postwar period (1945) showed the remarkable recovery after the World War II. The attention of the Japanese was towards industry and economy forgetting the influence of American force or other force. The survival of industry in the holocaust of Atom Bomb was important to them than anything else. In a short period they have showed their dedication and set the example in front of the world that how a nation can be rebuilt in no time. The nation Japan can be destroyed by missiles and bombs but the art of Knowledge of Japanese techniques can not be destroyed. It was supreme and it will remain so as is proved by the done of 21$^{st}$ century.

Chakravarti Rajagopalachari was the Governor General of India, Jawaharlal Nehru, Prime Minister and Sardar Vallabbhbhai Patel, the

Home Minister. Prime Minister Nehru was immensely popular with the masses, but Patel enjoyed the loyalty and the faith of Congressmen, state leaders and India's civil services. As Patel was the senior most leaders in the Constituent Assembly of India, he was directly or indirectly remained responsible in a larger measure for shaping India's constitution and as such he was known as the "Bismarck of India". Pakistan was not happy with the Kashmir situation. The Hindu King did not thing to join Pakistan although majority citizen of Kashmir were Muslims, even though their forefathers in most of the cases were being Hindu Kashmiri Pandits. Pakistan was restless although its military set up was not fully equipped to go for war. However, Pakistan was determined to attack Kashmir and Pakistani invasion of Kashmir began in September 1947, Patel immediately contemplated to send troops into Kashmir. But he was prevented by Nehru and Mountbatten as Kashmir's monarch had not yet acceded to India as per British declaration. Patel waited till Kashmir's monarch had acceded to India when it was too late. Srinagar, the Baramulla Pass and a vast territory was occupied by the invaders in the mean time. Patel started the operation along with the Defense Minister Baldev Singh to get back the Kashmiri territory. Patel strongly advised Nehru against going for arbitration to the United Nations because Pakistan was wrong while India was correct in invasion as the Kashmir being acceded to India by the King of Kashmir as per declaration. He did not want foreign interference in a bilateral affair. To stop communal violence, Gandhi went on a fast-unto-death. Peace restored with UN intervention. This was history. Kashmir problem even after sixty years of independence was not solved.

# [13]

## Jawaharlal Nehru (1889-1964):

Nehru was born on Nov'14, 1889, in Allahabad of India. In 1919, he joined National congress and joined Indian National leader Mahatma Gandhi's independent movement. Nehru became independent India's first Prime Minister. He died on May 27, 1964 in Delhi, India.

He was an international Politian professing with a socialistic bent of mind. In the words of Rubinstein—"Two paths were open to the newly liberated countries-the Capitalist path and the Socialist path." Nehru was an advocate of the socialist path and under his leadership there was the possibility for Indian to develop along socialistic lines. "About two decades ahead, 1927 when he made a visit to USSR, he rolled out India's economic policy. He thought of introducing planned economy, institutional process of industrialization, principle of development of science and technology, and the sanctity of secular spirit. He was honored internationally as he was one of the founding father of the non-aligned movement. Nehru made India a force to recon with in international politics. But however, his administration was criticized by the leftish critics for the fact of slow progress of development of the country. The Indian people were treated as before as the rule of British, that had created serious doubt about the benefit of Independence. It was because in most of the cases people confronted with the same civil servants, who were engaged in the British Rule, the same policemen who treated them with the same scorn and brutality as under British Rule.

If the largest Democratic country India and the oldest Democratic country the United States work in cohesion, the world may be benefited for the sake of humanity in the 21st century. Because of technological up gradation, the world has now reduced to a unit of a family. The ancient Greek philosopher thought of Democracy for the cause of the citizen of the particular country while today, it is necessary to think for a Democracy which will think for the citizen of the world. However, the term democracy appeared first in ancient Greek, where a political and philosophical thought had evolved a system of government at that time by dint of which political sovereignty was rested with the people. Freedom of speech, freedom of political expression and freedom of press were the backbone of democracy. Besides these, any democracy ensures equality before the law, civil liberties and human rights. India followed the Parliamentary form of democracy where parliamentary representatives had been recognized as the people's elected legislatives members for a fixed time period and the function of the government has been executed for a specific time period through a ministry under Prime Minister. While the United States followed the Presidential form of Democracy where President is the supreme authority to form the government, but India followed the Parliamentary form of democracy. However, the real test of a democracy is not in what is said in the Constitution of any country, but in reality how it functions on the ground. The purpose of the government was to serve the people, to look after the welfare of the people in communication, service, health, education, food, sports and culture & amusement above all security of its citizen. After 9/11 attack in US, the President of America designed the plan to destroy the attacker and dismantle its infrastructure and accordingly President ordered the American Army to start the operation in Afghanistan, and the fight continued since 2001 onwards for the protection of American citizens. But in India, after 26/11, the same kind of action did not follow when 185 people were massacred by the terrorists in Mumbai, because, the Indian Parliament did not approve such kind of operation, while being adversely the opinion of the majority country of the world body who were in opinion of direct action to dismantle the terrorist center at Pakistan.

Indian Democracy is concerned with the Indian people who were idealized with the philosophy of the doctrine of Tolerance while American Democracy is with tat for tie for cause of justice. Indian Democracy was originated by the theory of Ghandian Philosophy of the virtue of Tolerance, while American Democracy is the foot print of the Late George Washington based on the virtue of tat for tie in bringing justice in the war of independence struggle. It is difficult for any Indian government to take any drastic step in any matter but it is not difficult in America because American Citizens are accustomed to face the struggle of national adventure. Indian democracy is vitiated by caste, community above all by the sentiment of religion. Education had reached to villages true but did the level of education realize the importance of democratic franchise? All political parties choose a candidate based on religion and caste and not on merit. Americans were successful to fight against the Red Indians for unity of the United States, while the philosophy of Gandhi, the virtue of tolerance and non violence succeeded to achieve Indian Independence but failed to keep the Unity of the country, the Independence being achieved at the cost of the division of the country. Ancient Greek Democracy was in the look out to bring a better life in any Sovereign country. Every leader of every sovereign country wishes to sustain a better life in the country. To-day communication has improved, distance is no longer a factor, and people can travel from country to country, continent to continent without much difficulty. The disease like Aid or any other disease affected with unknown virus might originate in a particular region but it can be spread through out the world in no time. So time has come to think for every region of the world and not to think for the country of its own.

Kashmir, a name every where in the world history but the place belong to India and Indian sub-continent, is a test of Indian democracy and fight against the terrorism. On hearing the rumors that Maharaja Hari Singh of Kashmir had asked for annexation of Kashmir to India, militant Muslim and Pakistani Army attacked Kashmir from West and made rapid advances into the Baramulla sector. Maharaja Hari Singh of Kashmir asked the government of India to intervene. But government of India could not intervene unless Jammu and Kashmir officially joined the Union of India. As the Pakistani force reached the outskirts of Srinagar, Maharaja desperately needed military assistance. After the completion of the agreement of annexation signed by the Maharaja and Lord Mountbatten, the Indian Army along with the National Conference volunteers moved to drive out the Pakistanis.

The war lasted till 1948. India moved the issue to the UN Security Council, although the leader of National Conference was not in favour of India seeking UN intervention. It was certain that Indian Army could drive out the invaders from the entire State very soon. UN passed the resolution imposing an immediate cease-fire under the supervision of United Nations. Military Observer was asking the government of Pakistan for the withdrawal of force from the territory of Jammu and Kashmir and also asked the government of India to hold a plebiscite to put into effect 'on the question of Accession of the state to India.' However, both India and Pakistan failed to comply with the UN resolution. Pakistan did not removed army from Azad Kashmir and India could not do the plebiscite although India carried out elections in Jammu and Kashmir except Azad Kashmir after five year interval.

# [14]

1January, 1948, Kashmir problem lies under the jurisdiction of Untied Nations (UN) Security Council. On 1 January, 1949, a ceasefire between Indian and Pakistani forces left India in control of most of the valley, as well as Jammu and Ladakh, while Pakistan remained in control of part of Kashmir including what is now Azad Kashmir. Pakistan claimed it had merely supported an indigenous rebellion in Azad Kashmir and Northern Territories against repression. On 5 January, 1949, UNCIP (United Commission for India and Pakistan) resolution stated that the question of the accession of the State of Jammu and Kashmir to India or Pakistan will be decided through a free and impartial plebiscite. Both the countries accepted the principle but failed to implement the same in spirit due to the difference in the interpretation of the principle. On 30 October, 1956, the State Constituent Assembly adopted a constitution for the state declaring it an integral part of the Indian Union. Indian the then home Minister Pandit Govind Ballabh Pant, during his visit to Srinagar, declared that the State Jammu & Kashmir is an integral part of India and there can not be any question of plebiscite a fresh to determine its status a fresh. A period of eight years elapsed as such. In 1964, a mass upsurge occurred in Kashmir Valley when the holy relic is found missing from the Hazratbal shrine, which was recovered later on 4 January 1964. Taking the advantage of mass agitation, Pakistan attacked Kashmir sending few thousand armed Pakistani infiltrators across the cease-fire line in August 1965. It developed into a full fledged India-Pak war and came to an end on 23 September with immediate ceasefire. On January, 1966, by an agreement 'Tashkent Declaration' both the countries agreed to revert to the previous 1965 position. In the seventieth period there had happened mass movement in East Pakistan (present Bangladesh) for the independence of the country. India helped to liberate Bangladesh by sending Indian army there when Pakistani army surrendered. In July, 1972, India and Pakistan had agreed to sign Simla Agreement and also agreed to respect the LOC (line of control) and that the final settlement of Kashmir would be decided bilaterally in the future.

Pakistan, right at the beginning became a NATO member for the sake of its security and since then remained as a close ally of US and always supported US in the fight against communism during the continuation of cold war between two super powers. In view of alliance partner US always supported Pakistan in the affairs of Kashmir. But since 1992, it appeared, there is a change of opinion of US in the matter of Kashmir. US had realized that India would never compromise on its unity and territorial integrity, while by the turn of the events Kashmir become a part of India. US government understood that any practical compromise had to necessarily take into account the ground realities and the tremendous changes that had occurred since 1947. US is now convinced that the U. N. resolution requiring a plebiscite in Kashmir, which the US had strongly supported in the past, were no longer tenable and it now favoured bilateral negotiations to solve the problem within the framework of the Simla Agreement of 1972. Now the US administration faithfully committed to sustained engagement with both countries, the focus is now direct to indirect intervention for promoting a composite dialogue between India and Pakistan. The US intervention would come only after the consent of the two countries. The former President Mr. George W. Bush disliked direct mediation; he was in favour of solving the matter between the two countries mutually. But US would never give up keeping close watch because of the fact that both are nuclear power, out break of war would bring disaster. US government believes serious and purposeful dialogue would prevent any unwanted incidents if not complete solution. Although Pakistan is an ally to US but Pakistan had open up terrorist centers and also providing others safe shelters to train militants. Once US encouraged the growing of terrorist centers to fight against communism but now the trained up militants of these centers would not only work against India but to other places too. The ideology of all militant groups is not same. Pakistani militants might be against India, Taliban might be against the force of Afghanistan but al Qaeda must be against US, and other European countries for the fact the militant organization al Qaeda had been formed by Laden to fight against US, the goal was one world one religion, Islam. The militant activity in Pakistan is disturbing for US although Pakistan is an ally of US. Pakistan is officially working with NETO force against terrorism in Afghanistan but the question arises to what extent Pakistan is responding to the on going 'Global War' against terrorism. How clean Pakistan is on the going terrorist activity in Kashmir? This entire factor compelled the US government to alter the US stand on Kashmir

# [15]

India achieved Independence 14<sup>th</sup> August, 1947 under the Leadership of Gandhi and India opted for "Democracy" Why? Why did not a Rule of autocracy? It was the atmosphere of democracy prevailing in the globe. By the time the world had seen the French Revolution and how the King was killed and Forces of King were massacred. The world had witnessed how the 13 States of America revolted and fought the War of independence for long seven years under the leadership of George Washington. Under the prevailing situation India never thought of auto-critic Rule under one leader or under a group of leaders. It is certainly under democracy as prevailed in the United Kingdom, the Lord of India, and the Master of India who taught the few Indians the Rule of democracy under Parliamentary Form of Democracy. India accepted the same prevailing democracy with little modification although a large number of princely states ruled under autocracy were prevailing in India at that time.

**Ancient India verse Modern India:**

The ancient India was a land of Monks, who were said to be literate in religion and who were teachings the ideals of life by creating learning centers mostly in temples situated mostly inside dip jungles and others were illiterate who prefers to earn money by the playing of snakes with songs. In course of time learning University such as Taxashila, Nalanda like University were created and teachings based on religion were continued. Indian peoples were educated with certain virtues. The society was accustomed with the rituals of untouchability and familiar with the custom of burning newly married widow at the death of husband in an atmosphere of loud sounds of drums and beat where the hurt burn cry of widow is submersed under the sounds of drum and the society called the occasion of 'Satidaho'. During that period India was ruled by Kings and Princes spreading over 530 or more units of states. Kings were luxurious and little concern with the distress of the people or the infrastructure of the state. Every member of the king family were considered as the God gifted people and deserves to be respected and honored in the society. Thus India was a land of Kings and servants. King has the right to order and the servant (people) has the utmost duty to obey the order as if it was order of the God. Thousands of years Indian society passed their life like these and earned the reputation, India is a land of Saints. But prejudices like burning of widow were there. The teachings of religion were not against it. It was the Rule of British that compelled the religious Hindus to stop such rituals. Indians were living in jungles, there were beautiful places in the hills as well as in the river side, and they don't know the importance of these places. It was British who developed these places. Most of the hill resorts and most of the sea beach were the creation of British Empire. Indian leaders closed their eyes with the good works of British, because British had to go and the power had to be left with Indian leaders. Therefore exposure of British in front of public was nothing but enemy. In the atmosphere of non violence, there was no frontal violence but the mind of every Indian was full of violence. No government can work with peace under an atmosphere of suppressed violence in the minds of the people. British left, India divided. Where is the peace? What was status of every citizen? Where is the prosperity and happiness in every family of India? Rather people to people difference and distance had increased. There is religious difference, rich and poor, higher caste and lower caste, State verse State, Central party verse Regional party where the Indians stand to-day.

Looking to the atmosphere of communal flare up, rioting, killing and kidnapping, Indian leaders realized their mistake and consoled the Indian people to keep the rest of the Indian Union united, making it a living place for all irrespective of caste, creed, religion or color apart from the protest from many corners of religious groups. To-day Indian

Union is threatened, threatened with religious sentiment, threatened with caste-ism. Suspecting danger the Allahabad High Court has come out with an ordinance against the holding of procession on the basis of caste. In another day there may be procession on the basis of religion. Did Indians fight for Independence of creating groups like these? The humanity of Indians degraded because of division. The division has no end unless Indians learn to live in joint groups instead of groups in isolation.

**Who is to blame for this**, Indians citizens or Indian political leaders? Indians had made constitution of India where every individual were given equal rights. It is nothing but a misnomer. The principle of right accepted at the time of independence of India is not supposed to be denied afterwards. The division of India was based on the rights of religion, a separate home land for the Muslims of India. Now the Muslims who are living in India, the rights of Muslims as group can not be denied as such the rights of other groups, rights of reservation of seats for other caste and so on. As such the rights of individual should better be replace with the rights of groups, in the constitution such as religious group, groups of backward class, groups of schedule class and so on. Thus individual's right is less insignificant than the rights of groups. Hence India is a country consists of groups of individuals and not of only of individuals. It is the democratic rights of individuals groups and not the democratic right of single individuals although every individual has given a voting right. The division of India was based on the rights of religion, thus the sense of right of religion is injected in every mind. Each and every individual believing in particular faith would obey the advice of Religious Head by the customs and faith of religion. Thus our political leaders had created a situation, whereby a religious head become the most powerful person of the group. Of course this was not in India alone. The records of history shows that during the reign of Roman period, once the Heads of Church were more powerful as if the power of King was inferior to Heads of Church. How do our political thinkers think of one India one nation while they have infused the sense of religion, language or sense of right of caste on every Indians? It is heartening to see that the distance between people to people, on the basis of religion, language, caste and have or have not, have increased and destroyed the unity that prevailed in British period. Who will not think that the Indians were happy in the Rule of British as they could live as one entity as an Indian and with no other identity, religious or community and cherished under corruption free British India.

# [16]

**Functions of Indian Democracy:**

India is a country of religious saints and under the darkness of religion many inhuman superstation are functioning in the society. The burning of 'Sati', the sacrifice of human child at Goddess Kali's alter, were not the far away accounts of the Indian history. Even today big animals are sacrificed at the foot of Kali. The strong belief of religion has formed a strong religious entity who was guided naturally by the Heads of religion. Indian democracy has been polluted by the sentiment of religion. The merit and efficiency had taken the back foot in choosing an elected representative in our democratic system. The look out of the present Indian politicians are to capture Delhi by hook or crook and always attempts were there in the process of safeguarding their position in whatever conditions it comes in favor of them rather than addressing the core issues of the people. The patriotic spirit that prevailed once among Indian Politians is no more found to be visible. After 1990 a section of people are testing the flow of wealth, but in most of the cases the strength of wealth is utilizing in harnessing personal power, party power and not for the betterment of public in challenging the improvement of life system of every Indians. Political leaders have befooled the Indians at the independence movement of India by giving false assurance that life will be precious after independence of India. It is the Indian Political leaders who created a political system whereby the people are suffering at the hands of Indian political system in their hard earned independence of India. People are the victims of the Indian system of political administration subjecting to the big reasons of chaos and confusion. Thus both the center as well as the state government is contributing a lot to keep unrest in every state diverting the attention from the field of development and economic growth of India. Indians have a fascination for English as having the elite section of the society get familiar with English after practicing it in India in all official matters and in teaching Institute under British period of administration although English is a foreign language in India but people in general like it. The intention of Indian leaders to bring Hindi in the fore front become very clear from the activity of the government but knowing that the attempt of government may not be liked by the Indians, particularly by the South, the Leaders took a back door policy. Leaders gave importance to regional language just to get rid off English. But the policy appears to have putted a back fire. The importance of English is going to increase every day after the discovery of new science of computer. To-day in India in every urban city the number of English medium school had super seeded the number of regional school based on regional languages. There is heavy rush for a seat in any English medium school in Delhi. Every policy of India is a mistaken policy starting from the division of the country. British Ruled India restoring certain units. After the formation of Indian Union by the annexation of Princely states, no further change is ethically justified or traditionally justified. Indian people have given their consent at that moment of time for the formation of India. The area defined at that moment of formation of Indian Union was the actual area and subsequently the added additional area was the area of Indian Union. No body should have any write to modify the area or alter the area for the benefit of certain powerful person or for the benefit any political party. Actually it so happened. Hyderabad was divided into several states, Hyderabad, Karnataka, Maharashtra and later Maharashtra divided into Gujarat.

The regional sentiment with regional outlook, thinking in terms of community, in terms local language, grow faster in every mind of Indians submersing national interest. This was the creation of the policy of the center for an absolute command over administration. A broader mind took the shelter to a smaller corner of head and subsequently the cry for regional party got the priority in the minds of the people of India in every state. Building a regional party, a kind of satisfaction prevails in the minds of many that some one of these region is doing something good to this smaller region. Once the Indians thought of for the welfare of the people of the South-East Asia, later it changed into the welfare of the people of Indian sub continent. The idea of serving the regions was shattered by the division of India. Now one India is administered under different states safeguarding the interest of states. The people are tired of hearing the scam after scam. Naturally the cry for more power to states is increasing. This was because the people gradually losing their confidence over the expenditure of national interest. In the advent of the growth of regional sentiment, the demand for regional culture, regional language, regional boundary, had increased, consequently the central government now realized the effect of regionalism and tried its best to enhance the feelings of Indian-ism by high lighting the term 'Patriotism', a term which is likely to ignite a feeling among all Indians so that they should be patriotic to support the decisions of the central government though these decisions are not friendly to regional interest. It is the wish of the Delhi government to think in term of Hindi as Hindi is the national language of India although it is not so far practically accepted by all the states. India is now truly a victim of religion as well as a victim of regionalism. As India agreed once in the bifurcation of state, the demand for the creation of further state had went on as people were passing a strenuous life. Definitely it would be an endless demand. NDA Government divided Bihar, UPA government is now moving ahead for the creation of another state Talengana if it suits electoral gain. It is almost certain that the new State Telengana is coming as the 31st state of India as it would help to increase the number of congress MP. This is a painful situation; a state is formed looking to the benefit of a political party and not to the integrity of the state. The demand for the division of Uttar Pradesh government is already there. The process of division would continue as the government failed to preserve the Rule of discipline. The violation of basic principle is the root of destruction. The more the state, the more would be the regional sentiment. The bond of Indian-ism would go on decreasing. In the long run the unity of India will be in danger. Disintegration is a continuous process without end and that leads to destruction. A strong India can go for unity of Integration although integration is a harder reality. The survival of India lies in integration and not in disintegration.

Had the Indian could live under British, the Indians could be deprived of Indian wealth but the Indians could be rich by gaining a greater non perishable wealth. In Indo-British Rule, Indian could play a greater role in administration, in trade and business, but Indians have missed the train. In any international settlement, Indians could be looked upon as an honored, respectable citizen. The image of India in Indo-British Rule would be most significant and respectable in the international arena. It is insignificant whether India would be the guardian of the Globe, but India at least would be free from sectarian killing and free from corruption. India would be equal partner of the regions such as Canada, Australia and similar other region under British occupation. The population of British was insignificant compare to the population strength of India where Indian's command would prevail in the long run. After all Indians were lacking in administration and scientific knowledge. The help of British was a boon in disguise as it is seen in the development of Japan where the Japanese youth learn their scientific skill from the British. The present life of Briton in British Land is hundred times superior to the present life of Indian in India. The development of India in British period may not be at per with British Land but it would be comparable to a little extent but definitely not hundred times down the grade to the extent of present state of life.

The regional feelings had increased regional interest more than national interest. This was good for the region in the absence of central look out. But regional power carried regional dispute with adjacent states be it border dispute, or water dispute or any other matter. The power circle in Delhi apply its influence keeping in mind its party interest or interest of alliance. The treatment of central government depends upon its stability. Its behaviour is soft if it is weak but it behaves like a dictator if it is strong. This is the actual state of democracy. In the language of humble approach it is the reality of present and how the state and the central political parties have discharging their function in the present Indian democracy. With the rise of economy, the situation might have changed when the people would feel the life in India is better than any other neighbor country.

---

By nature Indians are come and quite. Even in distress condition people rarely comes out in the street to protest against the system of administration. Democracy and judiciary should work side by side. Functions of work under strict discipline bring back People's confidence. Democracy can only function when the state does not get involved in any judicial proceedings. Till to-day people have a faith over judiciary. But the people are rumbling in the functions of the judiciary for the fact that many millions of cases stay looming on the tables of various courts. Unless proper steps are taken, the people's faith is bound to vanish. It is not good to compare judiciary with that of Pakistan. It is because Pakistan is a country of military and democracy is only by name. Naturally judicial proceedings in Pakistan were not free from state interference. India on the other hand is a democratic country, no matter democracy is not correctly implemented or not. In fact, it is the duty of the state that judicial proceedings are free, fair, impartial and peaceful. This has not been happening recently and for any local or foreign observer, it would not be difficult to determine the façade of democracy that being presented to the Western media. The way the government is functioning, the public is gradually losing faith over the government and in hard reality; the situation might have been change for the sake of power. Over a period of time, it would not be unlikely that it would turn out to be a judiciary where corrupt and inefficient people are at the helm of power.

It was a known fact that Democracy was not prevailing in Pakistan or Bangladesh. The power directly or indirectly lies with army and army Chief. Accordingly Judiciary is also manipulated. However the people's cry is always for democracy but practically that could not be materialized yet for political and economic factors mainly. What was about India? India boastingly claims a country of democracy. Indian people's memory is not so dull that they would forget the happenings of 1974. In 1974, Indira Gandhi, the Prime Minister of India of that year, had gagged the press by imposing **a state of emergency** in the country. It had not only crippled India's economy but also destroyed the fabric of democracy. Of course very soon she realized the mistake and she lifted the emergency after looking to the mass protest. Was it not a black spot to Indian democracy?

Such dogmatist and obscurantist attitude has been prevalent in India as well as in the countries of South Asia. One wonders to think that how many generations would require departing before this system comes to an end. Democracy in India as well as in South Asia must also be looked into from a sociological point of view. Democracy was a system that was not known to the people of this Sub-Continent till the British Rule. A society where this system was not prevailing since olden days was seemingly not understood and welcomed by the people easily. It was particularly difficult for the Muslims who were Muslims by faith and believe in Quran. They were the ardent followers of Shariat Law as present in Quran. Law of administration is fixed for them by the law of Islam. The change of administrative law by the rule of democracy is very hard to accept for them. After all we are human beings we are following certain faiths of religion, and it is difficult to accept anything if it not permitted by the law of religion. Probably it was the reason due to which Muslim world is still now non-democratic. Well, opinion was there in, for or against. Thus indirectly religion plays a part in the administration of the country. There is no democracy in the Muslim Middle east but again democracy is also absent in Buddhist State of Sri Lanka. Democratic government means people's government. In Sri Lanka where is peace, there is terrorism and there is political instability. So to say, Terrorism, Tsunami and party politics has made life difficult and the system of democracy has turned into pseudo-democracy. In a poor country like Sri Lanka, the economy of the state always remained down; when the sufferings of the people had increased many folds. Under the painful strain of life, the virtues of religion remained only the source of consolation of life. The life of an individual either in Pakistan, Bangladesh, India, or in Sri Lanka is almost the same, and there was no less in sufferings of the common people. In the event of suffering losing all hopes over the government, the common people looks for help to al-mighty, the only guardian to whom they sacrifice everything for mental peace. So the effect of religion is more in the minds of the people of this region.

In 1974, after lifting emergency, the **freedom of press** got the highest importance in India. And since that time press and the different news channel got their right of freedom to a better extent. According to many intellectuals and sociologists, freedom of press is essential for democracy, because the press ought to act as watch dog for the deeds and misdeeds of the government. It is the press through which people could know what actually is happening behind the doors and simultaneously, press should high light the problem with possible solution. One major duty of the press is also to help the government in planning budgets and policies. But where morality of the people did not respond to function for the well fare of the people, then the man in power could easily buy the people of press. However, keeping in mind the changing international trends in the field of media, there was a change of mind of the people of press of this region. It is believed that the people cannot be barred from the exposure of the truth. Truth could not be hidden for long. Freedom of Press had disclosed the news of Scams after Scams. People could hear at least how the public money was misused by the government which was not known before.

The pluralist and secular society of Europe that we find today was not developed overnight. It required people to people contact for years together. Trade routes were the best opening for people to people contact. Europe's trade started among all the countries of Europe beginning with all known departments from science to commerce. This had opened up worlds of ideas and knowledge for Europeans and all was a result of people to people contact. Great Britain is a small country of few people. But the mind of the people of this small nation is not small but in contrary very wide. Its broad mindedness, bestowed in high morality, and exposed in their tolerant attitude towards foreign nationals, both tourists and residents has made it one of the most rich and dynamic societies in world today. In Indian democracy, the distance between people to people is increasing day by day. Firstly the issue of religion was brought in front, there created the two major groups, next the language, reorganization of states on the basis of language, next the division of states making the same people of the state enemy to each other, thus bitterness, enmity go on increasing day by day by the policy of the government. Where is the scope for ideas of worlds and world of knowledge?

# [17]

**Accountability:**

United States now becomes an ideal state of democracy, the system of accountability is very much there and that become a part of democracy. It was a known fact that at the outbreak of Abu Ghraib scandal, American Defense Secretary Donald Rumsfeld was taken to account by the Senate standing committees. What kind of accountability is maintained by the present government of India is seen by the public in the everyday news media, News by Times of India in particular. Few scams and scandals in the field of politics, finance, corporate and others that ragged the Independent India bring misery and frustration to Indians.

(a) **The Uttar Pradesh food grain Scam: (2003):** Food which the government purchased to give to the poor was instead sold on the open market making a deal of 35,000 crore corruption. In the allegation list the names of powerful person such as Kapil Sibal (now Minister), Mulayam Singh Yadav, Mayawati are found to be present.

(b) **CWG (Commonwealth Games:** It is one of the major political scam in India (2010). The name of Suresh Kalmadi, the former chairman of the organizing committee of the Commonwealth was accused for the scam. It involves number of corrupt deals. The matter is in the sphere of investigation under the cover of politics.

(c) **Adarsh Housing Society, 2002:** The Chief Minister of Maharashtra of that time allotted land to construct a cooperative society in the heart of the Mumbai City for the welfare of serving of the Defense personal and also of retired personals of defense. Instead of defense personal, the flats were allotted to top politicians, bureaucrats, and military officials who took the flats at low cost prices. The top organization like CBI, IT Departments is involved in the scam. Names of powerful personalities like Ashok Chavan, Sushilkumar Shinde and Late Vilasrao Deshmukh, are reported to be involved in the scam.

(d) **Chopper Deal Scam:** As per report, the Chopper deal scam involves Rs 74. 5 crore. The investigation was started a year ago against the Italian firm Finmeccanica which was finally culminated by the arrest of the Italian firm head. The former IAF Chief Air Chief Marshal S. P. Tyagi confessed meeting the middle man. But he declared he is innocent.

(e) **Tatra Vectra Motors Scam, 2010**: The scam involves an amount of Rs 750 crore. In 2010, Bharat Earth Movers Ltd (BEML) in collaboration with Tatra Vectra Motors under took a project of manufacturing over 7000 trucks. It was disclosed by the retired General VK Singh that he was offered a bribe of Rs 14 crore in his office. In exchange he was requested to clear the purchase of 1,676 substandard Tatra BEML trucks. This is how corruption was going on even in Indian defense.

(f) **The coal allocation scam:** (Also called Coalgate scam): It involves the loss of government revenue of Rs 185,591 crore. It is nothing but political scandal where the government's allocation of the nation's coal deposits to public sector entities and private companies between 2004 and 2009 were carried out in an arbitrary manner instead of auctioning it out to the highest bidder. The distribution of 155 coal acres was given to selected companies. The comptroller and Auditor General (CGA) has accused the government of India for distributing 155 coal acres to an arbitrary manner instead of auctioning it.

(g) **2G spectrum scam. (2008):** The Telecom Ministry in 2008 under the supervision of A. Raja sanctioned Licenses to many new Telecom Companies with none or little experience at a price set in the year 2001. This illegal undercharging to various telecom companies of the allocated 2G licenses for cell phone subscriptions paved the way for Scam. The report prepared by the CAG estimates the scam amount to the extent of Rs 176,000 crore while the CBI estimates Rs 30,984 crore. This is how the government is functioning and playing with government exchequer without giving attention to public works.

(h) **Devas Deal:** It involves man of high caliver who are working for the nation with full confidence of the people. They have nothing to do but to express their misery of fate. The former ISRO chairman G Madhavan Nair and three other scientists who had created the deal between the Indian Space Research Organization (ISRO) and commercial arm Antrix Corporation and Devas Multimedia, signing in 2005. The scam involved ISRO leasing the S-band transponders on two satellites, GSAT6 and GSAT6A, for broadcasting purposes to Devas Multimedia. But surprisingly G Madhavan Nair was barred from holding any government jobs since January 2012, until further review. It is shocking to ordinary people.

(i) **Vanishing Companies Scam (1998):** It was a scam of squeezing money of ordinary public. Over 600 companies on the Dalal Street disappeared after raising money from the public. A probe was ordered by P Chidambaram to look into the matter. After public anger, SEBI came into the picture. The probe of SEBI revealed that at least 80 of the companies had raised Rs 330. 78 crore. This is how government and private organization works without any accountability. Here lies the administrative efficiency of Indians. Was it a time right for the Indians to say goodbye to the British. There was lot of lacuna for doing corruption.

(j) **Satyam Scam (2009):** It is again shocking to see a personality like B. Ramalinga Raju, the Chief of Satyam Computers, a knowledgeable person of India, a pride of India, became so greedy to store huge money. It was not doing to his nature but the environment of scam that was prevailing in India without accountability tempted him to go for easy earning. It was one of the biggest scam in Indian corporate history. He manipulated the accounts which he later confessed but it shaken the Indian stock market. Satyam Computers Chief B. Ramalinga Raju manipulated the accounts very cleverly. The scam was due to misrepresentation of the accounts. The scam began with misappropriate books and inflated figures which led to a loss of Rs 8000 crore to company suffered by the Stayam chief.

(k) **Hawala Scam:** It involves an estimated amount of Rs 1000 crore. It is alleged that in the scam Indian politicians were receiving payment through four hawala brokers, the Jain brothers. The arrest of militants in Kashmir in 1991 led to a raid on hawala brokers which revealed evidence of heavy payments. Some India's leading politicians like L K Advani, Sharad Yadav, Madan Lal Khurana, V C Shukla, Balram Jakhar and P Shiv Shankar were alleged to be linked with the scam. Indians have no place, no person to go for faithful consolation.

Besides corruption scam, there is another type of intelligent corruption in the share market befooling the administrator because of their inefficiency in handling the share market. How the investor community could forget the unfortunate Rs 4000 crore of Harshad Mehta scam and over Rs 1000 crore of Ketan Parekh scam. India is a country of saints. Is it the teachings of our saints? It was because Indians do not know how to administer anything with efficiency. Had the British been here such things would never happen. The atmosphere of scam would vanish for ever from India. No body would dare to think of doing such scam. Did anybody hard of such scam in the land of Briton?

Since independence the number of scams and scandals India has witnessed can leave anyone dumbstruck, had the amount of money not involved in the scam, India could have not boosted its economy? As Gandhi rightly said, "There is enough to satisfy every man's need, but not every man's greed".

# [18]

Greek was the place where **the concept of 'democracy'** was originated. According to Greek the meaning of 'demos' is 'the people' and the meaning of kratein (=cracy) is to rule. In total the literary meaning of the two Greek words is "rule by the people". The concept of governance where all the men voted on all issues of governance is called the system of democracy. But there was too many difference with the present idea of democracy as because there was no representative in the Greek system, they directly ruled themselves making each man a life long member of the decision making body and also that was almost a total democracy except for the fact that women and slaves (over 50% of the population) were not considered citizens and were not allowed to vote. In spite of that no other civilization has come to close to Greek democracy in compare to modern democracy. Of course, similar to Geeks, the Romans were also thought of a democracy for the governance of the country. Considering a better system of governance, the Roman Empire (509-27BC) took some of their governmental ideas from Greeks but unlike Greek, their government was a representative Democracy, which had representatives from the nobility in the Senate and representatives from the commoners in the Assembly and Governmental power was divided between these two branches where they voted on various issues. The great Roman Statesman and political philosophers of the time thought of that governmental and political power should come from the people. Keeping that philosophy in mind it had started a new system of governance in the trend of democracy. The record of history indicated that the middle age, had invented many democratic ideas. These were evolved at that time, among that the religion of

Christianity had an influence over the society, which taught that men are equal in the eyes of God and that the idea of equality of men had set the democratic idea of equality in the minds of the people. By the time it had developed another system of governance called feudalism where it stressed that all people have certain rights and there developed a system of courts to defend these rights. The system of functioning of courts gave the idea of forming the judicial branch of American government along with many of the ideas such as Kings Councils, assemblies and parliamentary systems of governance. The function of democracy started in England in 1215AD where the Magna Charta opened the door to a more democratic system in England. In the process of democracy the Nobles forced King John to sign the 'Great Charter' that had created the English 'Parliament' or law making body where the written laws held a higher power than the king. The introduction of the new system had brought restriction to certain extent to Royal power where the laws had actually limited the power of the Royal family and simultaneously had given some of that power to the people, the Petition of Right stipulated that the King could no longer tax without parliament's permission and the Bill of Rights provided freedom of speech and banned the system of cruel or unusual punishment. Thus by the new system, Parliament was strengthened further and people got more right to express themselves. These progressive ideas of democracy were incorporated later in the government of the United States. The change of government became possible without bloodshed. Some one defined democracy in contrast to dictatorship or tyranny was an opportunity open to the people to control their leaders and to oust them without the need for a revolution. Democracy, the rule of people became open to public where the people were at liberty to choose one of the two ways of thinking of democracy, whereby one way of democracy was the Direct Democracy in which the eligible citizens might be chosen direct by people's vote who were to take active part in the decision making body of the government and the other was the Representative Democracy where political parties excised indirectly through elected representatives to form the government. The importance was the system of functioning of the governance and not the definition of democracy as such without giving the definition of true democracy, the equality, freedom and rule of law have been identified as the important characteristics of democracy since ancient times. It was better to explain in a representative democracy, every vote has equal weight; no unreasonable restrictions could apply to anyone seeking to become a representative. The freedom of eligibility of its citizens was secured by legitimized rights and liberties which were typically protected by a constitution of the nation. In the United Kingdom, the dominant principle was that of parliamentary sovereignty unlike the United States keeping independency of the judiciary. It was necessary for the neutral functioning of the democracy. Majority Rule was counted as a characteristic of democracy. Did the democracy allow the political minorities to be oppressed by the tyranny of the majority? The basic right such as freedom of political expression, freedom of speech and freedom of press were considered to be the basic criteria that being allowed to all eligible citizens. It was further suggested that a basic feature of democracy lied in its capacity of all voters to participate freely and fully in the formation of its government, who was to look to the life of their society. The emphasis directed to create a social contract with the collective Will of all voters. Thus democracy could be characterized as a form of collectivism because it was defined as a kind of government in which all eligible citizens have equal right to cast vote in the decision of making government that would affected their lives. Europe was in the threshold of democracy and the concept of democracy continued to be prevalent in Europe with the philosophies of an English man John Locke and a French philosopher named Jean Jacques Rousseau. They stated and explained the idea of governance under 'social contract' where the government's job was to protect 'natural rights' which included "the right to life, liberty, and the ownership of property." The philosopher Rousseau added a little more by saying that people should have input on how their government had run. However, such kind of School of thought had paved the way for modern day of American Democracy. In the Land of French the spirit of democracy had turn the atmosphere into a volatile movement and finally that spirit had transformed into a revolution by the turn of the century. Ultimately the French Revolution (1789-99) violently transformed the system of governance of the French from a monarchical state to social hierarchy. Actually the Bastille was built as a castle to protect the King and Royal family of French from the attack of England, but in the course of time it had turned into a state prison, one of the best prisons for upper class person, to be defined at, because of the standard of the facilities for the wealthy. In spite of its functioning as having being a state prison, the Bastille had retained the other traditional functions of a royal castle, and was used to accommodate visiting dignitaries. By the revolutionary turmoil, the absolute monarchy that had ruled French for centuries collapsed within three years. Thereby, French society underwent an epic transformation. Having suffered an acute economic crisis, the common people of France were very much angered by the incompetency of King Louis XVI and the King's limitless aristocracy. The accumulated anger of the mass had turned into an outburst of spirit of unknown strength and thus the Revolution began with the assault on the Bastille, and then an epic march on Versailles with the Rights of Man and Citizen. Finally a republic was proclaimed in September 1792 and King Louis was executed the next year. The causes of crisis was not one but many more and there was considerable controversy over the causes of the Revolution. According to a Marxist fellow material factors were responsible for revolution, such as the rise of population in the face of the shortage of food supply, the shortage of cultivable land due to multiple division of land area transforming it into small parcels. On the other hand many emphasized on the growing discrepancy between reality and the legally defining social structure where a men was distinguished by hereditary or acquired rank but again many believed over expenditure of exchequer in the American independence struggle was the vital reason out of many. At last France was transformed into a democratic republic in which the President was the head of state and the Prime Minister was the head of government where Legislative power was vested to Senate and National Assembly preserving multiparty system. The judiciary was being kept as independent of the executive and the legislature. The volatile situation did not ended so soon. It continued for the period of 1793-1795 when a reign of terror had continued having succumbed to the death of 16,000 to 40,000 people. The administration could not remain in control of the situation. It was only in 1799 by the emergence of the Consulate the great Neapolian Bonaparte, the situation came under control. The emergence of the United States of America was the out come of American Revolution, as one of the most remarkable Revolution in the modern event in the history of democracy. Thomas Jefferson, along with the Declaration of Independence in 1776, had produced a written document of declaration containing many ideas and ideals that were taken from the ideas of above mentioned philosophers, Locke and Rousseau. Jefferson borrowed the idea and ideals that all men are equal, all men have the right to life, liberty and property but he altered the right to life, liberty and property to "the right to life, liberty and the pursuit of happiness." His declaration also followed with the idea such as that all men should have the right to take up arms against the government if it did not respect these rights. In the French Revolution all these idea and ideals had emerged because of the matured thoughts of the great philosophers like Montesquieu, Voltaire, and Rousseau. They insisted and instigated that freedom would come only after the legislative, judicial and executive branches of the government were being separated. The people of France overthrew the King and had established the right through the "Declaration of the Rights of Man," which later changed to Locke's right to life, liberty and property to the right to "liberty, property, security, and resistance to oppression (Rousseau)." The powers of the King were being limited by the system of democracy, where the people have gained the right to express their demand to the government. After the French Revolution, the Rule of democracy began to spread all over to replace the Rule of monarchy. This had initiated a new movement all over the world, revolutions started against monarchies, to set up democratic government. Under the prevailing situation, before the end of the 19th century, almost all of the Western Europe had restricted the power of Kings and had given some power to the people in the constitution of governance. With the growing success of democracy in French and particularly in the United States, the people all over the world particularly in Europe became eager to bring democracy. Any newly formed independent country opted for democratic governance like that of United States as the United States became a model nation for the principles of democracy. The sequence of events that had led French Revolution was sparked by France's effective bankruptcy due to the enormous cost of wars for being helping the America to fight against the British Force for Independence of America. The cost was due to the challenging of British naval and commercial power in the Seven Years' War along with the loss of France's colonial possessions in continental North America and the destruction of the French Navy. However, subsequently French forces were rebuilt and joined the American Revolutionary War with success but at the cost of massive exchequer. The Public anger was due to France's inefficient handling of financial system that had made unable to finance the debt compelling the imposition of in equitable system of taxation. In the situation of economic crisis, the King called an Assembly of Notables in 1787. The people suffered a lot for the existing financial scarcity. Royal court at Versailles remained indifferent to the causes of hardship of the lower classes. In the atmosphere of strong protest from opposition, King Louis XVI, absolute monarch of French had preferred to remain in silence. Opponents in the parliament successfully thwarted King's attempts at enacting any reforms and few of those who were opposed to Louis policies further defamed the royal authority by circulating pamphlets with false information in the attempt to stirring up public opinion against the monarchy. Thus they were successful to bring resentment in the public mind. The anger spread with varied resentment, resentment of royal absolutism, resentment by peasants, laborers and the bourgeoisie toward the traditional seigniorial privileges possessed by the nobility, further the resentment was aggravated on seeing the Catholic Church's influence over public policy and institutions. People were shocked with the firing of finance Minister by King when people showed their anger against the King for firing the finance Minister, Jacques Necker, who was popularly seen as representatives of the people. Actually, Louis XVI ascended to the throne amidst a financial crisis, when the state was nearing bankruptcy and the state was in financial obligation stemming from enrolment in the American Revolutionary War. According to Finance Minister Necker, who argued that the country could not be taxed higher and that tax exemption for the nobility and clergy must be reduced. In the face of volatile situation, the King announced the calling of the Estates-General for May 1789, the first time the body had been summoned since 1614. The weakness of the King exposed and people demands got the priority. In the mean time, Necker had earned the enmity of many members of the French court for his open manipulation of public money. On the other hand the members of the royal family, Marie Antoinette, the King's younger brother the Comte d'Artois, and other conservative members of the King's Privy Council urged him to dismiss Necker as financial adviser. On 11 July 1789, in order to get public favour when, Necker published an inaccurate account of the government's debts and made it public, the King lost his temper and fired upon him and completely restructured the finance ministry. That had started the rebellion. Immediately after that, the Assembly, meeting at Versailles, went into nonstop session to prevent escalation of rebellion. Soon the activity of Revolution was started in Paris; very soon it had taken a different turn and riots, chaos, and widespread looting spread to the City. The French Guard, who was armed and trained soldiers, sided with the mobs. On 14 July, the insurgents went to capture the large weapons and ammunition cache inside the Bastille fortress in secret; these weapons were preserved for the safety of the royal family, which carried the symbol of royal power. Very soon the situation went out of order. At last after several hours of combat, the prison lost its control. The mob finally returned to Hotel de Ville (City hall), accused the mayor Jacques de Fleshless of treachery and butchered him without mercy. The king, alarmed by the violence, backed down. The king visited Paris, after three days on 17th July where he accepted a tricolored cockade (Long live the Nation and Long live the King). With the break down of administration, the random acts of violence and theft broke out across the country. Fearing the safety of life, members of the royal family, had fled to neighboring countries. The news of futile attempt of counter-revolution with the military support of foreign monarchs, public resented with the outburst of anger. By late July, the spirit of popular sovereignty had spread thought-out French. The spirit of revolution spread from city to rural areas, militant groups were trained with arms to fight against foreign invasion. More over wild rumors caused widespread unrest and civil disturbances that contributed to the collapse of law and order. On 4 August 1789, a new decision was taken, the National Constituent Assembly abolished feudalism and hence forth, nobles, clergy, towns, provinces, companies and cities lost their special privileges. On 26 August 1789, Assembly again published a declaration, the "Declaration of the Rights of Man and of the Citizen", a statement of principles. The unrest had continued national cockade had been trampled upon, a large crow of women marched to the Hotel de Ville (City hall), demanding that the city officials must address their concerns. They vehemently announced that they were the actual victims of economic situations causing shortages of bread. In addition, they demanded an end to royal efforts to block the National Assembly, and ask the King and his administration to move to Paris as a good faith in addressing the widespread poverty. Finding no reasonable answers from the city officials, a large contingent of women exceeding 7000 marched to Versailles, carrying with them cannons and a variety of smaller weapons. Twenty thousand National Guardsmen under the command of La Fayette, who were posted there to keep order failed to maintain the order of peace. Without losing time, the mob stormed the palaces, killing several guards. At last finding no other alternative, King acceded to the demand of the crowd and the monarchy was relocated to Paris. There had occurred change of power; the Revolution caused a massive shift of power from the Roman Catholic Church to the state, although the people had a good respect and honor for the clergy people from the time of Christianity. It had happened earlier that taking the advantage of the goodwill of the people, the Clergy people of Church acquired land from the public from time on ward. By the time the Church had become the largest single landowner in the country, acquiring about 10% of the land in the kingdom. On good will gesture from time immoral the Church had been exempted from paying taxes to the government, where only a fraction of the income of the Church were redistributed to the poor in the name of society works. The power and wealth of the Church was highly resented by the people in general during the time of economic scarcity. With the rise of resentment toward the Church, the National Assembly was compelled to enact economic reform curtailing the Church's authority to impose tax. A major decision was taken on 2 November 1789. According to that decision the property of the Church was declared as the property of the nation and the property was kept at the disposal of the nation henceforth. Monks and nuns were asked to change their activity of life. As a result large number of monks and nuns were encouraged to return to private life. The clergy men were asked to be the employees of the state. In nut shell the state authority had denied the authority of the Pope in Rome over the French Church. Many devoted person refused to accept the change. For the cause of wide spread refusal, the new government had compelled to bring legislation against the clergy people, "forcing them into exile, deporting them forcibly, or executing them as traitors." There actually occurred a fight of bitterness between common men and Clergy people and there created a volatile atmosphere. During that period a Reign of Terror continued in French. Extreme efforts of de-Christianization had ensued, including the imprisonment and massacre of priests and destruction of churches and religious images throughout French. To bring the volatile situation of French under control, the new government decided to celebrate the victory of revolution. 14 July 1790, was celebrated as the anniversary of the fall of Bastille. There also had required an over all change of military set up. In late 1790, the French army was in considerable disarray as the earlier military officers were largely composed of noblemen, but the new military soldiers were recruited from the lower classes. There was a conflict of the ego of status where the conflict of aristocracy disturbed the force in general. The process of democracy advanced a step further and in 1792, the monarchy was abolished and the country French was declared a 'Republic'. In the change of the turmoil of monarchy, the other members of royal family tried to take the military assistance from the other Kings of European state to revenge against the revolution. Suspecting the King Louis XVI conspiring with the enemies of French, the Assembly without losing further time passed a resolution on 17th January 1793 to execute death sentence against the King, who conspired against the public liberty and general safety and that was executed on 21st January 1793. But the things did not settle so easily. The new regime had to meet opposition from the royalist. The army tried its best to suppressed riots and counter-revolutionary activities. Finally the army and its successful general Napoleon Bonaparte had gained control of total power. By the turn of the events the Modern American democracy became a democratic republic or a representative democracy. The colonists of the United States were included in the republic in order to have a fair system as the colonists of the United States were being tired of taxation. The system was improved so that the people had more say in the rule of the country. In order to avoiding power to inefficient ordinary people, the Athenian form of democracy was avoided, as they feared it might have given the people too much power and that would lend the control of the government to the uneducated masses. The system was a representative democracy which involves elected representative rather than direct. It was a system of government to rule by the people. As the representatives were elected by the voters of the constituents, they would better represent their constituents. The US government was divided into three branches to keep corruption in check. These three branches were the Executive, Legislative, and Judicial branches where no one branch contains absolute power. A system of checks and balances were incorporated in the system of democracy to protect the principles of democracy so that the government was turned to be a people's government.

# [19]

## Indian Economy:

The historic record shows that the Indus Valley civilization (2800 BC-1800BC) had the evidence of well-planned streets, drainage system and the system of water supply. All these reveal that the citizens had the knowledge of 'urban planning' and urban sanitation. Maritime trade was in operation where South India traded with Southeast and West Asian countries from early times until the fourteenth century A D. making Malabar and Coromandel Coasts as the important trading centers. However very soon it was ended when the area was taken over by the local Parsi, Jewish and Muslim communities. However, by the end of eighteenth century, the British East India Company established its dominance over Indian political scene by defeating the other European powers. Thereafter there occurred a determinative shift in India's trade. Calcutta became the economic hub of British India and increasing industrial activity was seen during World WarII when the economy was reduced almost to zero during war time. Decrease in production of food crops led to numerous famines. The economic condition was one of the reason for which the British was willing to give up the rule of British India to the hands of Indians. But very soon industrial know how was started in the United Kingdom that had brought the industrial revolution by making a significant growth in production and trade in England and very soon the technology spread to Europe. India was unlucky in two fronts in getting its independence firstly it was deprived from knowing the industrial know how and secondly the administrative efficiency. However, at the end of British Rule, India inherited an economy that was present in the poorest of poor country, with no project of industrial development, no incentive scheme in agriculture to feed a rapidly growing population, a largely illiterate and unskilled labour force and without any an accountable infrastructure. The rate of growth of the Indian economy in the first three decades after independence was miserable. There was famine after famine, people are dying without food. This was the condition of India after independence. Since 1965, it was suddenly high lighted in India and abroad that there was miraculous achievement in India in the agriculture sector and proclaimed as success as "Green Revolution in India" where the use of high-yielding varieties of seeds increased production by the addition of fertilizers. It was nothing but the chance of outbreak of another famine was stopped but truly the economic condition of India was bad to worse.

**Green Revolution:** India is a large country with vast area of agricultural land but yet the food production was insufficient to feed all its citizens. This was because the well irrigated and permanent irrigated area was only 17% in 1951. The major part of area was dependent on rainfall and, consequently, agriculture suffered from low level of production. Thus attempts have been made to irrigate the land by the use of river water instead of depending on rain water. The record of history estimates that famines in India were very frequent during the period 1940s to 1970s. It was due to the faulty distribution of food product, where farmers did not receive the true value of their labour-activity injected for the production of food, while again the majority of the population also did not get enough food. All that was occurring due to hoarding and corruption remained unseen. The result was miserable. People becoming a victim of malnutrition and starvation having being born in a land of saints, a land being of covered with hills, sea, rivers and minerals. Government had no incentive to give loan to farmers to encourage production as the officials were lacking in management and the government lacking in future planning in the multitude of area of the vast country like India with vast population and with ever rising population. The small and marginal farmers found it very difficult to get finance from the government or loan at cheap rate from the banks. Consequently the farmers became an easy prey to the money lenders. This was India after

Independence and the achievements of our Indian leaders what they committed to the Indians at the time of independence, a happy Ram Rajya (a happy land in ancient history of India where people lived in happiness under the kingdom of Ram). Keeping the trend of traditional agricultural practices of low productivity, the government had no alternative but to import food grain from other country to feed the growing population and thereby drained away the scarce foreign reserves. The world's worst recorded food disaster occurred in 1943 in British-ruled India which is known as the Bengal Famine, where an estimated 4 million people died of hunger that year in eastern India (which included today's Bangladesh), the Bengal, the cherish land of East India company, the Land where the British stalwart Clive established the British footing and finally created Calcutta, the Land of the second City after London of the British Empire. When the British left India in 1947, India could not forget the memories of the Bengal Famine. It was therefore food security was one of the main items kept alive in free India's agenda. This awareness led, India to haunt for food and the result was the "Green Revolution" in India. The period continued from 1968 to 1978 and that had changed India's status from a food-deficient country to one of the world's leading agricultural nations. But the ever growing population at a much faster rate than food production could not show the spectacular economic growth in India but only it had stopped the repetition of feminine in India. The economy of the country went down to down reducing near to zero foreign currency. The thinking of 'Green Revolution' was an accidental phenomenon due to the effort of few individuals out of the complete purview of the government, a dream of greater production with high yielded seed, created a hope of running the government few more years with false assurance of better life in future. Government was happy with party power and urban population who were the spoke persons to say anything against the government, their mismanagement, and corruption. The use of high-yielding varieties of seeds, the use of chemical fertilizers and the utility of a regular irrigation collectively provided the opportunity to increase in crop production needed to make India self-sufficient in food grains, making a system of improving agriculture in India calling it a revolution to feed millions of hungry people of India and rightly called it 'the Green Revolution' as it happened in the green field with the growth of green plants of crop. Since 1968, the experiment in the field of agriculture using high-yielding wheat was continuing, the name of Norman Borlaug, M. S. Swaminthan is worth mentioning. The joy of greater production by the use of high yielding seeds, regular irrigation, chemical pesticides brought a enthusiasm among farmers, who were deprived from the facilities of education, electricity and even drinking water so to say the minimum requirements of living a life, who had found an opportunity for better living by earning more by the greater production of crops and that had resulted a revolutionary progress in food production in India making India self-sufficient in food and saved the millions of hungry from dying. In the matter of Green Revolution, there was series of research, development and technology transfer. The credit goes to particular few genus, Mr. Norman Borlaug was the one who may be called the "Father of the Green Revolution" as he was the person who might be credited with saving over a billion people from starvation, that involved the development of high-yielding cereal seed grains, modernization of irrigation infrastructure, hybridized seeds, synthetic fertilizers and pesticides to farmers. However, the term "Green Revolution" was first used in 1968 by the former United States Agency for International Development (USAID) under the guidance of William Gaud, for carrying out successful research works initiated the spread of new technology to other country. Norman Borlaug began his research work in Mexico in 1943. The year 1961 was the crisis year of India, there was no food in India to feed the hungry billions of people; India was on the brink of mass famine. M S Swaminathan, the Indian Minister of agriculture invited Mr. Borlaug to India who landed in India over riding all bureaucratic hurdles imposed by India's grain monopolies. Punjab was selected as the first site of experiment to try the new crops because of its reliable water supply and a history of agricultural success. That was the successful beginning. India began its journey of Green Revolution in the program of plant breeding, irrigation development and financing of agrochemicals through the excited army of rural farmers. Research work continued. India soon adopted a rice variety (IR8 variety) developed by the International Rice Research Institute (IRRI) that could produce more rice per plant. In 1968, Indian agronomist S. K. Datta enhanced the IR8 variety a step further whereby the yield of rice increased 5 tons per hectare with no fertilizer and almost 10 tons per hectare under optimal conditions, the meaning of which was that the production of rice becomes greater by 10 times the yield of traditional rice. The success of this variety of rice was spread throughout Asia making India in the forefront in bringing the "Green Revolution". In the year 1960, rice yields in India were about two tons per hectare, but it had risen to six tons per hectare in the later years making India one of the world's most successful rice producer countries. At last the government found the necessity to encourage the farmers to increase their production and had given them an opportunity to a greater portion of their products for sale in the market. The new incentive in agriculture had increased the yield of rice and wheat and this made the country in attaining food self-sufficiency. New varieties of wheat and other grains were instrumental to the green revolution. Looking to the development in the research activity for higher production of crops in India calling it a "Green Revolution", the other developing country were encouraged to follow the similar path to get a sign of relief. It was because every country has its ever rising population in spite of maintaining a skeleton of family planning; the government needs food to feed them. More over, it was the Asia or the African countries where there was no development or less development in spite of their huge minerals because of lacking in scientific knowledge, lacking in skill of technology, lacking in innovation, came forward to get something positive from another developing friendly country being suffering with the same phenomena of feeding the hungry mouth. In the year 1960, the Government of the Republic of the Philippines with Ford and Rockefeller Foundations established IRRI (International Rice Research Institute) making coordination with India to look for research activity for greater production. They came with success in breeding production and became a new cultivar, showing a success in the annual rice production where the crops yield increased from 3. 7 to 7. 7 million tons in two decades making the country a rice exporter for the first time in the 20th century. But there was negative effect too, good number of fish and frog species died by the environmental change due to heavy use of pesticide. Similarly attempts were made under new project in Africa using the breeding concept of Mexican and Indian but the project culminated with performance of less success. The reasons might be environmental factors, such as the non-availability of water for irrigation, the high diversity in slope of the land area besides other factor of corruption or lack of infrastructure.

But the then government of India could not utilize this euphoria of greater production for a better economic growth. The other sectors of agriculture such as farming etc . . . . as is done in Australia could not be materialized probably because of administrative inefficiency, planning adequacy and other factors.

1. By the time government was perturbed by the negative effects of the high use of chemical pesticides and fertilizers on the soil. The revolution tempted the farmers to use the land for two or three crop by rotation every year. Very soon, the farmers faced with the problem of production of lowering yield. The quality of land had gone down and yield suffered. The reasons might be many, due to heavy chemical fertilizer inputs, land has changed its character, the soft land become hard and carbon content had gone down, that had made a loss in the quality of land for better production. Excess use of fertilizers might have made the soil infertile.

2. Pest which is used for better production is suppose to be control by bio degradable methods was not materialized, the reason might be the abundant use of Pest in large quantity, the result was negative as the pest become resistant to many pesticides and at last the chemical pesticides became non effective. More over the growth of weeds lowered the production. Not only that heavy use of chemical pesticides, insecticides and fertilizers, has killed many birds and friendly insects and thereby the yield suffered an indirect loss. Anything carried out against nature, results in a negative effect. The large scale use of chemicals might be a future threat to Indians too. These chemicals which are used in farms go down along with rain water and likely to contaminate the ground water which might affects the health of present and future generation of the human being living in the region.

3. The fact is now clear, the techniques of Green Revolution heavily depends upon chemical fertilizers, pesticides and herbicides, some of which were developed from fossil fuels. Thus agriculture was getting reliant day by day on petroleum products. The theory of Malthusian catastrophe predicts that a future decline in oil and gas production would lead to a decline in food production.

The people of Punjab were not only a stalwart in army for the protection of the country but also a saver of the country. The Indian state of Punjab pioneered green revolution. It transformed India into a food-surplus country. It had used high yielded seed crops along with chemicals and pesticides. Again the state had witnessed serious consequences of intensive farming using chemicals and pesticide making the people victim of cancer. A comprehensive study was conducted by Post Graduate Institute of Medical Education and Research (PGIMER)and that had underlined the direct relationship between indiscriminate use of these chemicals and increased incidence of cancer in this region. An increase in the number of cancer cases had been reported in several villages in Punjab. Every good works followed with negative footings as like happiness followed with sorrow in a cycle of life.

# [20]

Australia is a country of agriculture including beef cows and calves in planty for the growth of economy. It produces plenty of agricultural products and exported plenty of products at the same time to keep its economy strong and sound. It earns about $155 billion a year making a share of 12% GDP. It has plenty of farms and farm lands covering about 61% of Australia's land mass. The government has classified the land area based on the rainfall and they utilized the area for better output. The zone of Tasmania (a high rainfall zone) along with the narrow coastal zone is used principally for dairying and beef production, the pastoral zone (a low rainfall zone) is less fertile and here large scale pastoral activities involving the grazing of beef, cattle and sheep are carried out for the production of mutton and wool. South Australia is in the process of viable land for agriculture. Thus each and every parts of land are utilizing for a better production of agriculture in a most scientific and discipline system. Subsidiary industry out of agro-product such as Cattle and calves, Wheat, Milk, Fruits & Nuts, Vegetables, Wool, Poultry, Lambs, Sugarcane etc. were produced, exported and also consumed domestically and not to talk of Cereals and Oilseeds besides the huge output out of industries of Lamb, Sheep and Pigs. To keep the economy sound and stable, constant care and nourishment of the agricultural land is a necessity. It is seen since 1984 there was a decrease in the agro-product in Australia and that had made an effect in the decline in total employment in the agricultural sector making thousands unemployed. The major issues facing agriculture in Australia are also to some extent like that of India which is drought for the cause of bad weather, short of water, and low soil fertility. Overcoming all the obstacles under the efficient administration of the government of Australia, the agricultural industry is made as one of the most trade-exposed sectors of the Australian economy. In Australia there are areas which are the land mass of large deserts. There are areas which are facing with irregular rainfall. But for the development of agriculture, irrigation is necessary. They have estimated the requirement of water in every sector, water in agriculture, water in dairy farming, water in pasture industry, water in cotton, and sugar industry and accordingly the administration had generated water and utilized water for sustaining the every sector of agriculture.

India is fortunate enough for the existence of many rivers and less of desert areas but yet, the administration could not utilize the natural wealth for development of agriculture and agro-industry. The euphoria of 'Green Revolution' died down with the emergence of negative effect. There was no development of the subsidiary industry in relation to 'Green Revolution' to sustain the economy. On the other hand India remained limited with the production of rice and wheat only. The vast additional sectors such as grazing of beef, cattle and ship and the subsequent industry out of these were not looked into. Very soon India came back to the category of poor country. Where is the efficiency of administration, will it not remind the Indians, efficient administration is a prime necessity to run a country for the betterment of the people. Will it not justify the fact that India, a country that had remained in dark under the shadow of teachings of religion in the control of body and mind discarding the economic growth for thousands of years, should wait to learn from the British the art of 'the Rule of Nation' for a while before asking for independence.

# [21]

**Rising Japan:** While at the same time Japan, a country that was totally destroyed by the dropping of Atom bomb, regained its economy. After having a debacle in 1945 by the destruction of atom bomb, where Japan had faced with 3 million war dead and the loss of a quarter of the national wealth, how did Japan become the second largest economy in the world by 1980 is a glorious guide to under developed nations and India in particular. The economic miracle was due to the atmosphere of Cold War that existed between the two super powers US & Russia after the World War II. After World War II, the United States thought it wise to rebuild Japan in order to slow the expansion of Soviet influence in the Pacific. The United States was concerned with the growth of the economy of the Japan because an unhappy and poor Japan was not sustainable for improving the relation with Japan and to make Japanese happy. The inner fear prevailed for the undisclosed fact was that an unhappy and poor Japan might have turn to communism and if that did truly happen, the Soviet Union would get easy control over the vast Pacific. The economic development of Japan as such was a headache for the United States to keep the region under control. The economic miracle was spurred mainly by adapting a Japanese economic policy through the Ministry of International Trade and Industry (MITI).

The late 1940, Japan was threatened with economic ruin by wartime expenses, and in Post-World War Japan was dipped in inflation, unemployment and shortages in all areas. Under the then circumstances Japan could not stand on its own. The United States, under the auspices of the Supreme Commander of the Allied Powers

(SCAP) came forward and played a crucial role in Japan's initial economic recovery. It was believed that economic development would democratize Japan and that would make the people happy, when the happy people would never wish to choose the path of reemergence of militarism, and foreclose communism. With the approach of military hostilities in the Korean peninsula, United States further inclined with Japan, but fortunately in 1950 Japanese economy boosted a sharp rise because of the U. S. governmental monetary help, a large sum of money as a "special procurement" package which amounted to rise 27% of Japan's total export trade.

The period 1937-1940, was the period of war years, Japanese economy showed rapid development. The production indices showed highest increase in machinery (252%). There was a vast expansion in automobile industry. Out of 11 major auto manufacturers, 10 came out during war years and one the Honda came out in post war period. Three of the ten, Toyota, Nissan and Isuzu manufactured trucks for the military when the other foreign company Ford and General Motors were driven out of Japanese market by legislation. During the period of Cold War, the government of United States allowed Japan to export trucks to US to enhance Japanese trade. After 1945, Article 9 of the Japanese constitution forbids Japan from rearmament and Japan had to live under the umbrella of U. S. military protection. That stimulates the Japanese to concentrate on non military products and mainly of electronic products, products like Camera & Photo-industry so as to carry out economic expansion. They are confident of their performance as they were being superior to all other Asian and European whites. Since 1950 Japan's economy progressed at high speed leading the country to attain a comfortable height. The SCAP completed its function and departed but the Japanese economy remained strong and sound. By the late 1960, economic miracle had happened when Japan had risen from the ashes of World War II to achieve an astoundingly rapid and complete economic recovery by stimulating private sector growth. P M of Japan sort out a policy of understanding between the Bank of Japan and the City banks whereby industrial conglomerates get loans at ease to pursue a policy of industrialization. President Johnson hails the Japanese Prime Minister Havato Ikeda as a man of miracle and calls "the single most important individual architect of the Japanese economic miracle," who pursued a policy of heavy industrialization. The country's laws also led to the reemergence of conglomerate groups called "Keiretsu" who efficiently allocated resources and became competitive internationally. Keiretsu went ahead toward strategic industries such as shipbuilding, electric power, coal and steel production locking out foreign companies from Japanese industries. Keiretsu also devised a policy of long term stock dividends for economic growth. The rapid economic growth of "Golden Sixties" paved the way for second decade to enhance the Japanese economic miracle. In 1965, Japan's GDP was about $91 billion, in 1980 it raised to $1. 065 trillion. P. M. Ikeda had undertaken an ambitious plan "income-doubling plan". To materialize the plan he lowered interest rates and taxes to private players to motivate spending when government rapidly opened the scope for investment in Japan's infrastructure, such as in building, highways, high-speed railways, subways, airports, port facilities and dams. Each of these acts continued the Japanese economy to set up an economic model. Having his success in infrastructure he pushed his government towards trade liberalization. Ikeda integrated Japan's economy globally by joining the GATT (1963), IMF & OECD (1964). The time Ikeda left office, the rate of GNP was 13. 9%. Japanese Prime Minister was a man of exception. In India we could not come out with such a man of miracle.

# [22]

**India after 1970:** Here lies the difference of planning and administrative efficiency. In the period of seventh to eighth, India's economy and political system encountered a severe crisis at the time of Indira Gandhi and her Congress Party rule. At that time there was no economic progress as Gandhi and her Congress Party paid more attention to how to remain in power rather than solving India's economic and social problems. The year, 1975, was a year of political chaos, year of emergency in the country. During this time, economic growth stagnated and widespread corruption became the norm. By the collapse of the Soviet Union and the Gulf War in the period of early 1990, India's economy began to worsen and economy was faced with high inflation, and unemployment. The country reached to the rim of poverty with the lowest foreign exchange reserve. The collapse of the Soviet Union significantly affected Indian's economy as because the Soviets were the India's major trading partner in the supply oil at low cost. The cost of oil is also compensated to some extent by the revenue earned by the Indians working in the Middle East but the Gulf War sent thousands of Indian workers back home resulting a huge loss in India's foreign reserve. The government was left with no other alternative but to change its closed-door economic policies in 1991. The present economic growth of India is nothing but an accidental growth. To sustain the growth it requires all round cooperation irrespective of the difference of political ideology but of course of corruption free.

As of 2010, India imported about 70% of its crude oil requirements. There are places of Oil and Natural gas fields which are located offshore at Mumbai High, Krishna Godavari Basin and at Cauvery Delta, and onshore mainly in the states of Assam, Gujarat and Rajasthan. India imported $82. 1 billion worth of oil in the first three quarters of 2010. Definitely it had an adverse effect on its current account deficit. There are plenty of places in India where exploration for oil could be continued. The geographical position of India indicates there might be oil in the West as well as in the East. Middle East countries are floating on oil which is situated on the West bank of Arabian Sea, while India is lying on the East bank, possibility of oil is there. On the East small islands of Malaysia and Singapore have high quality oil, there is likely hood of oil in Andaman and Nicobore island of India too. Exploration works, indicated the presence of oil and gas in many areas like Barmer, Jaisalmer and the Bikaner basin of Thar Desert. It is time to proceed to extract oil and save huge oil expenditure to save the country from economic downfall. It not only the foreign expertise but the Indian youths trained in expertise must be engaged in the field works who would never hesitate to devote the full energy for the country's best of the economy. Oil exploration with earnest endeavor will explore the India's hidden treasure. India has spent thousands of years in the study of body and mind but not the material without which there is no growth of economy. A country without the strength of economy has no power to raise voice in any affairs. Religion has given us many virtues, the virtues of tolerance, discipline, ideals of regular life but all these virtues could not diminishes our urge for a better prosperous life. That is why Indians are going after money through the secrets of corruption.

Corruption is the biggest problem in the path of progress for India. The Right to Information have considerably reduced corruption and opened up avenues to redress grievances. A cumbersome bureaucracy siphons off spending budgets and a little is reached to the intending recipients. This is the character of our powerful Indians what we had inherited from our ancestors where they devoted their life in the teachings of religion in the control of body and mind. But the visual fact is that an Indian living in abroad never wishes or rarely wishes to do any such mischief or say a lie in any eventuality. This indicates fault not lies with the human nature but it lies with administration. So today Indians must repent that Indians achieved independence too early before learning and getting the secrets of skill in the system of administration.

There are reports given by Swiss Bankers Association suggesting that India topped the world wide list for black money with almost $1,456 billion stashed in Swiss banks. The amount is quite a substantial amount rightly 13 times the country's total external debt. Indian government can not remain silent without taking adequate measure although the authenticity is in question. Apart from investigation we have to think of our moral degradation and it requires through research to find out the reasons. Qatar's oil and natural gas wealth is now visible in Doha, making Qatar the economic center. It was the success of Sheikh Hamad bin Khalifa, who did not allow the officials to siphon money and send to Swiss bank as that is alleged in India. The city Doha is developing very rapidly and it is the sincere attempt of the Qatari government to diversify the Qatari economy in order to move away from the dependence on oil.

After liberalization Textile manufacturing industry became the $2^{nd}$ largest source of employment after agriculture. It provided employment to over 20 million people. Information technology and business process outsourcing become the fastest growing sectors in India to earn foreign exchange for India. The growth in the IT sector is attributed to the talented youths of India, who had showed their ability in specialization, skill and capacity in adapting speaking in English with fluency. The foreign consumers are utilizing a large pool of low cost, highly skilled educated Indian workers to outsource their operations. It is remarkable to note that Indian IT industry has increased the country's GDP from 4. 8% in 2005-06 to 7% in 2008. It is also significant that in 2009, seven Indian firms were listed among the top 15 technology categorize as outsourcing companies of the world.

Now the economy of India is the tenth-largest in the world by nominal GDP. And again it is the third-largest economy by purchasing power parity (PPP). It is now one of the G-20 major economies and a member of BRICS. At present India is the $19^{th}$-largest exporter and $10^{th}$-largest importer in the world. India's economic growth is not stable because

India's GDP grew by an astounding 9. 3% in 2010-11 has slowed down to around 5. 0% for the 2012-13 for various reasons where domestic politics and huge corruption in many sectors are the factors to be counted.

The Indian economy for the period 1947-1991 was based on mixed economy which involves the combining features of capitalism and socialism. It failed to expand the post-war trade. Inefficient administration under the few Indian Officials during independence-era had brought corruption and total breakdown of the system. The disciplined administration that prevailed under British was totally destroyed and most of the officials who were entrusted with duty were doing their work with a secret understanding. Thus atmosphere of corruption was prevailing in the country.

In 1991, India adopted liberal and free-market principles. Under this policy it was easy to set up new industry. The finance Minister Dr Manmohan Singh liberalized the economy to international trade. There was huge collection of foreign exchange under the leadership of Prime Minister P. V. Narasimha Rao for the period 1991-1996 and development in national infrastructure such as the 'Golden Quadrilateral 'project' were under taken later by the Prime Minister Atal Bihari Vajpayee. The country's economic growth progressed at a regular rapid speed.

India's economic growth and prosperity after economic reforms of 1991 lies mainly on few factors (i) Increased foreign direct investment, (ii) Youths of India's expertise in information technology and lastly (iii) A greater degree of domestic consumption because of a growing middle class population. Foreign direct investment and IT (information technology) helped to produce thousands of new jobs and thereby swell the number of middle class. It would not be unfair to say that India's growing middle class become the backbone of its economy. The growth rate is not stable as the GDP is going down. However, administrative inefficiency had down graded the rate of growth of economy and in effect brought the virus of corruption at every stage of Indian economy. The change of economic policy is emerging with the change of developing strategy and also with the change of national security in consideration of the world economy. The economy is also related with the huge expence of country's security in view of a new threat of security concerning the development in weaponry and political instability of the neighbor countries. In India the growing political unrest makes the people inactive in the sphere of despair, making the economic growth further down. A faithful, healthy environment under good governance can only bring confidence among the masses to incur a higher growth rate. Any where in the world the history dictates that the masses are the architect in the growth of the nation, be it economy, administration, or security. The rule of autocracy is still there and the world is observing the fight in the Middle East how the autocracy and the peoples' Will (Democracy) are taking its shape, be it a religious fight between Shia, Sunni or Iran, Israel or Israel and Arab. But in the long run which is expected the sovereignty of people that would prevail with the distribution of wealth instead of concentrating the wealth in the hands of few individuals. Even in the name of democracy if the wealth is concentrated in few hands, people would not tolerate the policy for long. Education is opening the boundary of the mind sets of Indian, although it has to go a long way to over come the rivalry of religion, castes, and the policy of accumulating money in few hands for the cause of enjoying a better life. What the British had seen, a country India, what was a country of beggars, chimers, snake-players and monks dressed with dirty clothes and dirty dusts proclaiming themselves as the disciples of God, is no longer in existence, these peoples also have their brain and body if nourished in right way could reach to any height. There was a time when people could go from a temple to another temple in the streets of jungles taking the leave for months or years together, that has now replaced with cities and capitals where people could move by planes in no time. The saints and monks have thought of us how to survive in life in the midst of jungles among living animals and how to reach heaven in the ancient times, and in the recent times our political leaders have shown us how to fight against the foreigners, be it a fight in the attack of bomb or be it a fight in the control of anger in the form of non-violence to get rid of foreign rule but they either have forgotten or discarded to teach us how to fight against the crisis of economy in the atmosphere of ever rising increase of eating mouths in the scarcity of limited food and materials. Mahatma Gandhi, the father of present Indian democracy had showed us the way to a little extent how to live with cottage industry but in compare to the demand, the out put was insignificant and in compare to business, in the field of international market, its value happens to be of no value amounting to zero as a result the country met with famine one after another sacrificing hundreds and thousands without count particularly in the villages of rural areas. But in contrast to the Indian leaders, the political thinkers of Europe never left behind to learn the new technology of machines and tools of industry that being first came into United Kingdom, by sending their young boys and girls, the country Japan, being devastated by Atom Bomb and people suffering with fall out of nuclear bomb where the political leaders never hesitate to send their youths thousand and thousand in number to the United Kingdom after making a deal of agreement to learn the new technique to bring up the up-dates of industry in the land of Japan like that of the industrial revolution in the Europe to enhance the economy in stead of giving upper hand in acquiring political power and fighting against them with bombs and bullets in secret and converting them to the status of enemy of the nation. We achieved independence, got the administrative power to rule the country by demolishing the beautiful Indian sub-continent in the fight against the capture of power, be it religion, caste or whatever the weapon suitable good for acquiring power. Who knows had the industrial revolution been happen, the cry for separate homeland, deprivation of lower caste and law of protection in the constitution for backward class, trials or kinesis of language of mother tongue would not arise. Apart from all success of our independence by dint of our political leaders, the present Indian youths failed to assimilate the success of past in the atmosphere of corruption, unemployment, accumulation of money in few hands and ransacking the country with the acts of terrorism. It is the age of globalization; India should think every affair in wider prospect of international application. The Indian brains if not tested before at least this time have been tested in the field of Computer Technology, the Indian youths, the Indian IIT students become the first choice for recruitment in the service of IT as the desire expressed by the Micro-Soft Giant Bill Gate. Besides these the IBM, the pioneer of Computer Technology, and also the other industry mostly built by American Companies are in search of Indian IT Engineers to proof beyond doubt that these Indian boys has something of great potentials. The new electronic is developing in Japan, a little of which is borrowed by the youths of South Korea. Now we could see in South Korea wire technology fast developing super seeding America, the country who is in the technology of high rising building but also in other new field, the field of Robot technology although its wider application is not yet realized but very soon it might be an important means in affairs of life. In the field of hard wire we have many more things to learn from our neighbor country Taiwan. The knowing of any technology is not sufficient enough in the hard competition of making industrial products for the sake of business to make profit, but investment in planning to acquire knowledge from any corner of the globe through research is also required. The role of IBM Company in the initial stages of doing research in search of knowledge of IT sectors brought the intelligent students from good institutes present anywhere in the globe with high salary making a brain drain in the soil of United States. Similarly, the rising of Samsung Company has sat another example where it has utilized the best technology being generated by the system of research work carried out almost in every developed country.

The avenues are plenty, plenty in tourism sector too. A small nation Singapore, what they are not doing to increase the tourism industry in a disciplined system of planning and what not. This has helped the other sector as well. The markets of Singapore are flourishing like anything. There is heavy rush in every market, the quantity of sale and purchase are heavy, the flow of foreigners is enormous. All are busy in the performance of their own sphere of works in the dynamic small city of Singapore. As the life is easy with high income, the people find the pleasure of life forgetting the quarrel. A satisfied mind behaved gentle and talked sweet being freed from the strain of anxiety. Thus all in totality the span of life, turned to be a period of happiness as if a right of birth of life, remaining in high thought of morality. In India there is no dirt of tourists' spot of beauty; it requires the planning to make the spot beautiful, entertaining and spectacular in the eye of high technology of 3D, 4D, 5D and so on and in the development of infrastructure to make the spot easy in communication of comfort. There is vast Sea Coastal Area ready for entertaining Beach in the

South, West and also in the East. There is no dirt of Hills, hills in south leads to ooty, Ladak in the North including Simla, Mosuri, and Darjeeling and Shillong in the East, who can say the beauty of any hills would be less than that of Switzerland, only it requires attention, planning and development and not to speak of innumerable hills be it in Assam or any other place of Eastern India or Northern India, the development could create many unparallel wonders of amusement. In the security sector, Indian contribution might be essential, profitable and beneficial in the arena of domestic sector as well as international sector. On the consideration of population, India stands next to China. Indians are the citizens of India but they are also the citizen of the Globe. If America, having being the 1/4th of India's population strength could take part in any affairs of the security of the Globe, why India did not? In true scene the world is belong equally to all its citizens. So the maintenance of the security of the Globe also rests with India as well because the 2nd highest number of its citizens is living in India. The World organization UN is also partly belongs to India. We do not want to bring here weapon or tools of weapon, but we would talk of men power, the strength of army, which is required for the maintenance of peace and stability. The number of Indian artillery is next to China as the population is high, what is the harm to build up an army unit of equal strength in the sphere of unemployment to support the UN under the UN patronage bearing the expenses. This would not only provide employment to Indian youths but also India would rest with respect and honor and indirectly the service of these huge number of Indians in the UN would make India a nation of power. In Afghan war, Indians are not a party to NATO Force and Indian army did not play any military role there. Time will say the right or wrong, good or bad for the Indian Army to participate in the Afghan War to control terrorists. God has given us land, minerals and man-power. It is the bounden duty of all Indians to utilize all these for the benefit of mother India. If it is not used for right purpose in right time, it would be an act of sin. In the language of Gita, the holy book of Hinduism, the Lord Krishna said to Arjuna-you are a Khatria, the duty of a Khatria is to fight to establish the rule of justice without looking in front the persons who are of your own people. Arjun heard the advice of Krishna, fought the battle and established the rule of justice. A solder has to do his duty. In India we have huge strength of youth, but could we utilize these youth for rightful purpose. These youths are Indians but they have every right to act in the welfare of the Globe, in the act of maintaining the security of the Globe. But instead most of our youths are looking for job; few are getting jobs those who are fortunate enough but the majority of them remained unemployed. Again few of them are self employed by dint of their own efforts but again majority remained unemployed. Where they would go, they are forced to come to the street to agitate for reasons or no reasons, and thereby they become the political victim and become a strong force of political party. A Government is also the guardians of these youths like that of a father who is to act for the welfare & happiness of his children. Thus proper utilization of these youth forces would definitely come under the jurisdiction of the government. Unless the youth forces are utilize right way, the violence, agitation and street fight would continue. Youths must be used for youthful purpose in fighting the enemy, in the prevention of insurgency and so on. The question of sending Indians in the war of Afghanistan was something of political nature but the force of youths should be a force of UN. It would be the responsibility of the UN to utilize the force for the benefit of the Globe. This was a scheme why did not formulated here by the Indians in the opportune moment of Afghan attack by the Force of United States in combination with NATO Force and others under the cover of UN for the utilization of Indian youths for gainful purpose of maintaining peace at present and future by the virtue of love & tolerance of the Indian tradition with all neighbours. However the best is known to our Indian Philosophers. Peace only with love and tolerance is not always fruitful as India is already experienced with China creating the slogan of Hindu-China Bhai-Bhai after Independence of India but everything was shattered by the invasion of China towards Arunachal extending to Tejpur of Assam. Peace with love and tolerance get strengthens by the presence of force of military strength. Mahatma Gandhi, the father of India as well as the father of non-violence movement in India never said not to use force in a situation where non-violence has no meaning. That is why Gandhi gave his consent to British to recruit Indians in the British army to fight against enemy in the Second World War.

# [23]

**Sharia Law:** The new concept of Bin Laden who had opposed the democracy of United States was something different to bring peace and happiness among the people particularly to Muslim people of Middle East. According to him people must be the follower of Sharia Law. It is nothing but the religious law of Islam. As it is originated from Quran (the holy Book of Islam) and Sunni (the system set by the Islamic prophet Muhammad), it is regarded as a divine law in the Muslim world. It deals with all topics what are essential for life system. It deals with topics-secular law, including crime, politics, economics as well as personal matter such as sexual intercourse, hygiene, diet, prayer and fasting. The law lies in the jest of attaining the long standing goal for Islamic movement in the Muslim world. Although many differ, differ in the interpretation of Sharia Law with differing perspective in each interpretation, but all are in consensus with the divine law as it is the reflection of God's will for mankind. Sharia must therefore be in its purest sense, perfect and unchanging. Bin Laden believe in Islam, he had full faith on God and he follows the ideals of Islam-(i) one must be faithful in duty, (ii) One should have the virtue of obedience to God, (iii) One should devote himself for struggle in the path of Allah. He also believes in the imagination of one Muslim world.

Osama bin Laden, born 10th March, 1957 and who died on 2nd May, 2011 at Abbottabad of Pakistan at the age of 54, having being a national of Saudi Arabia, he was born as Muslim and wants to live as a strong follower of Islam. He was the founder of al Qaeda, the jihadist organization. **[Bin ladden, was the founder of al-Quaeda]**

It was the organization that had carried out the September 11 attacks on the United States. However, he was a member of the wealthy Saudi bin Laden Family. How he had risen to a number one terrorist in the world? He began his study in Saudi Arabia, but at the age of about twenty two he left the country and went to Pakistan to join Mujahedeen forces to fight against the Soviets in Afghanistan. But he was against the US influence in the Saudi Land. Osama bin Laden, the al Qaeda leader was motivated by a belief that US foreign policy has oppressed, killed or otherwise harmed Muslims in the Middle East. "They hate us for what we do, not who we are."—was the belief of Bin Laden, who tried to restore Sharia Law, a law in belief to him would set things right in the Muslim world. He helped to strengthen the Mujahedeen by funneling arm, money and fighters bringing from the Arab world. It revealed from the biography of Bin Laden that in 1979, after completion of college education at Saudi Arabia, he went to Pakistan, and joined Abdullah Azzam in order to help and strengthen the Mujahedeen group by giving money and machinery from his own company to fight against the Soviet war in Afghanistan as he believed in heart that a great injustice had been committed against the people of Afghanistan. During the period of 1979 to 1989, the United States provided financial aid and weapons to the Mujahedeen through ISI under a nick name 'Operation Cyclone'. Although the money and weapons are provided by the United States, the training of militant groups was given by the Pakistani Armed Forces and ISI. Bin Laden thought it wise to meet Mr. Humid Gull, a three-star general of Pakistani Army, who was also the head of ISI agency. Accordingly he improved personal relation with him for future militant training and militant activity. By 1984, bin Laden and Azzam (a secret militant fighter of Afghanistan) established a militant center naming Maktab al-Khidamat at Afghanistan. In order to strengthen the organization he made the arrangement to funnel arms, money, and fighters what was being supplied from the Arab Land. Thus a strong jihadi fighter group was being formed under the training of Pakistani Arm Force. Bin Laden also established camps inside Khyber Pakhtunkhwa in Pakistan and given training to all volunteers coming across the Muslim world to fight against the invader Soviet regime. All these activity made him a militant hero in the Arab World.

By 1988, difference of opinion between Bin Laden and Azzam had split up Maktab al-Khidamat. Azzam was a strong supporter for Afghan fighters and he wanted Bin Laden along with Arab fighter be integrated among the Afghan fighting group instead of forming a separate fighting force. But Laden wanted a more military role; the al Qaeda must be an organized Islamic militant group where its goal is to lift the word of God, to make his religion victorious. Its membership requires certain ideals: Listening ability, good manners, obedience, and making a pledge to follow one's superiors. In 1988, he founded al Qaeda and gained popularity in the Arab world. Saudi Arabia, a close friend of United States brought restrictions over Bin Laden for his subversive activity for which he was banished from Saudi Arabia in 1992. However he shifted his base to Sudan. Again he had to leave Sudan in 1996 under US pressure over Sudanese government. He shifted to Afghanistan and there after establishing a new base, he decided to take action against the United States, initiating a series of bombings and related attacks. The research revealed that al-Qaeda was formed on August 11, 1988, at a meeting held on in the presence of many senior leaders of Egyptian Islamic Jihad. It was kept secret because the organization would take up jihadist activity elsewhere after the Soviets withdrawn from Afghanistan. Following the Soviet Union's withdrawal from Afghanistan in February 1989, Osama bin Laden returned to Saudi Arabia in 1990 as a hero of jihad. Arab world regarded him as hero here because he had brought down the mighty superpower of the Soviet Union. During this period there was conflict going on in the Arab world. Invasion of Kuwait took place under Saddam Husain. Bin Laden met Saudi King and Defense Minister and offer his help and requested them not to defend on non-Muslim assistance from the United States and others. But Laden's offer was rebuffed, and Saudi monarchy invited the deployment of U. S. force in Saudi territory rejecting the request of bin Laden not to bring US force in the holy land of Mecca-Modena. Bin Laden began to criticize the Saudi monarchy in public that compelled Saudi King to take action against him to silence him. This is how in 1992 he went to live in exile in Sudan. Laden took shelter in Jalalabad of Afghanistan. There he forged a close relationship with Mullah Mohammed Omar. According to 9/11 Commission, bin Laden and his organization was significantly weakened after being expelled from Sudan under US pressure. The other intelligence sources argued that the expulsion left bin Laden without any option other than becoming a full-time radical, and the other 300 Afghan Arabs who left with him subsequently became terrorist. **[United Airlines Flight 175 crashes into the South Tower, by date 9/11/2001]. The sayings of Bin Laden were like this:**

"God knows it did not cross our minds to attack the Towers, but after the situation became unbearable-and we witnessed the injustice and tyranny of the American-Israeli alliance against our people in Palestine and Lebanon-I thought about it. And the events that affected me directly were that of 1982 and the events that followed-when America allowed the Israelis to invade Lebanon, helped by the U. S. Sixth Fleet. As I watched the destroyed towers in Lebanon, it occurred to me punish the unjust the same way: to destroy tower in America so it could taste some of what we taste and to stop killing our children and women."

[Osama bin Laden, 2004. ]

Bin Laden was a rich man, a multi millionaire, hailing from a very influential family of Saudi Arabia, a follower of Islam why did he became an aggressive man to constitute al-Qaeda, a jihadist organization to attack US although he announced it to set example to show the US, how they could provide the U. S. Sixth Fleet to Israelis to invade Lebanon in the act of destruction of towers in Lebanon. Yes, the conflict of Arab-Israel might influence the young Arabs but above all that was the attraction of dedication to the religion Islam. He was not alone; he was compelled to go away from Saudi Arabia, the birth place and organized al-Qaeda in Sudan and later in Afghanistan and Pakistan. It involved many countries, many organizations and many youthful youths ready to sacrifice life for the cause of nation and for the cause of religion Islam. The world is peculiar where we find human habitation but the human beings varied by color, size and structure and get accustomed with the language, religion and customs prevailing on the very land of Earth. In the advent of opportunity the human beings of different regions become friend and exchange the love of brotherhood to make the world beautiful for them. But in the event of disparity, people become enemy to each other, the people become blind under the strong belief of religion keeping him in dark and dipping him in the darkness of religion when he could not see any kind of humanity other than the good of the people of same faith. In extreme cases, people could not tolerate the existence of the faith of people of other religion. Why? A student becomes a brilliant or addicted by the teachings of a teacher. Similar is the case that had happen by the teachings of a religious teacher. The teachings of a particular faith might be polluted by the presence of the people other faith. The world had seen many religious leaders who had came to this Earth to preach religion for the welfare of the mankind. Who were they?

**Ethics of Islam:** It is to be seen that most of the educated and elite of non-Muslims gentry who have read Islam knows that Islam teaches peace although apparently it appears Islam teaches violence, Islam teaches terrorism. To visualize life in Islam, one has to leave the luxurious and sinful life and devote himself fully to Islam to realize the sole (a part of Allah) in them. Islam is in hot debate in America. America is a country of cold weather and the people are habituated with alcohol. Drinking is legal but not over drinking because over-drinking goes beyond control and many innocent lives were lost due to this evil. Many family lives were destroyed, over drink makes a man drunk when he commits many nuisances in the family as well as in the society. As the alcohol does harm not only an individual but also society, therefore it is not allowed in Islam.

American believes in freedom of sex. A girl gets pregnant without marriage. What about the baby who has no father. The child can not foresee a happy life. Did the girl a mother or a criminal? Did the society have not taken the right of innocent newborn baby by giving liberty to sex? That is why Islam does not allow sex without marriage.

According to Islam killing one innocent life is like killing the whole of humanity and saving one life similarly measures as saving the whole of the humanity. The non-Muslim elite of America know that the so called Muslims who are involved in terrorism are not the followers of Islam. They are taking their revenge through terrorism under the cover of Islam. Killing an innocent life, whatsoever be the circumstances, is not a Muslim by Faith.

But even then many questions arise in the open air. After 9/11, did any one could see anywhere near six million Muslim-Americans condemning it? It was only a small handful of Muslims speaking out against 9/11 attack. Similarly the case of 26/11 Mumbai terrorist strike, where few Muslims condemned it and only a handful of Muslims speak against it, become a subject of discussion among fellow Indians. No one wants to admit that Islam has been a violent Religion since its principle is based on peace.

# [24]

**Partition & the City of Calcutta:** Now Calcutta (Kolkata), a place may be called a place of fortune as well as a place of miss fortune. It is because Calcutta was a place, a religious place, a place of village without any infrastructure of road, rail or anything of living standard, all on a sudden transformed into a superfine city, a city of Capital of British Empire by dint of its fortune but again it went down by the destruction of human habitation due to the arrival of lakhs and lakhs of refugee beings assembled here beyond the capacity of the city bringing the unrest in the youths and the city witnessed a fight for survival for better living, bringing an witness of tragedy of miss fortune. The city Kolkata is located on the east bank of the River Hooghly, a channel of the Ganges, about 154 km upstream from the Bay of Bengal that was the India's largest City and once the capital (1772-1912) of British India. Kolkata assimilated European influences during British rule and that had created an amalgam of culture the expression of which had found in the life and works of the 19th century Bengali elite.

The Writers' Building

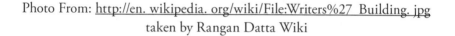

Photo From: http://en. wikipedia. org/wiki/File:Writers%27 Building. jpg
taken by Rangan Datta Wiki

**The Writers' Building**: The achievement of British in India was due to the activity of East India Company of British Land. The man behind the flourishing of British Empire in India was Clive, the great, who came to India as an employee of East India Company and with the assignment of a writer of the company. Calcutta was made the Capital of British India at the beginning, and the building from where the capital's activity were carried out was called 'The Writers' Building' in honour of the memory of the Clive as a writer of the Company. However, the same building, of course modified, and was used since independence as the States' nerve center with the same name of the building. The building is now acting as the secretariat building of the State Government of West Bengal in India where more than 6000 employee is working for routine works. The historical fact recorded the building located on the northern shore of a water body locally called Lal Dighi was designed by Thomas Lyon in 1780 with an impressive façade of Neo-Renaissance style. A statue of Britannia atop the main entrance is kept in shinning. It is a witness of great political significance and memories of the Indian Independence movement.

Calcutta was a place of art and culture and the elite residents maintained a level of vitality and political awareness over passing the rest of the country. In short, Kolkata still remains an enigma to many Indians and also too many foreigners. It arouses an abiding nostalgia in the minds of many who have live there once. But for many it brings a hope of uncertainty of despair. The above Writers' Building is the witness where three teenagers, the three musketeers, Benoy, Badal and Dinesh dressed in European costume, entered Writers' Building on 8th Dec. 1930 and shot Simpson dead. Will there souls would get peace seeing the present day affairs of Kolkata where the news is flashing in the news paper of almost every day killing and murder, corruption in the handling of public fund. Where is the greatness of Bengalis?

**The Partition of India:** The Partition of India had deprived Kolkata half of its hinterland and burdened it with a vast refugee population. This has made Calcutta dead. The pictures are the witness of the foresighted visions of our leaders. It was the leaders of India who guided these people to come forward to fight against British. Let the British go, you will get a beautiful country, where you will enjoy 'Ram Rajya', a country existed in Hindu epics where exists only happiness, endless happiness, no strain, no pain, a dream land of heaven. Is it the fruits of their promise? It was nothing but the betrayal of truth for the capture of power. Jinnah came forward with two nation theory. British accepted the theory and placed before the congress. The leading personality was Sardar Petal who was the most senior person, above 73 of age. He pleaded for the acceptance of the two nation theory by the division of Bengal and Punjab because the leaders could not wait any longer as they had struggled harder for independence in spite of the adverse opinion of Gandhi. Power of Ruling India became dearer to them than the sufferings of the people because they might not get the chance to Rule India in their life time as the leaders get aged. The Leader Ho chi Minh achieved independence for Vietnam by Liberation Movement carrying for 35 years. American Air strike 150 Fighter launched from US Seventh Fleet carriers to bomb Vietnam could not deter Ho Chi Minh from the decision of the liberation of United Vietnam. Despite the mobilization of 500. 000 US troops, US military plan failed to defeat North Vietnam, making the leader

Ho chi Minh victorious to get the United Vietnam. But in India, the Indian Leaders succumb to the demand of Jinnah, a leader of insignificant strength compare to the mighty US, and accepted the two nation theory without giving a befitting reply. Why? Is it not for the power of chair? Punjabis were massacred in Delhi; the Bengalis were reduced to beggars, had the United Punjab or had the United Bengal be an independent country, which would be freed from religious sentiment, who could say both the country would not be happy?

The intellectuals of Calcutta failed to foresight the present situation. It has created a bad precedent of what the Gokhla said once "what Bengals things today, India things tomorrow". Calcutta never thought to be a state of dust bin of huge refugee. Calcutta's death has brought a day of tragedy to all Bengali. Once the Bengali of Calcutta who led India, in ideas and idealism, are now dead, the name Bengali even to Indians, now a word of terror, because either it carries the news of large scale child death at the birth in Hospitals, epidemic of cholera and polio, corruption in miss use of fund or the message of strikes, and political murder forgetting the appealing sensibility for Bengali Hindu refugee who being the front runner of in the independence movement of India under the guidance of the then Bengal leader, are now sometimes tainted as infiltrator, a travesty of truth. The success of independent movement is strongly associated with the memories of last century and Calcutta is the city of witness. Coming to the city of Calcutta, a victim visualizes the earlier picture of Calcutta. In 1966, development office for the city declared "Calcutta Metropolis in crisis". The existing urbanization was limited to colonial economy as imposed by the English and de-linked from the development in the rural areas. The great famine of 1943 took a toll of 6 million lives and pushed hundreds of people to seek relief into the city and its suburbs. In the years immediately after Partition, people began to come to West Bengal due to threat of life for the cause of partition of the country on the basis of religion. From February 1950, after the riots in Bagerhat and Barisal, the refugees entering West Bengal were mainly agriculturists and artisans. Amrit Bazar Partika reported on March 23, 1950 that large-scale movement of Hindus from villages in districts like Dacca, Chittagong, Rajshahi, Mymensingh, Bogra and Rangpur have started. In fact every Hindu in Eastern Pakistan is trying to move out. The rioting and insecurity of life compelled the people to move out either by rail or by walking barefoot. A large number of people thereby had crossed into West Bengal. One arm of this multitude crossed the rail station at Darshana and entered the state where they were temporarily sheltered at the camp in Barnpur. The second arm, coming from the South Western areas of East Pakistan, ended at the camp at Bongaon. The platforms of Sealdah station were often the epicenter from where the refugees were either dispersed to camps or who managed to find their way into the teeming multitudes of the anonymous city. The public space of Sealdah station became their first halt into an uncertain future. These people were compelled to leave Islamic East Pakistan (East Bengal) where many of them were lost their life in rioting and burning of their houses under military in disguise. Refugees were unwanted people both to India and West Bengal as well. At first the policy was just offering casual relief, hoping that the refugees would go back. When finally a reluctant State and Central Government woke up to the fact that the refugees were here to stay, the main thrust of rehabilitation policy was to 'disperse' them outside West Bengal. Naturally, the educated middle class refugees resented this. They were vocal in their hostility and considered it their political right to be gainfully resettled in the city.

The sayings were somewhat like that "Where are the Bengal leaders? Fight for self Rule, fight against British, where are you, you thought to be intelligent, and made us fool but you no more could make us fool by sending us far away and making the path easy for dying. We are not going anywhere; it is our right to live here and right to die here."

Rather than waiting passively for government help, they began to self rehabilitate themselves by taking over marshy land in and around Calcutta to build squatter colonies. By 1955, these colonies were mushrooming in and around Calcutta at a tremendous pace.

However in 1951, West Bengal was flooded with a fresh and larger influx of refugees. June 11, 1958, Amrita Bazar Patrika in a report stated that 21 lakh refugees were in scattered colonies and no plan has been made for rehabilitation. The old boundaries of the city suburbs has increased to accommodate wave after wave of population-abandoned lands, fertile lands, rice fields, marshy lands, ponds, lakes, jungles and gardens all took in the rising tidal waves of population.

On looking to the deplorable conditions of the East Pakistan refugees and the treatment given to them, the young Teresa had forgotten her age because the cry of her inner mind understands to serve these destitute young little children and she immediately devoted herself after taking consent from Rome, fully forgetting the right of Rome, she became an Indian by heart and mind and sacrificed her life without thinking for a moment for a little pleasure of her own life that an unknown spirit had given her a power to become a virgin mother comparable to any virgin God. The prize of noble laurite to her is too small a gratitude to the dept of her sacrifice.

"By bold, I am Albanian. By citizenship, an Indian, By birth, I am a Catholic nun. As to my calling, I belong to the world. As to my heart, I belong entirely to the Heart of Jesus. Small of stature, rocklike in faith, Mother Teresa of Calcutta was entrusted with the mission of proclaiming God's thirsting love for humanity, especially for the poorest of the poor.

This luminous messenger of God's love was born on 26 August 1910 in Skopje, a city situated at the crossroads of Balkan history. Later she came to Calcutta and set to living for doing service to man kind. In 1952 Mother Teresa opened the first Home for the Dying in space made available by the city of Calcutta. With the help of Indian officials she converted an abandoned Hindu temple into the Kalighat, Home for the Dying and a free hospice for the poor. She renamed it Kalighat, the Home of the Pure Heart (Nirmal Hriday). Those brought to the home received medical attention and were afforded the opportunity to die with dignity, according to the rituals of their faith; Muslims were read the Quran, Hindus received water from the Ganges, and Catholics received the Last Rites. "A beautiful death," she said, "is for people who lived like animals to die like angels—loved and wanted."

Mother Teresa, (a noble laureate, an Albanian Catholic nun) was surprised on seeing the distress of the children of Hindu refugees of

East Pakistan in Kolkata (Calcutta) and there after she decided to become an Indian by changing her citizenship in order to give a long service to the children of these refugees. She founded the Missionaries of Charity in Kolkata (Calcutta) in 1950. She dedicated her mind in the act of selfless service and remained in service for long 45 years to serve to her best to the poor, sick, orphaned and dying children of Kolkata till her death.

## Bombay Harbour:

Bombay is acting as a Harbour since 1731 when ships were resting there in good numbers. Communication of the countries of Middle East with India through sea was the route of trade where Bombay was the gateway and as such its importance as Harbour was all the time the most. We know there are countries in the Middle East where there is nothing but oil. The nation Japan so strong and sound economically but the country possesses little of minerals. While India is a country full of minerals consisting of rivers, Hills and planes, if the minerals of these regions were utilized scientifically under modern technology, there would be no reason of remaining any kind of shortage in this land of purity. The land was definitely worthy, that is why the growth of people had taken place in this region at the earliest. To-day the knowledge of science guide us how to use each and every mineral for the good of industry and beneficial for the country. The main industries of India are now said to be concentrated in the area of textiles, chemicals, steel transportation equipment, cement, mining, petroleum and machinery products. Besides these the source of foreign exchange lies in the skill of utilization of technology of software by the Indians to all the emerging industry and by the export of industrial products mainly to United Arab Emirates and United States. However, both the new partner China and Iran are expected to join in sharing the industrial product in large quantity. The country India is a big Country big in size and large in population as such it requires oil and other necessary materials for running its industry for the economy of the country. The oil deficiency is materialized by the supply of oil from the Middle East at the expense of monetary exchange at high rate exhausting the hard earned foreign exchange. India should think for generation of its own oil by extensive search around its territory for oil exploration. Essential goods such as crude oil, machinery, fertilizer, iron & steel and chemicals are imported. There are countries who were in business trade with India, supplied these materials. The countries like China, UAE, Saudi Arabia, United States and Switzerland are the five countries that were doing business with India, from where goods were imported. After a gap of long period India showed for the first time after Independence a little progress in economic front while currently the economy of India is the tenth largest in the world by GDP and third largest by purchasing power parity (PPP) making India as one of G-20 group of major economy and a member of BRICS. To count with by 2008, India had established itself as one of the world's fasted growing economies. The earlier record tells us Indian Economy for the period 1947-1991 was based on mixed economy and there was wide spread control over any kind of industrial expansion for the Pattern of socialism in order to make the equal distribution of wealth. The controlling of the growth of industry had restricted the flow of money to the hands of the public making the country poor, a country of poor people. Having the administration being remained confine to a very limited executives, the government lost the control of ruling a vast country like India efficiently, consequently, the unskilled, untrained people, who were lower in morality, recruited for the cause of administration. The untrained people were being unable to bring discipline in the policy of administration; the floodgate of widespread corruption finds its root in all sections of administration.

In 1991, Dr. Manmohan Singh, the then Finance Minister of India adapted the principle of free-market and liberalized its economy to international trade. The post-British Era mechanism of strict government control on setting up of new industries is abolished. The system helped to set up industries and the country's economic growth progressed at a rapid pace with high rate of growth making large income for the people. The future of India lies with present trend of increasing growth rate. Professor Peter Rodriguez (PhD, Virginia) of Princeton University said that the communist command economies of both China and India were responsible for their many years of slow, tiny growth, and that things changed when communist ideology and tight restrictions on business were replaced with a more opening free-market system.

The days went by, in a strain of miracle, the government of India were compelled to change the policy of the nation, a liberalized Trade policy of business, a free trade business instead of restricted business so long maintained, brought a spectacular change in the economic front. The neighbor Pakistan, the most near and brother country of India instead of extending hands of friendship took the grievous path of cruelty to destroy the growth at the bud by designing the highest crime of cruelty of attacking the commercial peak center Mumbai, on 26th November by sending militants in secret under Muslim Radicals in the cover of Terrorist. The issue was jealousy and Kashmir was in inner mind. But the true teachings of Islam are peace with love and solve the problem by wining the hurt. The constant antagonism against religion would definitely bring religious radicalism instead of brotherhood of humanism. England and French fought for centuries but what was the result? French socked in poverty by extending all out help for the liberation movement of USA, who is fighting against British, the arch rival of French, revolution erupted, Lewis VI, once a beloved king was killed by the people of French bringing resolution and similarly, England lost its territory of 13 States in USA. The days of rivalry once ended after losing a lot. What the friendship had brought for them? The bond of friendship, made them an alley to fight together against Hitler, and also made them a close friend to accept the common currency 'Euro' for common benefit of their economy. The friendship made them intimate brother by lifting the harder restrictions of visa, and also made them co-worker in the search of better avenues for their young ones opening their entry anywhere in any institute for each of the country. Could we not the two countries of India, Pakistan emerge out from the battle of Indo-Pak conflict thinking for the future of all youngest of both the countries equally?

By 26/11 terrorist attack, the damaged Oberoi Trident Hotel, a luxurious center of foreigners to reside in Mumbai, and the Hotel Taj of international reputation for business mostly remodeled in the fashion of 21st century were attacked by terrorists under the patronage of Pakistan to down grade the Indian business is an incident of record and an example of how the human emotions work out of jealousy and enmity. As the government of Pakistan is suffering under the strain of military, under the threat of radical Muslims who dare to utilize religion for any militant or mischievous work for the gain of personal power as social worker, no body could divert the attention for betterment of the economy of the country to ensure a better life style for the citizens of the country. The government failed in the economic front and consequently, the people were restless for better amenities and for minimum requirements of life. To remain in power under the volatile situation of the country, the government has no alternative but to focus the Kashmir issue prominently and befool the common people bringing the religion in front in every matter as the origin of the country was based on the religion and against the religion of Hinduism. This was the principle of any government of Pakistan to remain in power.

India and China both are showing economic progress. Both the countries have huge population and both the countries have successfully utilized their man power to a little extent. Therefore it is expected in future that there would be a competition between China & India in the economic front in rise of GDP, the index of growth. China is doing better in the economic front and now showing higher GDP compare to India. It is highly appreciable to see that China's economy is the second largest in the world after that of the United States. A major component supporting China's rapid economic growth was the export of China. Of course economist differs in their individuals' analysis and they possess different opinion, some one supports economic growth in India's favour. In 2003, Goldman Sachs predicted that India's GDP in current increasing rate would overtake French & Italy by 2020, Germany, UK and Russia by 2025, and Japan by 2035. Such a growth is nothing but a boon for India. If the imaginary success turns to reality, India would stand as 3$^{rd}$ largest economy of the world behind US and China. India would be an economic superpower when India would play the major role in the Global Economy in the 21$^{st}$ century. India knows its problem, the militants are hiding in Bangladesh and Bangladesh knows her problem, the problem of poverty, the economy of the country. A good relation will benefit both the countries. The improvement of relation between Bangladesh and India will not only reduce the insurgency, but will increase travelling without permit in a course of time. The fear of theft in the boarder region would reduce making the safety of trade route between the two countries. In the Eastern sector of India rather it would open up increasing trend of trade using Chittagong Port between the two neighbor countries involving the number of states of India in the Eastern sector. The business of trade would bring economic development for both the countries. The business activity of Chittagong Port would enhance the state of economy of the country of Bangladesh to a great extent, as that of Mumbai Port of India on the Western sector of India. There will be improvement in average earnings of the people of the country of Bangladesh.

It would be beneficial for the country and its people for the fact that (I) it would enhance employment rate for the people of Bangladesh. The increase in the growth of business and firms would increase the internal need for more people leading to increase in the rate of employment significantly, (ii) Economic development would enhance the standard of living of the people of Bangladesh making in effect in the lowering of poverty rate, (iii) The rise of gradual increase of profits from small business and firms due to economic development would bring a better confidence in the minds of business people of Bangladesh to devote more energy in the efforts of business for making better profit. Government will be in comfort to collect more taxes from the people who are in better economic growth sustaining stability with the rise of economy of the nation. The government would be happy to collect taxes. The extra money collected by the government as such could be utilized in financing various projects as and when required for making development of the Nation. The primary need for development is the construction of infrastructure and thus the money could be spent as such. In the end there remains the possibility of further development for the country and thus it is crystal clear that the country's development is impossible without neighbor's cooperation but to keep on power or capture political power it is sometimes necessary to make the neighbor a country of enemy or exploiter for the convenience of getting vote from illiterate masses. The irony is that the people of this region have given the right of voting but they have not given the knowledge of understanding of the value of voting. It would be a long time to achieve it. Thus the improvement of business relation of the two nations is a well coming trend and essential achievement without which economic progress is a far cry.

# [25]

India is now the greatest democracy in the world and India is concerned of its greatness and responsibility. With the call of its conscious of greatness it has involve the nation in doing a commendable humanitarian works for the down trodden people all over the world. If it is going to be one of the global powers, it must think equally to be capable of a fittest partner in solving global problems with responsibility and dignity keeping the human value above all politics. India things the world should accept it as a permanent member of UNO instead of opposing it for mere political reasons. Before independence India was a land of illiterates and a land of snakes and charmers. Although India was ruled by many Kings and Princes spreading over 530 or more units, the development was practically zero. Kings were mostly busy in personal luxury & enjoyment and a little of concern with the sufferings of the common people or with the development of the infrastructure of the region. The virtue of tolerance prevailed in the minds of common people that being derived from the life long practice of Hindu religion either in Temples or in the house of Gurus prevented them to take the courage of disobedience or to raise any kind of protest against the King as we find to day in the democratic system of government. However, after independence majority of the Princely States had merged to form one entity under the patronage of far sighted Indian political leaders and also to a little extent out of fear to survive in isolation as a single unit of King, where the mind set of hungry, distressed people completely being changed due to long struggle against the British Rule. Although in the atmosphere of communal flare up, rioting, killing or kidnapping, the Indian leaders had acted like veteran statesman and kept the Indian Union, as a living place for all irrespective of caste, creed, religion or color apart from the protest from many corners of religious groups, the complete discipline in the administration could not be brought back, the unrest could not be eliminated. To-day Indian Union is respected as a country of honor and dignity in the international arena where it overcame all kinds' of ethnic conflicts when India rightly proclaim to be a member of UN to do its best for the people of the globe. Now India is a Country wishes to extend its hand to help the people in distress, to extend its support to any country suffering under natural calamity. Apart from its humanitarian help to its neighbor states Pakistan at the time of earth quake, (in the region of its Kashmir valley), Bangladesh at the time of cyclone and storm, SriLanka at the time of ethnic conflict, Marissa at the time of administrative collapse by the foreign intruders, India had extended its hands to UN at the time of world conflicts in any regions of the world and never hesitated to send Indian Arm Force at any places for rightful purpose but of course denied to send Indian Force along with NATO in the Afghan War. Who can say its role in Somalia was not praise worthy to bring peace and order in the country? The American Marine Force had killed the rioters as the very principle of America is to give punishment to the wrong doers without compromise but in doing so the Marine Force had inflicting heavy causalities among the innocent masses. But on the other hand the principle of India is to settle the matter amicably without killing. Indian Army had taken up a principle, the principle under which they had been taught and brought up so long—a principle of administration under tolerance. Instead of killing the rioters, they contacted the local warlords and militia commanders and had set up an atmosphere of 'ceasefire' after an understanding with the local leaders, elders and other leaders. Of course, the army never had to compromise with the turn of ambushers where Army had never hesitated to slaughter them en mass. But simultaneously, the army extends the arms of sympathy for every victim by declaring grants. Thus the army brought the situation under control by declaring hefty ex gratis to kin of the dead of Somalia's citizen apart from the supply of package for food and medicine to the victims.

India is a country of new democracy wanted to adopt democracy that was being followed in the most civilized nation of United Kingdom and also had chosen to follow the ideals of democracy that had been followed with success in the United States of America in spite of its hurdles of existing non-democratic country all around of its boundary. India feels its democratic ideals would be strengthening by becoming a member of UNO. India would be favorably approved by other country if India happens to be a member of UNO. In the middle of conflict, American President Bill Clinton had the strength and courage to abruptly pull out the American troops from Somalia even after spending billions of dollars, when the gangs of militia were set free for creating chaos through out Somalia inflicting heavy injury to innocent Somalis. India on the other hand did not withdraw the army rather India had given its service under the direction of UNO to bring peace in Somalia. India always believes peace in mutual understanding. Peace through the principle of keeping a balance between killing and forgiveness was the motto of Indians and that principles of ethics were followed in Somalia. The countries of vested interest might have work in disguise to prevent India of becoming a member of United Nations, but India would rightly justify its membership of the United Nation by dint of its woeful service to any country at the time of urgent necessity.

The people of the world are in belief that India is the greatest democracy in the world. It is also in the news of few foreign countries that India is doing a commendable humanitarian works for the downtrodden people all over world. India is going to be one of the global powers and they believe that India is a capable partner in solving global problems with responsibility and dignity keeping the human value above all politics. But it appears practically that the world is not accepting India as a permanent member of UNO. It is truly clear that India has only a few of the friendly country, who favors India. A country becomes a close friend of another country if the friendship is beneficial to either of its economy or defense security or both. So it is crystal clear that India has few friends. The reason behind in the lacking of the friendly country was in the matter of economy and also in the matter of defense of the country.

# [26]

Muslims were allowed to live in India even after the formation of a separate state for the Muslims of India, not only that they were given the equal rights and also additional right, the right of independent religious right, the right of independent Muslim law instead of one uniform law of the country while in Pakistan the Hindus were denied the right. Dalits were given the privileges for a time period to develop and rise to the status of other casts. The additional rights did not satisfy the Muslims as well as the Dalits. They preferred to stabilize their status first and then wish to exert further for additional right remaining indifferent to the development and economic success. Of course in a situation of scarcity, the community right or religious right get the priority. Keeping the demand of right in mind they prefer to caste their votes in favour of a candidate of their religion or caste and not on the consideration of the merit of the candidate. It is undoubtedly a set back for the Indians to bring true democracy in India. It definitely indicated India had to do a lot in order to bring true democracy in India. People of India did not know before independence what is democracy. What was the necessity of establishing a democratic government in the country of India when the principle of democracy was unknown to the Indians? The political leaders explained to the public that the term democracy appeared first in ancient Greek, and since then the different countries of the world were gradually changing from the rule of kingdom to the rule of democracy. They said in summary, democracy can be defined as a political process of administration of a country by which all citizens have been granted equal opportunity for enlightened understanding, effective participation, voting power and control of agenda for perpetrating well fare of the people and development of country. They further said the ideal character behind the term democracy lies in permitting every citizen to participate in the sovereign power of the state. What was the necessity of establishing a democratic government in the country like India? To answer the question, the leaders said it was a necessity for the formation a civilized society of equality. It was democracy which could prevent the government from oppressing its citizens. The democracy can prevent the Rulers, who had adopted autocratic systems because of unrelenting pursuit of ideological, religious or nationalistic motives of depriving the public of fundamental rights. Democracy was not only a governing system but also it had provided guarantee for citizens' constitutional and human rights. Participation in the process and implementation of the process were also part of democracy. The activity like public education, plans and policies, decision making process, or voting right of equality, restoration of each citizen's fundamental right, etc were all some kinds of democracy. It was only a democratic system of government, which could ensure an individual's freedom of thought and freedom of speech. For sustaining a civilized life, a human body needed food, shelter, health care, and love & entertainment. Can an autocratic rule satisfy the demand? Studying the development of the French Revolution, the democratic system of UK and the recent democracy of US, Indian leaders and Indians believe that it is only a democratic government in India that could full fill all its need. As the comcentration of money and wealth in the hands of few individuals is anti-democratic, the ownership of Land with few individuals is also anti-democratic. God has created us with equality, then how an individual get deprived of Land, money and wealth. Is it not the states responsibility to look to each individual's progress of knowledge, prosperity and happiness of his life? Land Reform was one of the essential items to bring democracy in the developing country. It is also believed that a true democracy only could eliminate hunger, poverty and save lives. To bring an effective democracy a liberal Land reform policy was required and that could be implemented with the spirit of sacrifice. According to George W Bush if the country could be rid of its tyrant, the people must be free in mind and democratic in spirit. The people in every country under the influence of culture tend to be democratic as the unity of culture increases the love for fellow citizen. Indians perform much festival such as Festival of Colors, Festival of Durga Puja, Kali Puja, Ganasha, Romzan, and Milatsarif like festival to exchange love and affection among fellow citizens bringing a unity among them. The intellectuals, the religious Heads, the patriotic politicians should think of festivals where people of all religious faith could freely participate to make merry making so as to bring a bond of love and unity of understanding to full fill the true ideals of democracy. So long the ideals of democracy are not based on humanity, but on caste, religion and wealth, it can not be called a democratic country from the law of ethics of humanity.

Nazi German became democratic after Hitler; fascist Japan became democratic after 2nd world war. But in Haiti, democracy could not be established even in the period of a century in spite of the repeated attempts of the United States for various reasons. In most of the developing countries, land was one of the most important assets in the economic sector and political power. In Pakistan, maximum portion of land had remained concentrated in the hands of small group of local elites. When elections were held, the candidates were no other than the local landowners or their agents. In India also, there were few regions in Uttar Pradesh or Bihar where the power lied with the landowners and hence landowners were the political candidates in the name of democracy. The farmers who worked on the land for generations were not the owners. After the 2nd world war, the United States had implemented the land reform in Japan, South Korea and Taiwan and established democracy. Without economic expansion, the establishment of true democracy was difficult. The right of Dalit for reserve seats is for the economic backwardness of the region. On the other hand without democracy improvements in infrastructure and increase in per capita income were also difficult to achieve. If the citizens of a country had a wish to spread democracy, a set of important conditions had to be emulated in the country at first. Such as the limit of population growth, increase of GDP, increase of self reliance, enforcement of equality of laws regardless of class or tribe or religion, which would have ensure a stable and democratic government. Democracy in terms of socialistic pattern would help to ensure equality in the distribution of wealth, but practically it lacks to bring a better economy for the nation because of less individuals' effort as it was seen in Russia where economic downfall was the main root for the disintegration Soviet Union of Socialistic Russia. Democracy in terms of capitalistic pattern would help to bring economic progress for the cause of individuals' greater incentive for industrial product where the individual will be the absolute owner of the wealth. The principle is a greater knowledgeable person is a greater wealthy person because his skill of knowledge would help him to earn more. But the drawback of capitalistic pattern of democracy lies in the concentration of wealth again in few hands. Our political thinkers have taken these into account and that is why India is a country called Socialistic Secular democratic country. It sounds nice but in the last 60 years people of India has seen democracy in India based on money and power besides religion and caste.

The United States always advocate for democracy and extended its hand for spreading of democracy. For the spread of democracy it believed in the following five general principles. (i) Free and fair election process, (ii) civil liberties, (iii) functioning of governments, (iv) Political participation and political culture (v) faith in the right of equality. The US commitment to democracy was tested in the Middle East and China, Bush said, "Our commitment to democracy was tested in China. That nation now had silver, a fragment of liberty. Yet, China's people would eventually want their liberty in pure and whole. China has discovered that economic freedom leads to national wealth. China's leadership had also discovered that freedom was indivisible and that social and religious freedom was also essential to national greatness and national dignity." Democracy means freedom, freedom in speech of expression, freedom in individuals' thought and mind and that spirit would lead the humanity in the path of new innovation for a better world.

# [27]

Indian National Congress Party was established in 1885. Since then it conducted the independence movement, and even after independence it govern the country continuously except two terms each of 5 years interval. The allegation against the congress party was countless but the people find no other alternative but vote for congress for the governance of the country. Now people might think otherwise because people are suffering with poverty, lack of facility of proper education and above all with the sufferings of daily life for long. The news of corruption, the news of scam after scams has vitiated the minds of common citizens. The wealth is there in few hands but the common people are deprived of the benefit of wealth. A good party would not remain good, unless the activity of the party are good for the people and unless people are happy to support it. There are many good parties of other countries where the party showed its ups and down by its performance. However, Congress Party of India was comparable to that of Labour Party in Great Britain, the Social Democratic Party in Germany or the Democratic Party in the United States of America in its political ethics of functioning. In Indian democracy, currently, it is seen, the evolution of few national party with little of national philosophy and innumerable regional party without any ideology to profess except the regional benefit who were competing election to enter into power politics. The case of Congress Party was different because, this was the party that led the movement for freedom, the party that united India and brought people of different religions and languages into a single political identity where it was correctly recognized as a unity among diversity. Once the Party was consist of men and women of high personal integrity and few of sectarian integrity. When confronted with the congress of today, the conduct of savagery such as the question of massacre of Sikhs in 1984, rampant corruption by officials and administrators discarding the growing evidence of corruption, an Indian who knows the earlier history of congress can not but be stuck by the loss of ideology. Despite the fallout, the earlier history would still remember the Indian National congress as one of the great political Parties of the modern world. With the glorious record of past achievement, the congress of India, what is comparable with that of Labour Party in Great Britain, the Social Democratic Party in Germany or the Democratic Party in the United States of America was in the attempt to bring equality of the citizens of the country. Since its formation, the congress Party was functioning with an ambition to build a Great Nation of India embracing Indians of all kinds. In the first few decades of its existence, it produced some impressive and outstanding leaders. They were those of great Bengalis, Surendranath Banerjee and Bipin Chandra Pal in Eastern India, Bal Gangadhar Tilak and Gopal Krishna Gokhale in Western India of Maharashra. Also there were other congress leaders in the Indian National Congress from North and South India as well. The then independent movement had showed that Indian National Congress was inseparable with Mohandas Karamchand Gandhi, who had returned home from South Africa. Gandhi had already established himself there as a leader of oppressed people by the weapon of non-violence. He successfully carried out a mass movement in South Africa without taking any arms in hand. With the arrival of Gandhi, the Independence movement of India got fresh stimuli. The movement so long was concentrated on major cities but now it had spread from urban to rural area through the publicity of regional languages instead of English. The movement spread from Presidency cities to small-town of British India, where Clerks, workers, lawyers and other residents flocked to the nationalist cause giving a mass base movement of unprecedented character. His vision was to remove the divisions within Indian society. His principle was to abolish untouchability in the Hindu society and to embrace Muslims, Christians, Paresis and Sikhs in the congress in the Independence movement. His ideals often were not implemented in practice, and that created resentment among Dalits and Muslims emerging rival leaders like B. R. Ambedkar and M. A. Jinnah. Apart from that, it must be concluded that the Congress leaders in Gandhian era were not successful to bring equality which had caused the division of India and formation of Pakistan. It must be said that Gandhi was against the division of country but his voice was over turned by the emotional speech of Petal in the Congress Assembly meeting that determined the final decision in favour of Partition of the country. However, in the long run, Gandhi failed to prevent division. Gandhi also failed earlier against Netaji Subhas in the election of Sita Ram Pottavia, but he never gave up his fight. Gandhi was the undisputed leader of the whole country. Gandhi's opinion was the opinion of the people of India. But here in the decision of partition of the country he gave up the fight. Was it not an injustice to the people of India?

# [28]

By the creation of Pakistan and subsequently naming its capital as Islamabad keeping in conformity with Islam and Islamic country, Pakistan had increased the distance of separation with India and thereby the under current bond of love and affection gets deteriorated and finally that led to the creation of mistrust in the minds of Hindus and Muslims of the two nations. Under an atmosphere of communal feeling and rioting, Pakistan was created in 1947 as a separate home land for the Muslims of India. Pakistan declared the country would follow the Rule of Islam and in its function it considered India as an enemy country which was exhibited by his activity of the last sixty years. Of course it was an easy process of instigating the people against India and gather vote in the election process. The more the anti-India slogan, the more is the number of votes for any political party and that sets the competition among political parties to abuse India, the more the best. The past history shows, the election and setting of government is nothing but a political chaos because no party was based on ethics and ideals except of slogans of abuse of anti-India that made the opportunity for the military to take over the administration. Pakistan actually could not enjoy the 'Rule of People'. It was the Force of Military who was ruling the country directly or indirectly. Had the thinkers of the Nation thought to establish a friendly relation with India forgetting the territorial dispute, dispute of Kashmir, the permanent peace would have been prevailed making the economy of the region in the path of progress, and reducing the sufferings of the people to a great extent. The people of the two nations were the people of the same country, a few years ago, enjoying the same climate, same culture having with the same ideals of life although differ in the path of prayer to all mighty being accustomed with the thought of different religion. Religion was not a fixed set of mind; it changes with time with the change of mind. The Sweat Valley of Pakistan, a strong hold of Taliban and al-Qaeda, was once a place of Buddha religion, but today all the inhabitants are Muslims. Who can say religion will not change with the change of time and change of mind. Human beings are not immortal. Every one is the children of God and every one should pass a peaceful and comfortable life. The growth of economy of the region would not only develop India, Pakistan but even the whole of South East Asian's countries. The nations of Europe were also fought against one another but today they were living under common currency 'Euro', moving freely with easy permit without the barrier of boundary of territory. Could the two nations India-Pakistan do the same instead of thinking the reverse of destroying the Indian commercial center Mumbai by the attack of Taj-Hotel and others or sending militants in disguise to Kashmir to create unrest for the demand of Kashmir? The good, friendly & hearty relation would made the Kashmir dispute non existence, the demarcation of border would vanish as that had happened in the many States of Europe, and a day might come when both the nations would live as a country of confederation. Religion can not be a barrier for living together of the two nations. Let the manifestation of mind be changed in its own way in the love of almighty; let the people be free to do their prayer to their own way without bringing any obstacles in public and in street. The formation of SMI, student organization of Muslims in India and its collaboration with terrorist organization in Pakistan in conducting terrorist activity in India have aggravated the relation between Hindus and Muslims in India. Definitely its effect had reflected in the voting pattern in Indian election of politics and it would influence the voting pattern in future too. It was the reason for the formation of Political party either with agreeing with the principle of Hindutva programme for getting the vote of majority Hindus or disagreeing with the principle to get the votes of majority of Muslim people. The creation of such divisive force (SMI, student organization of Muslims in India) by the secret act of Pakistan might have bring unrest in India when the government of Pakistan would feel a sigh of happiness on seeing the unrest and destruction of the Union of India but the people of both the regions would remain in dark, suffering with poverty and would burn with the fire of enmity. The religious thinking sets the mind for thinking in terms of religious community and so on instead of thinking for the poor or downtrodden people who were suffering not only from living in distress condition, inadequacy in education, and lacking in service or any other acts of society, irrespective of caste, religion or community. If the human beings accept that all human beings are the children of almighty, then service to anyone irrespective of any of any religion is a service to God. The success of rising the sense of service to humanity in the minds of religious leaders, terrorists, or militants would vanish the attempt of bomb blast or terrorist strike because the victim of blast or strike would be no other than a children of God. The act of killing of any children of God is nothing but an act of sin. Again the service of teachings to any children of God is nothing but an act of purity. The future development of the region depends upon the economic success of the region and not on religion. A progressive mind set would never say vote for the people of community or vote for the people of same religion. A narrow mind set would bring in front the vicious atmosphere of hatred and enmity where a Dalit would vote for a Dalit, a Hindu will vote for a Hindu, a Muslim will vote for a Muslim and thus voting would follow the community and not the person, the merit of the person. In the recent past in UP, there were also votes with Dalit people to be casted with community. Thus the democracy of India could not be counted as a country of true democracy; it is still in the infantry stage in choosing the members of Parliament on the basis of merit instead of caste or religion. The partial solution lies in the act of sincerity of all right thinking people in the endeavor of eliminating the cast politics or religious politics. As the realization of democracy required certain political processes and behaviors and the establishment of certain institutions, who would be acted to reduce the difference in inequality in the society, the responsible government in power would not or should not remain indifferent in the formation of such institution for the sake of great Indian Democracy. Apart from the existing drawbacks, the Indian democracy since 1952 conducting elections under an Independent impartial Organization called Election Commission after a gap of five years in general, establishing voting centers in every corner of hills and planes of India giving the opportunity to caste votes by every matured citizens of India without fear to choose their leaders. The democratic process granted freedom of speech, freedom to participate in establishing independent political and social institutions, freedom to make use of all liberties in the course of their political and social activities. The voting pattern, such as the selection of candidates on the basis of religion, and caste are the signals in the functioning of Indian democracy, which can not be called an ideal democracy. However, India would get impetus from the other countries, the leaders of those countries who had already faced the upheaval task in bringing democratic government in their country. But who could say vote of election of illiterate mass, most of them being passing a strenuous life, could be purchased easily by money. Will it bring a true democratic government in India? But the relief is that even in Europe, democracy faced with election fraud, democracy faced with partiality of vote, discarding the right of franchise of female candidate, in UK female was not recognized a voting person at the beginning in the election process. After French revolution, the thinking of the people went to a sea change. The Rule of autocracy was suspicious of undisclosed threat as because 'The Rule of People' was the cry or secret wishes of the people. However the gradual transformation from autocracy to democracy was going on. The spread of democracy had continued in faster rate in Europe after Napoleon, even though democracy was being consistently hollowed out and rendered mock by election fraud. But the constant attempt of United States in the preaching of democracy succeeded in installing democratic government in the European states to foster human rights and global peace. However, democratic stability did not prevail in many countries right at the beginning because of uncertainty in the new system of ruling involving many people at the seat of power. Cronyism, corruption and intimidation imperiled the stability of country like Ukraine, Serbia, Moldova, Indonesia, Mexico and Bolivia but failed to threaten the foundation of United States and French. United Kingdom followed democracy with utmost devotion, a country what was called the bestowal of civilization keeping queen as the symbolic head. The system of administration utilized in the United Kingdom had not only established the human civilization to the highest order but also upgraded the human value.

**End of hostility Brings peace and prosperity:**

Human civilization is a continuous process to explore the ethics of humanity. Hostility is a human nature but human nature changes with the knowledge of humanity, how could we know? The evident of history is the only guide that influences the humanity to reach to the goal of peace and prosperity in sustaining a better life in the Earth.

During the period of Ottoman Empire (1299-1923), Turks and Greeks lived together but after undergoing independence war a new state Turkish Republic was formed. Since 1923 both the countries looked each other as hostile neighbor and a source of threat prevented them to normalize the issues relating to social, political, or economic issues till 1999. The disputes were related to the status of the Aegean Sea and the Cyprus Issue. It was something like that of Kashmir as between India and Pakistan. Probably, the all powerful God was not happy with their dealings. Devastated earthquakes had happened in the regions of the two countries in 1999. The people of the two neighbors realized that they were the children of God they have to live together and they have to die together and continuation of hostility has no meaning. In July 1999, the two countries had entered into a relation of new era of promising in building trust and collaboration forgetting the last long-lasting period of tension and mistrust between the two countries. The impact of sufferings due to earthquakes of 1999 had brought the Turkish and Greek peoples together and provided a stimulus to the intense diplomatic efforts for the improvement of bilateral relations. The significant attempt in this respect was the establishment of the Turkish-Greek Joint Economic Committee and Turkish-Greek Business Council for providing opportunities to explore the possibilities of expanding trade and economic ties and joint projects. The subsequent improvement of relation encourages in the intensification of the people to people ties and cultural exchanges between the two countries. It was necessary because without the approval of the society people, no government can proceed further to normalize relation. Thus the decrease in the hostility at the social level provided the scope for increased rapprochement between the two governments. The friendly relations between Turkey and Greece based on mutual understanding, respect and trust had not only increased in the initiation of new projects of economic development but also enhanced a stability and security in the region.

This is an evident of history that sets a guide line for India and Pakistan to normalize relation for peace and prosperity for sustaining a better life in the Earth, where a neighbor has to live or die together.

The creation of Pakistan by Jinnah having the call of direction action day on 16th August 1946 was based on religious strength even though he wished a friendly relation between India and Pakistan on the point of humanity after the formation of Pakistan. But since the creation of Pakistan, the country was ruled by military. A military Ruler never can think of peace and prosperity by any other means except the military action. Kashmir was the cause of concern for Pakistan and directly or indirectly it was also a concern for the whole region. The concern of Pakistan for the people of Kashmir is due to its keenness of religion, on the other hand for India Kashmir is a test of secular integrity of India to protect each and every citizen of India irrespective of religion. Aegean Sea and Cyprus were the issues in between Turkey and Greece for sixty years, which are now no longer any issue in the midst of people's cooperation and trust of faith for the welfare of the people. The military ruler of Pakistan have encouraged the militant activity and terrorist activity against India for more than thirty years after the formation of Bangladesh but without any fruitful ground reality except the increase of miss-trust between the people of the two countries. The policy of military vengeance has now created problem in Pakistan itself where the girls and ladies of Pakistan are going to lose their freedom of expression, education and movement under the threat of shariat Law, even in the modern age of 21st century. The technology of the current century has integrated the distant countries superseding the barer of boundaries. If Pakistan had increased the activity relating to the cooperation of people of the valley forgetting the increase of territory, it would have increased the economy and the stability. The might of people's friendship and cooperation is superior than military might is only can be understood by a Civilian government and not by a military administrator. India had shown the maximum restrain in the event of 26/11 Mumbai carnage in spite of the killing of high profiles of 180 human beings belonging to the citizens of the different countries of the world. Internationally Pakistan is being humiliated and graded as a terrorist sponsored State short of a declared terrorist sponsored country. The citizen of Pakistan has now realized the effect of lasting military rule and continuance of patronizing terrorist activity further being complicated by the Taliban activity of Afghanistan. Taliban are mostly Pashtun origin. All the Pashtun dominated areas of Afghanistan are in revolt against US Force. Pakistani side of the boarder is occupied by Taliban. The whole region of this area is antagonized by religious slogan, which is looked dearly by the intellectuals of Pakistan. Further rise of strength would lurk the possibility of a unified Islamist ruled Pashtun State threatening the unity of both Pakistan and Afghanistan. This has tempted the cry for rule of democracy. The re-appointment of the former chief justice, Iftikar Chaudhury, who was dismissed by Pervez Musharraf in 2007, was highly hailed by Pakistani public. Mr. Chaudhury fought against Musharraf regime's corruption and contempt for the constitution. Even President Zardari did not agree to re-appoint him. He might be afraid of his right of Presidency. The amnesty under Musharraf regime that had led Benazir Bhutto and him return from exile might be in the shadow of question. The emergence of Democracy has brought a light of hope of prosperity and stability in the region of Pakistan. But that the hope of stability and democracy had been shattered by the assassination of Mrs. Bhutto. Whatever kind of governs exists in Pakistan directly or indirectly it speaks the voice of military and not the voice of people.

**Welfare of people is better done by the cooperation of people and not by the religious antagonism:**

It is seen that a country is developed by its technology, industry and exploring its minerals and not by preaching of any religion. Of course, it is believed that religion brings a kind of purity of mind and a discipline in personal life. The history says religion of a place changes with the change of time. In the western world of Europe Christianity spread in the time of Caesar but a change of religion in same region took place in large scale in the period of Ottoman Empire of Turkey. In Asia in the Indian Sub-continent, change of religion also had seen, and also that had happened in the earlier period of century. The present Swat valley of Pakistan or the present Passwer of Pakistan was a center of Buddhist religion and now these places were the center of Islamic fundamentalists. Kashmir, a place of importance, a place of dispute between Pakistan and India was a place of Kashmiri Brahmin Hindu Pandits but now it is a Muslim majority State. A religion can change custom and community but not the constitutional character of a human being. The economic status of a country can even change the constitutional character. A flourishing economy of a State can change food habit of taking nutrient food which may change the composition of hemoglobin of the people of the state irrespective of caste or religion. It is only people's coordination that can bring a change in the economic status of a state. Economic integration would have united the world to make it a beautiful place to live in just like that had the integration of communication brought through internet at every house. Contact of people to people, country to country, exchanging of goods, technology, known and unknown ideas are the tools of development to bring justice in the effort of bringing welfare of the people of any state. People's cooperation is superior to religious affinity in the development of human civilization.

# [29]

Americans are in favor of promoting Democracy by wining the heart of the people by giving material aid as well as by granting aid and also by diplomatic skill instead of military Force. The idea of promoting democracy using military as is done by the US President Bosh to bring democracy in Iraq had been rejected by the majority people of America. The President of America is all powerful, but if his activity was not with wishes of the people, the President could not remain in power to hold the post of highest honour. Bosh was defeated in the fight of election of American Presidency against Obama. The majority people of America believe that the goal of overthrowing Iraq's authoritarian government by force in order to bring democracy was not the correct approach. War could not bring democracy by suppressing the voice of the people by the strength of military rather it would create terrorist and militants. American citizens want to hand over the power of administration to the hands of Iraqi people. Now American people want no more war and no more death of American soldiers in the foreign soil. Majority of Americans were in favor of withdrawing troops from Iraq by accepting an Iraqi constitution even though it did not fully meet the democratic standard. Very few percentage of Americans were in believe that the more the number of democratic countries, the more safety is for the world. This belief of thought was not true proved practically. There was no guarantee that a democratic government would be friendlier to the US and would abide by the US policies. Although the majority people believed that democracy was the best form of government, even then all countries were not ready for democracy. Saudi Arabia, one of the best friends of America did not like 'The Rule of Democracy'. Apparently, American had supported any country in promoting democracy, but Americans were not in favor of imposition of democracy. The people of America did favor the US government in promoting democracy through the act of skillful diplomacy, or by granting aid or by technical assistance in conducting elections. Very few people of America were in favor of putting greater pressure on countries like Saudi Arabia, Egypt or Pakistan to hold elections to become democratic. But Americans speak out against the violation of human rights be it the government of Burma, China, Egypt, Iran, Pakistan, Russia or Saudi Arabia or Sri Lanka in recent time and asked the respecting government to respect human rights. America never hesitated to bring resolution in the UN against any country for the violation of human right. Many journalists compare the democracy of India with that of America while one was the oldest, and the other was the largest. The democracy is already established in America and the fruits of democracy is enjoying by the citizens of America since a century while implication of democracy has started in India under all obstacles and in a state of trial in the field of scarcity of basic amenities of human life. Many good or bad ideals would come in front by comparison of democracy with the democracy of other nations, According to the 2008 index of democracy, which was based on the performance of certain indicators, such as the measure of electoral process and pluralism, civil liberties, the functioning of government, political participation or political culture, India appeared to be not a full democracy but a flawed one. But still India is born with the ideals of democracy and accordingly, India has framed its constitution keeping in mind the constitution of the greatest democratic countries of UK, US and French. The democracy in Sri Lanka, Thailand, Philippines, Indonesia, Malaysia and Brazil if measured, were also found to be rated as 'flawed democracies'. But in term of rating, the position of India would be better and would be very close to the nations of 'full democracy'. India's scores record is sufficiently good in the index process of political participation and political culture, but in the back foot dragging behind in the measure of corruption, lacking in governance and government accountability.

The country Canada came into existence only about hundred years before of Independence of India. Canada has already set the record of example in the implementation of democracy. Canada's Parliament constituted in 1867, continues to be a vibrant country of democracy. In Parliament, the representatives examine the issues on routine basis, based on the policies and laws of the country, and made the government accountable for its action of misconduct. India wanted to be a nation of great democracy setting the example of ideal democracy in the world, but it could not do so for many greedy politicians having with sectarian mind set. More over at the very beginning of its independence, India faced with the challenge of division of the country and subsequently with huge task of the exchange of population deepening the financial crisis of the new democracy. The policy of equality could not be implemented in the atmosphere of economic turmoil and mistrust of fellow citizens. The existence of Islamic Pakistan, a religious state at the door step was also a hindrance for the implementation true democracy. Education as well as economy of the country was in bad condition of the new democracy since the beginning and continued to deteriorate by the years extending to 1990 bringing frustration and division among the people of different religion and race. Above all, the greatness of Indian leaders lied in the formation of constitution of India where equality, fraternity and brotherhood had been rightly inscribed in the preambles of the constitution. In1990, after the policy of liberalization, the economy of the country had improved satisfactorily and it is also expected in the course of time it would supersede in the rate or development to many more countries and proclaimed itself a country of great democracy and set its position parallel to the United States provided it could develop infrastructure, and bring the status of life to a respectable position.

French is a country who helped America in the declaration of Independence against British, the long seven years with arms, weapons, men and money out of enmityagainst British and itself dipped into extreme poverty. United States of America declared its independence at Philadelphia by ringing the bell of liberty on 4th July, 1776. In French the new King Lewis VI faced the volatile public who were suffering to the point of extreme not in any other luxury but in the scarcity of food, the ladies were more furious than gents because, the everyday handling of kitchen lies in the hands of ladies. These were the shocking days for the people in the country of French although, at present the City of Parish, planned in circle, stands unparallel in beauty as the queen City of Universe, could not remain idle in the brick of death, revolt, revolt to Hotel de Ville (City Hall), revolt to Versailles, revolt to Parish, city to rural and revolt continues for three years, King was killed, new system of administration following the ideals of Greek democracy, Roman federalism, had emerged enhanced with new ideals under the principles of great French Philosopher Rousseau, an intellect of Great Geneva of Switzerland, a center of creator of all new born thought like Red Cross, UN etc and great English Philosopher Locke what was called administration under democracy. After stability the government of French thought of her duty for the sake of humanity to enlighten the world and so the Statue of Liberty. The Untied States achieved its independence because of the constant cooperation of the government of French. In the American Independence struggle the involvement of French was so much that the administration gets dipped in economic disaster bringing the 'French Revolution' and brought democracy by killing the King Lewis VI. Thus the French rightly thought it wise to give the message of democracy to the citizens of the Globe by installing a Statue of liberty at the gateway of US at NY as a gift of greeting to the American citizen. And there had given an unwritten declaration to the world for peace such as "The message of Brotherhood, Fraternity and Equality are the principles of democracy." These principles of democracy would bring Global peace. People of the world had seen the holocaust that had occurred at Nagasaki and Hiroshima. Had the message of Brotherhood, Fraternity and Equality been heard, the holocaust might not have been happened.

The new 21$^{st}$ century is now again in the threshold of deadly nuclear weapons. The North Korea and Iran are also in the search of Nuclear weapons who declared that their national sovereignty is in danger. It is now the test of UNO how to bring the two nations in control by the message of love, fraternity and equality.

Of course, the success of India lies in bringing democracy in the midst of so many existing kings, who instead of opposing democracy for the fact of being losing the autocratic rule of kingship, supported the rule of democracy, even then everything was not good for the Indian democracy. It could not be ruled out that Indians achieved independence before learning the rule of administration. The presence of few ICS was not sufficient to rule such a big country India. No one can out right reject the reasons of down grading the Indian democracy. Veteran journalist M V Kamath had a different perception. The facts and figure had demonstrated that how in all areas of activity where merit and excellence had a role to play; the Indians remained far behind than the smaller nations of the world. He rightly pointed out that, how none of the 567 Indian Universities figure within the top 200 universities of the world. Likewise, none of India's 292 think-tanks figure listed among the 5,329 such institution of the world. Not a single Indian think tank has been named among the 30 of the world. He said that there are other parameters that are equally revealing. In India, people below the poverty line continued to be about 36%. By contrast, poverty in China declined from 30. 7% to 14. 3% in just nine years between 1978 and 1987. It was further down to 3. 2% in 2001. Even in Indonesia, the proportion of people in poverty dropped from 41. 1% between 1967-1987 to 11. 3percent in 1996. In India, the total number of farmer suicides in 1995 touched 270,940. The infant morality rate in India is still 48. 2% per thousand whereas it is 4. 2% in South Korea and just 2. 54% in Malaysia. Much of what is happening undemocratic in India could very well be due to the high percentage of law makers with criminal records or at least criminal charges against them. On July 13, 2012 of the 4,896 MLAs and MPs constituting the Electoral College for presidential votes, 31% had declared in sworn affidavits before the Election Commission that they had criminal charges pending against them. How could the Election Commission have allowed them to vote? However, the more important question is—how could they have been allowed to become lawmakers? It had shown the principle of law accounts nothing. What counts is the flawed discretion of whoever is in charge when a decision has to be taken. There is no denying fact that the Indian republic is in such a situation where the government has virtually no control over things. The lack of control is so evident that to-day India is no longer in a position to identify its citizens by issuing identity cards of citizenship. The country has allowed so many million illegal migrants to infiltrate across the international borders that it has no way of distinguishing between the citizen and the infiltrators. What is even worse, it has no control over the prices of essential commodities and as such no control over inflation. Government would evade responsibility by claiming that control of prices in the days of free market economy, is not the responsibility of the government. The other important responsibility is to control a large number of economic offenders. Manufacturers or industrialists who had no liability with the people but to hike prices on any pretext to make more profit are the powerful beneficiary who can donate money to the politicians at the time of election process. Government has no control over inflation as well as no control over money laundering. Who can give credit to government when the government had failed to stop over Rs 1,886,000 crore (figure quoted from published article in paper) being laundered out of India in just one decade. Control of infiltration across international border, control of price rise etc such other many thing were out of government control as the government was over burdened with huge problem since independence. Political leaders could not think of such problems beforehand. Political leaders never thought of improving economy beforehand. Japanese youth learnt the skill of industry from the British in British land even after the destruction of Japan by Atom Bomb in 1945. While Indian youths were not motivated by the political leaders to go to England to learn the industrial skill like Japanese youths rather the wealthy and influential persons went to England to qualify as ICS to become a key man in British administration. Political leaders were more in favour of getting the power of administration at any cost, be it inefficiency in the field of work, threat of rioting in the process of division of the nation, corruption or division of the country leading to economic downfall of the country. History will never forget the achievement of Indian independence at the cost of human tragedy.

# [30]

**The Past, Present and Future of Hindus of Bengal:** In 1947, Bengal was partitioned into the Indian State of West Bengal (1/3 rd of Bengal) and East Bengal(2/3$^{rd}$ of Bengal) that East Bengal became a part of Pakistan, a declared home land for the Muslims of India. Subsequently East Pakistan broke away from Pakistan to form the independent country of Bangladesh. Most of Sylhet district in Assam also become a part of East Pakistan and subsequently included in East Bengal. At last Independence of India came into being under the dominance of Northern leaders with the partition of India along with the partition of Punjab and Bengal. The ultimate aim was the dominance of Northern India over the whole of India. The Hindus of Bengal were befooled with the temptation of living in Hindu India under Hindu culture less a United Bengal under the British Presidency of Bongo-Bihar-Orissa would jeopardize the influence of the Hindus of Northern India. Communal politics were brought in front to divide Bengal. However after partition of Bengal, the West Bengal was thought to be a home land for the Hindus mostly as because East Bengal became the home land for the Muslims only although no constitutional provision was made for the living of Hindus with faith of Hindu religion in the remaining portion of Bengal. The religious sentiment provoked the minds of every religious community to acquire land for future safety and security. People were compelled to leave their home and hearths because of the politically religious decisions of political leaders. PM of both the countries meet together to reduce the tension, as a number of many communal riots broke out in different areas of India and Pakistan.

After partition, the reaming part of Hindu Bengal had flooded with uprooted Hindus of East Bengal. In 1952 Liaquat-Nehru Pact 1950 was formulated. Jinnah thought of a Muslim country out of India at the time of partition, but again Liaquat Ali by his clever diplomacy thought of a united Muslim Bengal even after partition of India. How? If the Northern leaders were sincere in there mind and action of spirit, and think for the good of all and Hindus of Bengal in particular after partition, the respected Indian Prime Minister Nehru would not go for a Liaquat-Nehru Pact. The very Pact gave the opportunity for the Muslims of West Bengal who left the country just after partition for the sake of life, came back and settled in West Bengal in safe and comfort and having with constitutional right, who can live here as a class one citizen unlike the Hindus of Pakistan. While not a single Hindu who came to India from East Pakistan went back to East Bengal. Here lies the supremacy of diplomacy of Pakistani PM. He knows no Hindu of East Pakistan would prefer to go back from India because of no Hindu would like to live there as they have no right to live there constitutionally, as having being Pakistan was formed as an Islamic state and a homeland for the Muslims of India only. But people of other religion can live there without constitutional right as a second class citizen. The Pact was formed in 1950 at the Capital of Delhi after long seven days of thought out decisions between the two PM of two countries. There was no protest raised from West Bengal or Assam as well. It was not that the Leaders of West Bengal or Assam have not understood the long term implications of the Pact but the Leaders were more patriotic and more wide in thinking on humanitarian ground. The Muslims who were compelled to leave West Bengal or Assam out of fear came back to their ancestral home because of Liaquat-Nehru Pact, was a sigh of consonance of peace to the hearts of every leaders. But it carried a long term political implication. Knowing it very well that the Pact would increase the Muslim population in West Bengal or Assam and that would bring back the religious conflict of pre-independence period in Bengal. Why the PM of Northern India did such a Pact? Is it only for humanitarian ground or for the underground cause of fear of rising Bengal supremacy as that prevailed in pre-independence period as the 'Rule of Bongo Bihar Orissa' of British Presidency. It carried peace and stability no doubt. But it had also carried an undeclared route of movement of people to a region of Bengal for sustaining a better life. A comparatively better economic situation prevailing in India at that time in compare to East Pakistan (Bangladesh) had encouraged the Muslim population to settle preferably in West Bengal. Thus the Hindu Bengal of Independent India by the period of sixty years has already transformed into a Muslim Bengal. Now no political party can form a government without the favour of Muslim community. It is therefore a spree of competition among the political parties who should be the first to give maximum facility to Muslim community. The days are not far a way a United Bengal under Muslims is coming into being. Indian leaders 'thinks ahead for short term gain, but Muslim leaders always think far head, the history says so. The implication of Liquat-Nehru Pact (1950) is equally disturbing for Assam if it is looked in terms of religious point of view. The point of religion undermined the ground of humanity as because the saddest story lies in the division of the country on the basis of religion. The Pact had equally increased the Muslim population in Assam and equally created the secret route of human transfer. As no body or no force on Earth can stop the natural flow of Sea water, similarly, the flow of human movement no one can stop. Did the Super Power Untied States prevent the flow of Marxian to the United States? Did the West German stop the flow of East Germans to West German by the creation of Berlin Wall? To-day the demograpgy of Assam is going to change. Now the division of state is going on in India for immediate political gain, several division had already being made by the time for political gain, but very soon a day will come for Indians to face the challenge of separatism when unity will break into regional security as division of state and formation of regional party is increasing day by day.

Liaquat-Nehru Pact goes like that. At the time of independence, many communal riots broke out in different areas of India and Pakistan. These riots were political riots to root out the religious community not liking to the declaration of the country as Pakistan was for Muslims, but of course India was for all although there existed a fear of uncertainty in the minds of Muslims just at the time of partition if the India become a Hindu State. Due to brutal killings by the majority community under political patronage, a huge number of Muslims migrated from India, and Hindus and Sikhs from Pakistan. Yet, killing and the mass migration failed to solve the human problem. Even after the migration, almost half of the Muslims living in the Sub-continent were left in India and on the other hand a small number of Hindus were left in Pakistan. The physiology of common people was that India is a secular country, all groups of religious people can live here but Pakistan is a Muslim country, it would be difficult for the people other than Muslims to live there. Therefore even after partition migration of Hindu community continued from Pakistan to India but the reverse flow tends to nil. This was the policy of Jinnah who predicted a situation, a day will come when the **Hindu people will well-come the Muslims to rule India** which they denied at the time of partition. It was the belief of Muslim leaders that if Muslims could rule India having being minority in the Mughal period, why not they would rule India now? To day also no matter minority or majority, the leaders of Muslims have created a situation to rule India. To day we could see in every state, it is the Muslims who were counted to form the Ministry. Let the Hindus form the government but the government would be run by Muslims from behind. This was possible because of the far-sighted policy of Muslim leaders of India.

The Hindus who were left in East Bengal, now Bangladesh, were unable to become an integral part of the societies they were living in. The people and government of their country looked upon them as enemy being a Hindu, a well-wisher of Hindustan according to their religious outlook. They were unable to earn of their loyalty. This problem escalated during the time and human slaughter continued time to time for any of activity in India related to religion such as the 'Stealing of Hazratbal' 'Demolition of Babri Mosque' etc. Liaquat Ali Khan thought of the plan of acquiring the whole of Bengal. He issued a statement emphasizing the need to reach a solution to the problem and proposed a meeting with his Indian counterpart to determine how to put an end to the communal riots. The two Prime Ministers met in Delhi on April 2, 1950, and discussed the matter. The meeting continued for days together. On April 8, an agreement was formulated, which was later entitled as Liaquat-Nehru Pact. This pact provided a 'bill of rights' for the minorities of India and Pakistan. According to the Pact, the following issues were decided to be addressed.

1. To alleviate the fears of the religious minorities on both sides.
2. To elevate communal peace.
3. To create an atmosphere in which the two countries could resolve their other differences.

   According to the agreement, the governments of India and Pakistan solemnly agreed that each shall ensure, to the minorities throughout its territories, complete equality of citizenship, irrespective of religion; a full sense of security in respect of life, culture, property and personal honor. It also guaranteed fundamental human rights of the minorities, such as freedom of movement, speech, occupation and worship. The pact also provided for the minorities to participate in the public life of their country, to hold political or other offices and to serve in their country's civil and armed forces. The Liaquat-Nehru Pact provided to control rioting or other elements with an iron hand. Both the governments decided to set up minority commissions in their countries to look to the reality of the matter to ensure that no one breaches the pact and to make recommendations to guarantee its enforcement.

   Both the leaders agreed that the loyalty of the minorities should be reserved for the state in which they were living and for the solution of their problems they should look forward to the government of the country they were living in. This pact was broadly acknowledged as an opportunity to improve relations between India and Pakistan. Muslim leaders were intelligent, think far away. Today Muslims were safe and powerful both in Bangladesh as well as in West Bengal of India.

India liberated Bangladesh at the cost of Indian army and taking the whole country under risk. India did it to keep Bangladesh at the control of India and curtail the power of Pakistan. At the beginning India kept its force in Bangladesh and the country was obliged to India. But Indian diplomacy failed, India compelled to withdraw forces from Bangladesh, the country became a friend of Pakistan. The army killed the Father of the Nation, Mujibur Rahaman. If any duty, the government of India thinks for the Hindu people of

Bangladesh, who sacrificed every thing for the cause of Independence of India, how did the government remain silent without interfering in the formation of their ministry? After all the turmoil of that region had already affected India who had to suffer to keep 10 million people of East Bengal in the soil of India till the declaration of Independent Bangladesh. Government changed, torture over Hindus continued, and India became again an enemy country. Now the change of government sometimes made India a friendly country or an enemy country. Where is the fore slightness of India? Bangladesh was liberated by India but that country speaks against India, against the Hindus. Is it the Indians' gainful diplomacy? India should not ask the British to go. Now it is the time to hand over the administration to Muslim, who can keep India united, who can rule India under strict rule of discipline. They have vision of administration proved by the record of history. The political party of Bangladesh never hesitates to torture the insignificant Hindus who were living there for any matter but for no fault of theirs. Burning of houses and throwing of Hindu Gods to water are the normal activity of torture after a certain interval in that country. India is nothing but an on looker because the government of India has exhausted the words of sympathy for these people. The days are not far away when every Hindu living there will declare voluntarily that they are now Muslims because they have to live till death. They have no voice, no safety, no security and above all no service to earn to live as long as they would live on the faith of Hinduism. Is it the vision of the Hindu leaders of Northern India to protect the Hindus of Bengal by division by the weapon of religion? There was no dearth of love for people to people but the sentiment of religion had infused in the minds of the people by the political leaders and destroyed the existing love and brotherhood among the people of different religion and different communities. The Leaders played their political game for power using the religion as their weapon of success and making the people of religious community as the victims.

## INDEPENDENT UNITED BENGAL OF SUHRAWARDY:

The Bengalis, the Kings of British Kingdom of Bongo, Bihar Orissa is shattered into the fight of self killing making two domains of West Bengal and East Bengal. Much of blood has flown over the Ganga and Buriganga rivers and now a rethinking was necessary to get back to the glory of Bengal. The record of history will tell how the Bengalis were befooled by the leaders of Northern India to destroy the command of United Bengal, the Bengal of Bongo, Bihar and Orissa. Love and affection of the Hindus and Muslims of Bengal have been polluted by the sentiment of religion. After partition of Punjab and Bengal, the immediate effect was massacre in Punjab, but the same kind of massacre did not happen in Bengal. Even after partition people could not forget the feelings of brotherhood. Slowly and gradually time to time rioting took place under the patronage of political leaders. Now what is the condition of Bengalis here and there? It is nothing but poverty, unemployment and distress of economic sufferings. People understand little of politics, their distress mind take the shelter of religion to consol the self. Having being certain of the division of India on the basis of the two-nation theory, the partition of the Bengal province along with religious line become almost certain. The Muslim leader of Bengal province Suhrawardy came up with a plan to create an independent Bengal state that won't join either Pakistan or India but thought to remain as United Bengal, an Independent Bengal. However, the plan went against the principle of Muslim League which was a political party during the British period. The demand of the political party was to create a separate homeland on the basis of two-nation theory for the Muslims of India. The plan to create an independent Bengal State was against the demand of Muslim League of India. However, the plan to create an independent Bengal State was well-come by Bengal provincial congress leader like Sarat Chandra Bose, the elder brother of Netaji and Kiran Shankar Roy. Many of the Muslim Leaders opposed it but again few of the leaders supported it. Barddhaman's League leader Abdul Hashim supported it. Imagining the turmoil of the citizens of Bengal, Muhammad Ali Jinnah also compelled to give a tacit support to the plan. From historical point of view Muslims were majority in Bengal since the period of Nabob

Siraj-ud-ulla, the feeling of suppression was there. More over the situation was excited with the two nation theory based on religion. The option to Hindus of Bengal was either to join the movement of United Bengal (Independent) or to join Hindu India.

However, other Congress leaders of Northern India and Congress leadership including Nehru and Patel rejected the plan of United Bengal. The Hindu nationalist party Hindu Mahasabha under the leadership of Shyama Prasad Mukherjee vehemently opposed the plan of United Bengal. The atmosphere of the country was explosive as the country is going to divide on the basis of religion. Mr. Mukherjee was the Chief of Hindu Mahasabha, a Hindu organization based on religious faith of Hinduism, relied on the majority of Hindu India for the protection of Hindus of Bengal. Keeping the strength of majority-Hindu of India in mind he strongly opposed the proposal of a United Bengal. Thus the Hindus of Bengal sided with Hindu India.

Many of the Hindu leaders could not visualize an independent Bengal. Rather they also opined that even though the plan asked for a sovereign Bengal state, in practice it will be a virtual Pakistan and the Hindu minority will be at the mercy of the Muslim majority forever. But they under mined the facts that the United Bengal would be a sovereign State with equal right of Hindus and Muslims where sanctity of religion would be a non issue. There are many countries in the Globe where different religious people are living happily without any religious feeling. Such as the Catholic and Protestant are living in most of the European countries, Shia and Sunni are living in the same country of Middle East. Muslims, Hindus and Buddhists were living in Indonesia in amity. A good economic state of the country never allows any favor whatsoever. Under the distress state of economic situation, the religion got the top most priority as soon as a country is formed on the basis of religion. As the demand of Muslim League under the command of Jinnah was for a separate Home land for the Muslims of India, the Hindu organization, Hindu Mahasabha under the command of Shyama Prasad Mukherjee also things like wise something for the Hindus of Bengal. The subsequent incidents of rioting, human slaughter and mass migration did support the decision of opposing the plan of a United Bengal? Did Hindu Mahasabha came to rescue the Hindus of Bengal to live in West Bengal with constitutional right of Hindus where the Muslims can not have the equal right as they got 2/3 of Bengal for their living. More over did the Hindu Mahasabha protested against the enactment of Liaquiat-Nehru Pact (1950) that goes against the spirit of Hindus of Bengal. Who was the friend? There was no friend and foe in this universe.

But in the plan of United Bengal no body was demanding a separate homeland. The religious sentiment prevailing in the country could not permit any body to think rationally for the Bengali as a nation. A United Independent Bengal would neither be a party to India nor to Pakistan. As a nation Bengali will live in the world with pride and honour. The root cause of disparity of people to people lies in the distress state of condition of economy.

According to the Vedanta of Hindu religious doctrine to get rid of the great deal of stress, the simple way out is to love people for what they are. Accept them. No expectations, no demands and no bondage imposed. Then you will be loved and adored by all! The Hindu people of Bali and Java are living happily in the Muslim majority of Indonesia.

After the division Bengal what had happened to the Hindus of East Bengal? Did the leaders of Delhi have any answer?

Did the Hindu think of, Hindu would remain majority in West Bengal? Did the Hindu could think of to form the government of them?

It is now Muslims are majority in other part of Bengal (Bangladesh) as well as in this part of Bengal (West Bengal).

What the Hindu Bengali has got by becoming a party to Hindu Mahasabha? Did the Leaders of Northern India have protected Hindus of Bengal? Did the Hindu leaders could stop the migration of Hindu from East to West? Who did the greatest blunder by doing the Liaquiat-Nehru Pact, 1950?

By doing the Pact why the Indian PM allowed all the Muslims, who left West Bengal just after partition in the juncture of rioting and human holocaust to resettle in West Bengal with full government protection and with equal constitutional right?

Did it not under mine the right of Hindus Bengalis?

While not a single Hindu of East Bengal who fled to India from East Pakistan, out of life security did not return to East Bengal (East Pakistan) because, they have no political right to live there as a right of equality as the country constitutionally belongs to Muslims of India. Did the Hindu Leaders of Hindu Mahasabha provide any constitutional guarantee for the dominance of Hindus in West Bengal? The Hindus of Bengal not only lost their majority but also lost their territory. To day Hindus are neither safe in West Bengal nor in East Bengal? If they were in United Bengal at least they would not lose their land and property and they would not be a refugee. Who is friend and who is foe? It is you to decide, it is not religion but the love, the true love of humanity. The love will develop the custom, the rituals and a belief of faith, a long association would command your ego to obey the rituals, the rituals of religion which can not bring hatred provided love is in heart.

The Hindu Muslim rioting in Bengal was not due to religious hatred but due to the command of administration where Religion was used as a weapon to acquire the command of administration. Had it been a United Bengal, the hatred of religion, the demand of territory on the basis of land area would not arise. Now also survival of Bengal lies in the Unity of Bengal provided the Bangladesh constitution provides equal rights to Hindus even though the process is much harder to achieve. The Delhi government never works in favor of Hindus of Bengal; it worked rather against the interest of Hindus of Bengal. It never protested against the division of Bengal before partition, it did not provided any constitutional safe guard for the protection of Hindus of Bengal, it provided shelter for the Muslims of East Pakistan who returned to West Bengal and Assam of India after partition instead of giving shelter to Hindu Refugees in West Bengal, the Refugees, who came here after being tortured in East Pakistan after partition, it did not provided the respectable shelter to the Hindu Refugees of East Bengal in India as is done in the case of the Punjabi Refugees of East Punjab who were being migrated from West Punjab, it did not gave protection to Hindus of East Pakistan after liberation involving the Indian Army and after being the emergence of Bangladesh. Now Muslims are dominating East Bengal as well as West Bengal. What kind of benefit the Hindus of Bengal had gained after being sided with Hindu majority of India except the exploitation. Had the Hindus of Bengal sided with Suhrawardy in the fight to form Independent United Bengal, at least Hindus would not be Refugee and converted to beggars as now in India under the Rule of central government of India. To day or tomorrow it is going to take its real shape, a Muslim Bengal just as the sea of water flows to the downward channels.

The demand for the **creation of a home land** for the Muslims of India and subsequently the acceptance of the demand without a single protest creating Pakistan, automatically created a undeclared right of the Hindu people over the rest of India, the Indian Union. How can the Indian Leaders equate the right of Hindus with the right of the people of Muslim faiths with equality? Having being acquired the right over India after being forming a separate homeland, how the Muslims acquired the equal right again over the rest of India? However, Muslims can live but the right of Muslims in the rest of India should not be detrimental in any way to the right of Hindus because the country, the rest of India belongs to Hindus by the right of Ethics of the Law of Division. In addition to this right, Hindus of Bengal acquired an additional right over the rest of Bengal left with India by virtue of the Law of Division. Did India, or Majority-Hindu India, or Hindu Mahashaba preserve or protected the right by any constitutional attachment? Why does the Hindu Bengal (West Bengal) should live in India under the grace of Delhi? Did you think under the present circumstances, the Hindus of West Bengal could live as Hindus with Hindu faith in course of time? Did India go any longer to protect the Hindus? It is now time to think for United Independent Bengal that proposed by Shawardy at the time of partition and supported by many Hindu Leaders.

The concept of democracy in the South Asian region has a remarkable history. This is historically known as **Indus Valley Civilization,** which thrived in modern-day Pakistan, was one of the earliest and largest ancient human civilizations alongside Mesopotamia, the Nile Valley, Anatolia and ancient China. It is very much known for its development in sophistication and urbanized culture at a time when there was no Islam in Pakistan. It had organized planning system, standard architecture and civic controls. It suggests the Indus Valley of Pakistan as possibly as one of the earliest model of democracy, the one which was being based on a "Rule by the people" and one that could even predate Greece. But democracy failed just after independence of India and the area went under the Rule of military. Since independence, Pakistan's democratic system has fluctuated at various times throughout its political history, mainly due to feudalism, political corruption and periodic coup d'états by the act of martial law. However an Islamic democratic system was introduced time to time. In practice, two kinds of Islamic democracies are found to be recognized in Islamic countries. The basis of this distinction has to do with how logically Islam is incorporated into the affairs of the state. It recognizes Islam as its religion. Introduction of Shari-law in its democratic system of Islam was encouraged. Of course it differs state to state. There are also states in the Muslim world which are secular democracies rather than religious democracies. The concept of Islamic democracy is vitiated by Sunni-Shia split. What is, wrong with Pakistan's Democracy, the wrong is with the governance. The voice of Army is superior to the voice of president as is found practically true. People have every right to look and judge the kind of democracy what is going on in the country. It is only in Islamic Pakistan among the Muslim world where a democracy at least by name is present. Zardari, a tainted man, who is the co-chairman of the ruling party, presides over the party meetings at the presidential palace and as such the President. He is not an elected president but he is conducting the party affairs amidst an act of controversy. Constitutionally, the president, he or she should not belong to a political party, and should not make political statements, and should not conduct him or herself in such a manner that can cause controversy. But after all he is a tainted man being charged with massive corruption. Thus democracy in Pakistan is only by name and not in worthy action with etiquette of Presidential honor. However in 2013, new President Nawab Sarif have emerged as victorious a democratically elected President of Pakistan, but it is a test of Presidency in a terrorist infected country under the command of Army like Pakistan to what extent the voice of democracy is truly heard and implemented for the benefit of the country and people at large.

**Sense of Perception:** In India brotherhood and tolerance is the basic character of the people. These characters had been developed due to age old practice of searching the peace and pleasure of mind in silence of the concentration of heart and soul in solitude. It reminds many the remark of an American who said practice "Brotherhood and tolerance" on both sides between Pakistan and India. The record of the history is that Hindus were tolerant by virtue of their religious faith and custom, but the Muslims were renowned for their might, vigor and aggression. A Muslim Ruler never compromises with the power of throne and in need assassin the own brother or even torture the Father as seen in Indian history. In regard to Pakistan it is understood, a country formed out of violence how it can teach the lesson of tolerance so easily. The virtue of tolerance is not to teach, it evolves from within. Geeta, the sacred book of Hindu Religion refers the Doctrine of Karma. The sense of tolerance and brotherhood is the philosophy of self perception. Every one can not have the same perception. Growing, learning, experiencing, is a long process, and in the end, an individual will know what perception is, and become one of the person of the virtue of tolerance with emotion of love of brotherhood.

# [31]

**Modern Concept of Democracy:** In the doctrine of democracy the word such as 'Liberty' 'Equality' and 'Freedom of speech' are very common. United States is recognized as a true democratic country in the 21st century. United States is a country of companies and companies are the back bone of the economy of the country, a country which is conducting the states through the Capitalistic system of state policy which is different from a socialist patern of democracy. To day US consists of many multi-millionaire and again many poor citizens who were unable to pay even the minimum money for health insurance which is the basic need of health treatment. Do we see democratic equality in the disparity of wealth in between rich and poor? We are living in society under community with freedom of liberty. A man is living with two wives and ten children (family of 12) while a man is living with one wife and one child (family of 3). The social benefit is 12 times for a family of 12 while the social benefit is 3 times for a family of 3. Where is democratic equality in granting social benefit? How freedom of democratic 'Liberty' could be sustainable with the concept of democratic 'Equality'? Does it not require democratic restrictions or binding curtailing the democratic liberty?

The concept of true democracy is open and boundless. There was a time when it is said to be termed as 'Roman Empire", 'Mughal Empire', or 'British Empire' to confine the area under Romans, Mughals or British where the respective rulers would look to the welfare of its citizens. These 'Empires' are now being shattered into small countries, some are again ruled under democracy and some are under an autocracy. The World had seen World War I and World

154

War II as well. The two blocks were created one under Communism (Russia) and the other under Capitalism (USA), the two super-powers of the world. The countries under respective blocks were always in fear of obliging the dictum of Super-power. Where does stand the concept of democratic 'Liberty'? The world had seen the 'Cold War' for a considerable period of time and now in the 21st century that has been eliminated. The Super-power Russia had broken and new Russia and US are looking for terms of friendship as there is no need of enemity and looking for the welfare of mankind. United States always ask for the establishment of a democratic government be it Pakistan, Bangladesh or Morisis. Sometimes democratic government is formed and some times not. Is it beyond the control to look after whether a country is functing democratically or not?

The present trend is for the formation of a democratic country, which would be good for the well fare of the people as the country would be ruled by the people, and for the people. A day may come when the people will ask for the formation a democratic World, which would be good for the well fare of the humanity comprising the people of the globe, a globe that would be ruled by people of the globe, by the formation a Central body like UNO, and that would be built by the people of the Globe. If the democracy is designed Islamic democracy, Hindu democracy, Christian democracy or Buddha democracy, it would hurt the humanity as that democracy is either reducing the democratic right or debarring the democratic right of the people of other faith. The World is beautiful if the people of the World are beautiful in mind and thought.

It is still a long way to proceed to achieve true democracy in the country of Globe. The principle of democracy is good for welfare of the society, welfare for human beings then how can it be confined to a particular country, or to a particular boundary? Time has come to see equality in democracy but also equality in wealth regardless of regions, states or country. The Earth is one planet, one region of space for human living and hence there should be Endeavour to look out for the creation of one central government like that of UN without boundary and restriction, where the human being would live with love, cooperation and affection without any addiction to colour, race or religion.

## Drawbacks of Indian Democracy:

India, a nation of 1. 2 billion population has turned into a nation of democracy and hence it rightly be called, the biggest democracy in the world. But there are pity examples of supremacy of political party that had truly degraded the value of democracy. Indian democracy for the last few years had undergone a sea change. In many cases democracy had failed to provide justice in the implementation of its function for the cause of its citizen. Rather it amounts to untold misery and killings of the innocents. The failure of the system cannot be accounted for the cause of one party or just for the politicians. Various other factors are responsible for the failure. Indian union is divided into many states and union territories governed by the regional or the national parties formally are being elected by the people. Now it appears that in most of the states people are unhappy as because the grievances of the people are not met as per requirement and sufferings of the people had increased. This situation has created an environment for the formation of regional party. Gradually the national parties of India are losing their popularity in the masses. The State has to function in coordination with the national party, who is holding administration of central government by the set up of the Indian democracy. A national party always favours a party of its own in the state who is obliged to do work at the pleasure of the center. The victimized citizens of the state find no other alternative but to vote for regional party. Thus the voting in favour of regional party is growing day by day. The final result is bad for the country. National party can not form a government without the support of regional party. For the survival of the government it becomes essential for the government to form an alliance with the regional parties jeopardizing all ethics of democracy. A minister of regional party doing corruption, making money for personal gain instead of public benefits during the discharge of his or her duty without any accountability or fear of anybody is very much evident now in public. It was because; the Minister knows the government can not go against him. This is the greatest drawback of the Indian democracy.

Most of the Indian people are religious and community friendly. People cast their votes mostly in consonance with the guidance of religious head or community head of any caste. In addition money and power plays an important role in the election process to win over the voters. Actual merit comes in front in rare in the political parties of India. The look out of the politicians are to capture Delhi by hook or crook and always attempts were there in safeguarding their position in whatever conditions it comes in favour rather than addressing the core issues of the people. Thus the people are suffering at the hands of Indian political system in their hard earned independence of India. People are the victims of the Indian system of political administration subjecting to the big reasons of chaos and confusion. Thus both the center as well as the state government is contributing a lot to keep unrest in every state giving less attention to the development and economic growth of India. Just after independence Indian leaders thought of dividing India into few regions for the benefit of smooth administration behind the underground political reasons. But that had created the sentiment of regionalism and later on division of States went on to the concept of creating more states for political gains. Accordingly India was divided into states giving a language to state. This leads to the division of Hyderabad into several states, Karnataka, Maharashtra and Gujarat. The regional sentiment had over ruled national interest. Subsequently the formation of regional parties continued with regional outlook. Once the Indians thought of for the welfare of the whole of the people of the South-East Asia, later it changed into the welfare of the people of Indian sub continent. The idea of serving the people of this region was shattered by the division of India. Now one India is administered under different states safeguarding the interest of states. In the advent of the growth of regional sentiment, all the facts, such as of the regional culture, regional language, regional boundary, got the priority of thought in the sphere of development and development on national sphere got the less priority. The central government now realized the effect of regionalism and tried its best to reduce the regional sentiment and enhance the feelings of Indian-ism by high lighting the term 'Patriotism', a term which is likely to ignite a feeling among all Indians so that they should be patriotic to support the decisions of the central government though these decisions are not friendly to regional interest. It is the wish of the Delhi government to think in term of Hindi as Hindi is the national language of India although it is not so far practically accepted by all the states. The regional feelings had increased regional interest more than national interest. It has created regional dispute with adjacent states be it border dispute, or water dispute or any other matter. The power circle in Delhi apply its influence keeping in mind its party interest or interest of alliance. The treatment of central government depends upon its stability. Its behaviour is soft if it is weak but it behaves like a dictator if it is strong. This is the actual state of democracy prevailing in India.

There is brightness and purity only in judiciary. Democracy can only function when the state does not get involved in any judicial proceedings. Till to-day people have a faith over Indian judiciary. But the people are rumbling in the functions of the judiciary for the fact that many millions of cases stay looming on the tables of various courts. Unless proper steps are taken, the people's faith is bound to vanish. In the language of humble approach it is the reality at present how the state and the central political parties have discharging their function in the present Indian democracy. With the rise of economy, the situation might have changed when the people would feel the life in India is better than any other neighbor country. It is also expected the conflict of power between center and state will die down in the years to come. Or otherwise!

Will it lead to further division? A broader outlook diminishes narrow thinking or regional thinking or religious thinking or thinking in term caste or community. If the Indian could live under British, the Indians could be deprived of Indian wealth, true but the Indians could gain a greater wealth. In Indo-British Rule, India could be the guardians of the Globe to handle not only the administration of India free from sectarian killing and corruption free India but also could be the executer of the Indo-British Rule and could be assigned with the administration of other regions such as Canada, Australia and similar other regions under British occupation. The population of British was insignificant compare to the population strength of India where Indian's command and domination would prevail in the long run. After all Indians were lacking in administration and scientific knowledge. The help of British might be a boon in disguise as it is seen in the development of Japan where the Japanese youth learn their scientific skill from the British.

We the Indians, the citizens of the present generations of India became the victim of the political blunder of Indians Leaders one after another. Our leaders gave importance to capture power from British hand instead of giving much more importance to the economic development of India. Had our priority been in economic growth, the distance between people to people would not arise. When the condition of economy of the country went down, every one became conscious for benefit of each ones' community, community on caste basis, community on religious basis for the sake of future of each community in a field of scarcity. Political leaders took the advantage to utilize caste or religion for acquiring power and made name for self, as a leader of community, a patriotic leader. Therefore the mistake lies at the root, the movement was political instead of economic front. The second mistake was in the division of country, on the basis of religion. Well, Jinnah might have his own thinking to divide country. Had the entire majority Muslims been supported the two nation theory, the Muslims would not stay in India, they would have preferably opted for Pakistan. Jinnah might have collided with British. British might have been correct to his policy in the old principle of ruling the country on the basis of Divide and Rule. The British might have thought of Ruling both the regions even after leaving India from distance in the event of division of the country and evolution of new problem of the country. But it remained beyond reach to understand, how the mighty congress succumb to the demand of Jinnah so easily without raising any protest. There was no example in this Globe that a country was divided without protest and without bloodshed. Not to speak of Ho Chi Min, or Sukarno or many others who never hesitated to sacrifice lakhs and lakhs of people to keep the country united. It was nothing but the immediate attraction of power. The only aim was to acquire the Chair of Delhi by removing the British. The 3rd mistake was in the declaration of Independence of India as Nation of Union of a secular country. When decision was settled to divide the country on the basis of religion and Pakistan declared a country of Islam, a country for the Muslims of India, how India could declared, the rest of India was not a country of Hinduism but a country of secular character.

With all respect to all leaders I should announce it was nothing but a foolishness of intelligence. Yes, Indian leaders wanted to make India a land for all irrespective of religion and caste or color like that of United States, a great Nation of Democracy. A country of Hindustan with Hinduism could also be a democratic country like United States with dignity, with character of Hinduism with equality to all. Jinnah was not a less international leader than any leader of India. He declared Pakistan is an Islamic country but the people of other faith of religion can also live there but not doing any harm, political, social or any other form detrimental to the nation of Islam. Pakistan may be a non democratic country, Bangladesh may be a poor country but they are living in the character of Islam as a citizen of proud nation. Indian leaders were always with the vision of democracy keeping in mind the symbol of the democratic country of United States in front as model country. But did our leaders thought of the geography of the nations of United States and compare it with the surroundings of India? America is a country in isolation, surrounded by Sea, sea in the East, sea in the West. But India is surrounded by the nations of country particularly by its own part East Pakistan (now Bangladesh) in the East and West Pakistan in the West, both the nations had declared Islamic country. How from ethical point of view a democratic country with secular character could survive, keeping an Islamic cry at the door step? It was nothing but a fallacy. Indian Leaders were neither sincere in their policy nor in their activity. If the Leaders were sincere to Indian Muslims why did they agreed to partion? If the Leaders were sincere to Hindus why did they allow the Muslims to live in India giving all rights? Jinnah was clear in his vision; he created Pakistan for Muslims of India. He was sincere to his duty to Muslims. The 3rd mistake was done after three years of the partition of the country. Yes, both the nations were disturbed by the holocaust of human killings, burning of houses, destruction of property and what not, the depth of which our leaders could not think of before. The leaders were happy with the Chairs of Delhi but they were insecure of their position because of political unrest among the masses suffered with killing, torture and burning. Finding an opportunity for the future command over the West Bengal and extending to Eastern India exceeding the regions of Assam, the PM of Pakistan came forward with a peace formula to India. He was successful to convince the PM of India, Sri Nehru, playing with the card of humanity for human distress. Thus Liquat-Nehru Pact came into being in 1950. By dint of this Pact, all the displaced Muslims came back to India and settled and enjoyed the all kinds of right of secular India. While not a single Hindu returned to East Pakistan because of future insecurity as the country was an Islamic country. Is it a gainful Pact of India? It opened the route for infiltration. Muslims who were suffering in economic distress in Pakistan founded their new home and shelter in India with economic, social and political right. Thus in secular India what we see to-day, it is Muslims in Pakistan, it is Muslims in every State of India. Thus political Party of India in every State and Political Party at center was very much eager to see the welfare of Muslims, because every vote is important for the power of Chair either the State or the Center. Therefore Jinnah thought it right in his mind, in future; Hindus of India will welcome the Muslims to come to the Chair of power. Liquates formula was the most clever formula to bring the Muslim Rule in West Bengal and Eastern India. Well, the Chief Ministers for the time being might be Hindu but they have to work under the direction of Muslim leaders till Muslims were the Chief Ministers. So what was the wrong with the Independent United Bengal of Sourab-uddin? Had it been there people would not have seen the massacre of human slaughter.

Our leaders are all powerful once but now they were not. They were democratic but inclined to Islam. In a democracy, the power rests with the number of votes. At the juncture of partion Muslims were insure in India because of the formation of Pakistan on the basis of religion while it was expected that the religion of the rest of India would be Hinduism. But the fortune was in their favor by the wisdom of Indians leaders. It was pity to think the power of Chair in term of religion, of course, the fault not lies with the common citizens, but the fault lies with the leadership. It was the leadership, it was the division of the country, and that had increased the distance of people to people. It will not go until the abolition of either of one religion. The day is not far away when every one will either learn or would be compelled to learn the faith of one religion as that had happened a few century ahead in Swat Valley or Afghanistan. It is good to think one country, one nation with one religion when the issue of economy would get the top priority which was overlooked at the beginning of the independence of India. However, the new policy of Center divide the state and command over it like that of British 'Divide and Rule' would enhance the change over. Each district will be a state, and the unity of India would be shattered into pieces. Ethically the Central government has no right to disintegrate a State into pieces for political, social or whatsoever the reasons because the formation of Indian Union was due to the union of Indian States and union of princely states. Once the Union was formed it became one single entity where every state or every princely state had lost its separate entity. Breakdown of single entity is unethical from philosophical point of view. Even constitutionally it is not permissible for the fact that as India can not change the basic principles of democracy,-Brotherhood, Fraternity, and Equality, similar to that one entity of Union can not be crushed into pieces, by the act of division of state for political gain although separate administrative unit being permissible, however the greatness of the Supreme Court, the highest body of India's judiciary, be rested with the Ethics of Law.

# [32]

**My Journey to Mumbai:**

It was my first visit to this historic city, a crowded city, a commercial city and the city is also being the Capital of the State Maharashtra. Modern Mumbai is formed out of seven small islands: It is a place where people from different parts of India used to come here for various purposes like trade and commerce, education, business and so on. It lies on the west coast of India making it a port of commercial importance. The convenient coastal location of the city has made the city a trading center to carry out trade with Middle East and Western countries. The day by day, the increase activity of trade and commerce has made the city a commercial Capital of India. Mumbai port is now handling 60% of India's maritime cargo. The trade activity made it a center of business and a center of meeting place for the people of all walks of life coming from all corners of Globe from West to East, or North to South. Simultaneously, it has grown up to a amusement center attracting regular crowds in watching film, and shooting in the beautiful site of Marine drive. Thus Mumbai becomes a dream city for many people although cost of living is very high. Big industrialist has found Mumbai to be their ideal place for business. For Hollywood industry Mumbai was a hot place and continued to be so in future too. The streets are marked with regular crowds watching the film shooting especially in the Marine drive. It has been recoded now as one of the populous cities of the world carrying 14 million inhabitants. In the neighboring suburbs of Novi Mumbai and Thane carrying 19 million people, and thereby it had exposed the danger of world's 4th largest urban agglomeration. After independence there had been lot of changes while Bombay was partitioned on language basis on fist May 1960. Gujarati speaking people of Bombay were pushed into the state of Gujarat while Marathi speaking people were kept in Bombay, when the area including Bombay is said to be the State of Bombay. With the rise of economy the employment opportunity in Bombay was increased which brought people from all states to Bombay. With the increase of population the urban area was also expanded, the limited South Bombay being extended to North-Borivali.

Naming: It is interesting to remember the pattern of naming and the pattern of growth of modern Bombay from historical of view. The analysis of naming of Bombay is such that the goddess of the villagers of seven islands was Mumba-devi, the Portuguese who was being the first occupied country to claim possession of the seven islands called them Bom Baie, meaning Good Bay, and the city was called Bombay and now the name has changed to Mumbai. The city was developed especially by Parsis of Mumbai, Gujraties from Gujrat, and the Marwaris from Rajthan who pioneered the growth. It was the Parsis who first build up the causeways, docks and ship building yards. In the later period, the people from all over India have migrated to Bombay to make the modern Mumbai a crowded city, the city which is now bursting into a breaking point. A lot of people are now leaving Mumbai to be freed from daily traffic jam.

The formation of modern Mumbai was started out of seven small islands with villages of Kolis, the local indigenous people of this part of Western India. Their means of living was from fishing and their goddes was Mumbai Devi from which modern Bombay was finally renamed Mumbai. **British became the Ruler of Bombay after getting Bombay as a 'dowry' gift from Portuguese.** There were seven islands when the Portuguese ceded these to the British as 'dowry' for the marriage of the English King Charles II to Catharine of Braganza of Portugal, in 1661.

**Solution of Traffic jam:** Taipei have utilized the service of Metro and light Rail system with advanced VAL and Bombardier while Japan used Bullet trains and popular flying trips to solve transportation of crowded cities. Shanghai had already introduced a revolutionary system of Maglev in the transport of passengers from air-port to shanghai. The best system for Mass Rapid Transit is managed in Bangkok by the introduction of underground Train (MRT) and BTS (Mass Transit System) Sky-train in the 21$^{st}$ century. Mumbai of India also would definitely require a similar measure like MRT and BTS to solve the transportation problem besides the control of population through out the country in a massive way.

Mumbai's Chhatrapati Shivaji International Air-Port is the main aviation hub in the city: Mumbai is India's financial capital of the country. As it generates more than 5% GDP every year, it becomes the economic hub of India.

Bullet or Maglev Train is the need of the day. Mumbai lies at the mouth of Ulnas River on the West coast of India. The earlier name of the area was Konkani. The local trains are the only transport available for the long distance commuters. Unless special and most modern communication system is introduced, the city will go down to down from economic point of view because people would get afraid to come to the city for the fear of traffic jam.

**Traffic jam:** As the Bombay was growing to be a center of financial Institute after Independence of India, service of Metro, light Rail system like that of Taipei or Bullet trains like that of Japan must be thought of. During the middle of eighteenth century, Bombay had emerged as a significant trading town under British East India Company. It was a base for Indian independence movement, where many vital decisions were taken in Bombay. By the time Mumbai become the nerve center of the commercial activity of India. It now the need is to improve its communication system like that of Japan, Taipei or Bangkok.

**My visit to attend a function of Republic day of India:**

I attended the function at the city of my resident at Dispur, the Capital of Assam where the Indian National Flag was hoisted by the Chief

Minister of the State. As usual parade was made and the day was observed with honour and dignity. But at the same time it reminds me the sacrifice of the forefathers of the refugees who are living in India, many of their kith and kin have lost their lives in the struggle of independence movement or even after independence that many of them lost their belongings and some of them even lost their lives as well, as they were the victims of riots, they lost their land too, as their land East Bengal being happened to be a part of Pakistan. Now they belong to India and protected under the shadow of Indian Flag. There are thousands of such kinds of people are living in India. After a long span of their lives overcoming all hurdles at the end they were faced with a question to themselves whether they are living here at the mercy of the State or at the mercy of the government of India or by the virtue of their political right or by dint of their birth right? Thousands of Sikhs sacrificed their lives in independence movement. But they were butchered few hundred in number only once at Delhi in 1984, and rightfully they are demanding the punishment of all the guilty. But in Eastern India including Assam, Bengal and other states, thousands of Hindu Bengalese of East Bengal is facing with the question of unlimited problems since their arrival in this land, although they were not butchered like Sikhs but they were humiliated by raising the question of their identity. Their identity is nothing more than 'Refugee', who sacrificed everything for the cause of independence and their rightful demand is nothing but "Right of humanity" and not quest of humility to the fact of identity, a citizen of India or more correctly an honoured citizen of India.

6th January 1950 was the date on which the Constitution of India came into force replacing the Government of India Act 1935 and since then 26th January is observed as the Republic day of India although India observed 15th August 1947 as the day of independence. The day 26th January is one of the most important days in Indian history as it was the day of enforcement of the constitution of India and making India a truly sovereign state. It was the day, the countrymen realized the dream of Mahatma Gandhi and remember the numerous freedom fighters who, fought for and sacrificed their lives for the cause of Independence of India. Dr. Ambedkar was the pioneer in making the constitution. Federalism and the British Parliamentary system jointly formed the basis of the constitution. Sir Anthony Eden, the Prime Minister of the United Kingdom (April 1955-January 1957) said, "of all the experiments in government, which have been attempted since the beginning of time, I believe that the Indian venture into parliamentary government is the most exciting. A vast subcontinent is attempting to apply to its tens and thousands of millions a system of free democracy. . . It is a brave thing to try to do so. The Indian venture is not a pale imitation of our practice at home, but a magnified and multiplied reproduction on a scale we have never dreamt of. If it succeeds, its influence on Asia is incalculable for good". Granville Austin, who was an American Constitutional authority, wrote that what the Indian Constituent Assembly began was "perhaps the greatest political venture since that originated in Philadelphia in 1787." On 26th, January on the day of Republic Day Indian Flag, are hoisted in all the states of India the Unity of India and represents the festival as the Symbol of Unity of India.

**Republic Day Celebration:** The Republic Day is celebrated all over India. Of course, the day is especially observed in the capital, New Delhi. The occasion begins with a solemn reminder of the sacrifice of the martyrs who died for independence and for succeeding wars for the defense of the sovereignty of the country. The day is also observed to award the medals of bravery to those who have exceptional courage in different situations. A spectacular parade becomes an attraction of the occasion. Every year a grand parade is held in the capital, from the Rajghat, along the Vijaypath where regiments of the army, the Navy and the Air force march past in all their finery and official decorations. Pageant of different states displays their activity that brings out the diversity and richness of the culture of India giving a festive air to the occasion.

**The Preambles of Democracy:** The Indians might be proud of sustaining democracy since six decades but definitely would not feel satisfied looking to the shortages in different sectors. India might be shown progress in economy but not in giving proper education to all the children, proper training to all the youths and proper adjustment at work to all of them to earn their living. It is still observed that most of the children are not going to schools. The people with lower income is poor, most of them live in huts and mud houses and many living under open skies. There are people starving and spending days without food. Many are weak and frustrated where most of them have been declared as Scheduled Caste, Scheduled Tribes, Backward Classes or Dalits who have been given separate colonies to live in and they are recognized unequal. Similarity is also shown with few Muslim communities too. Frustration leads them to become a terrorist party and friend of neighbor state Pakistan who indulge in terrorist strike to snatch Kashmir from India. There is patriotic song of unity but party tickets are mostly distributed on the basis of Hindus, Muslims, Sikhs, Christians and Dalits.

**Unity of Tricolor:** The Indian national Flag has united people of all states irrespective of Caste, religion and language and that is the greatest achievement of Indian democracy. The country has shortcoming in all fronts but the country is rich by the blessings of God. It is blessed with mountains, rivers, minerals, jungles, fertile land, gases, petroleum, coals, irons and other basics of progress. The country could not achieve the desired targets. It is because the people who had been occupying seats of power were not competent people. These people have made the democracy into a state of bureaucracy. It is not correct to say that these people are the true representative of the people. The political parties nominate candidates not on the basis of merits, but on other consideration. The candidates spent money in elections and when they are in power, they try their best at first to recollect that money and collect something more for the next election. Thus corruption and favoritism become day of administration. That is why there is huge corruption in 2G-Spectrum in Telecom, huge corruption in CWG (Common Wealth Game), Adarsh Housing Scam, Money laundering keeping huge amount in the Bank of Switzerland and also in every other sector beyond detectable sphere. There is democracy in the guise of party dictatorship and individual autocracy. The elected people are not working for the common people. That is the reason here in India rich are growing richer and the poor becoming poorer. 26th January is the day of introspection where the leaders should examine their activity in the sphere of development to remove the distress of the common people to make India really a democratic peaceful country, a country for all community and religion manifesting a country of 21$^{st}$ century of human civilization in the history of Mankind.

# [33]

**Culture of Religion:**

Human being is thought to be the highest creature. It is natural that a sensible individual will try to know the mystery behind birth and death as the time of death comes nearer. It is impossible to come to any definite conclusion but the facts of history gives us knowledge and power to analyze, criticize and reserve individual's opinion for the sake of others to get a mental satisfaction in the minds of a living body before losing the sense of realization of thought termed as the body of death if not the death of soul. The greatest weakness of human beings is the fear of death. But even then no body thought of dying soon. The birth of unknown spirit (the GOD) lies in the shadow of fearing death. The messengers of God had created Hindus (~8000 BCE), Buddhist & Janise (~400BCE), Christian (6-7 BCE), and Islam (~500-600 CE).

The earliest Religion Hinduism: (~8000BCE): **Krishna holding a flute is regarded as God in Hinduism.** The religion Hinduism is originated from (i) Sruti Vedas (Divine Origin), (ii) Smriti Vedas (Human origin) and Upanishad or Vedanta (The Doctrine of Universal soul is the keystone of the philosophy and thought of Upanishad). There was a time when nothing was known to human beings except his emotion of thought. That emotion tempted the human being to warship on his own way by emotional sound evolved from within which we today called (Divine Origin) and it continued generation to generation by the process of chanting regularly bringing an undeclared discipline in the process of search for peace in humanity. The subsequent development is the human creation. Those who are Hindus believe in 'The Three in one God' that is Brahma (creator), Vishnu (the Preserver) and Siva (the Destroyer). They believe in other aspects such as (i) Karma, (ii) Reincarnation and (iii) Nirvana.

Karma means performance of works good or bad. Good Karma will return one to the present world with good life. Reincarnation means rebirth as a person of higher status depending upon the performance of good Karma in the present world. Nirvana means, the release of the soul from the endless cycle of rebirth in the present world. Hindus believe in one God that appears in different forms. According to Hinduism, if people want to live a good life, they must respect creation and perform selfless service to humanity as a sign of their devotion to God. The functions of Hinduism are written in the holy book called 'Bhagavad Gita'.

According to Hindu culture, happiness lies in the service of others who are in distress condition. The rituals of worshipping many God, although Hindus believe in one God are not understood by the people of other faith. The Hindu religion explains clearly giving reasons in each and every case. The Hindus believe in reincarnation. The belief is that a person may reborn again and again into a different living things depending upon the person's own performance during his life time. If a man is a good person, he might come back as a rich and happy person, but if the person did not live a good life, he might come back to earth as a fly or small kit. The question of rebirth might have created a Brahmin, a man of higher caste by dint of good work or a 'Sudra', a man of lower caste by dint of his bad work. Thus in India, there are people belonging to higher caste and again there are people belonging to lower caste. The humanity is divided between castes. This is a drawback of Hinduism. Now India is facing the real problem with caste politics.

Buddhism: (~400 BCE):

After the battle of Krukhatra as described in Mahabharata, the people lost faith over the ruling of King by the strength of might. The practice of killing the enemy is replaced by the practice of no killing in the

Buddha & Jain period. From the outset, Buddhism was equally open to all races and classes, and had no caste structure, as was the rule in Hinduism. It appears an Indo-Aryan dialect was cultured to develop a language called Pali. In Hinduism, Gautama is regarded as one of the ten Avatars of God Vishnu. Asoka, the powerful Emperor, was the ruler of the Magadhan Empire. Initially he was thought of expanding his empire by the battle of Force, but he changed the idea and initiated the expansion of Empire by the attachment of love and faith after witnessing the brutal carnage at the battle of Kalinga. This event led him towards Buddhism and he built his empire into a Buddhist state, a first of its kind. He laid the foundation of numerous stupas and spread the teachings of Lord Buddha throughout the world. Emperor Asoka became convinced that Buddhism was a religion for all of the peoples of the world. Accordingly, he sent missionaries throughout the known world. Asoka also called the third council of Buddhism in 247 B. C. at Pataliputra for the purpose of determining the true canon of Buddhist scriptures and discarded numerous bogus monks from the Sangha. Buddhism spread to Northern India, present Pakistan, Afghanistan, and extended to the territory of Russia and China. Emperor Asoka sent his son, Mahindra, to Sri Lanka to spread Buddhism in the state. He succeeded in converting the King of Sri Lanka to Buddhism and soon, Buddhism became the state religion of the country. The Fourth Council took place in Sri Lanka, in the Aloka Cave near the village of Matale. It was in this council that decision was taken to write the teachings of Lord Buddha for the first time. The entire writing was collected in three baskets and given the name of Tipitaka or the Pali Canon. Another Fourth Buddhist Council (Sarvastivada tradition) was held around 100 CE at Jalandhar or in Kashmir.

From the seventh century, Buddhism went on a downward spiral in India, because of growth of Hinduism. The decline of Buddhist universities were replaced with Muslim religious institutions by the Muslim Turk invasions of northwest India.

**Spread of Buddhism in China and other South-East Country**: Buddhism started gaining entry into China around 1ˢᵗ century CE. In 4ᵗʰ century it spread to Korea, in 5ᵗʰ century (~538CE) it spread to Japan. In 8th century CE, the religion further spread under the patronage of Emperor Shomu to different small islands of South East Asia including Japan. In the 12th it further developed in Japan and in 13th century it spread to larger area of China. It also spread to Tibet.

**Christian Religion:**

(6-7 BCE) Jesus of Nazareth referred as Jesus Christ is the central figure of Christianity. The most Christian believe that he rose from the dead after being crucified. The holy book Bible is the sources of information regarding Jesus. Christians traditionally believe that Jesus was born of virgin, performed Exorcisms and Miracles, founded the church, proclaimed the SON OF GOD, but betrayed by his own disciple and was crucified, died at the age of thirty three and finally ascended into heaven. The soldiers crucified Jesus but Jesus states "Father, forgive them, for they know not what they do", usually interpreted as his forgiveness of the Roman soldiers and the others involved. It is believe that the man, Jesus sent by God to save human race from 'sins' it inherited originally from the 'evils' of Adam and Eve.

Jesus was causing havoc and problems for the Romans and the Jews. Pontius Pilate, the Roman Perfect of Judea, condemned Jesus and ordered, the CRUCIFIXION of Jesus. The Romans, who were the rulers at the time, sentenced Jesus to be crucified. At the age of 33, JESUS CHRIST WAS CRUCIFIED and DIED ON THE CROSS. Christians say that Jesus Christ was resurrected 3 days after dying, proving that Jesus was DIVINE. The day that Jesus was crucified is called "Good Friday" and the day he was resurrected is called "Easter."

**The ideals of Christianity are understood by the few words: 'We know that we have passed from death to life, because we love our brothers.' Anyone who does not love remains in death. Anyone who hates his brother is a murderer, and it is known that no murderer has eternal life in him.**

**What love is: Jesus Christ laid down his life for us all. And we ought to lay down our lives for our brothers. If anyone has**

**material possessions and sees his brother in need but has no pity on him, how can the love of God be in him?'**

**'If anyone does not provide for his relatives, and especially for his immediate family, he has denied the faith and is worse than an unbeliever.**

Although Jesus had died, his message of teachings had not died. It spread to Jewish communities across the empire by the energetic apostles, such as Paul and by the subsequent developed communications of the Roman Empire. The spread of Christianity was made a lot easier by the efficiency of the Roman Empire, but its principles were sometimes misunderstood and became dangerous to implement.

**Muslim Religion or Islam (~600-700 CE):** Muhammad (26 April 570-8 June 632) was the founder of the religion of Islam. He is considered by Muslims as the last prophet (messenger) of God. Born in 570 CE in the Arabian city of Mecca, he was orphaned at an early age and brought up under the care of his uncle Abu Talib. He later earned the reputation of a faithful merchant, as well as a shepherd. He was married at the age of 25 with a wealthy lady of Modena of age 40. He used to meditate in a cave surrounded by mountains. According to Islamic beliefs it was here, at age 40, he received his first revelation from God. Three years after this event he started preaching these revelations publicly. He proclaimed that "God is one". That to complete surrender to Him is the only way of life and that he himself was a prophet and messenger of God. Although he gained few followers at the early stage, he met with hostility from some Meccan tribes. The first thing Muhammad did to settle down the longstanding grievances among the tribes of Mecca and thereby he was drafting a document known as the Constitution of Mecca and the community defined in the Constitution was called 'Ummah' which had a religious outlook. Thus it effectively established the first Islamic state. In the 622 he migrated to Medina along with his followers to escape persecution. This event, the Hijra, marks the beginning of the Islamic calendar, which is also known as the Hijra Calendar. His followers after being eight years of fighting with Meccan tribes had grown to

10,000 when he conquered Mecca. He and his followers destroyed all of the remaining pagan temples throughout Eastern Arabia. In 632, a few months after being returned to Medina, he suddenly fell ill and died. By the time of his death, most of the Arabian Peninsula had converted to Islam, and he had united the tribes of Arabia into a single Muslim religious polity. The revelations were which Muhammad was being receiving until his death is the fact of verses of the Quran and that is regarded by Muslims as the "Word of God". Thus Quran is the basis of the religion "Islam". Both Jews and Christians saw Muhammad as a 'false prophet', who came here with sword and chariot and spread nothing of truth except of human bloodshed.

It is noticed in the history that religion became a political tool for the expansion of territory and business. There occurred more than 9 times crusades between the followers of Christianity and Islam. By the 8th-Century, just 100 years after the death of Mohammed, the Arabs had converted most of North Africa to the Muslim faith, crossed the Straits of Gibraltar, and overrun Spain. They also tried to enter France, but were decisively defeated by the Christians at the Battle of Tours (Battle of Poitiers) in 732 AD. It is seen by 700 years, from the 8th-to the 15th-Century, the Spanish Christians slowly pushed the Muslims back and, till the reign of Queen Isabella in 1492. While that 700-year battle was being fought, Muslims remained firmly astride the trade routes to the coast of China and the territory of the Far East. While Christians prevailed in Western Europe, the Muslims were growing stronger in Eastern Europe. Muslims also easily expanded to the North East crossing north India, present Pakistan, and Afghanistan up to the territory of China and Russia. The expansion was easy unlike the west because of the prevailing Buddhism, religion of no violence.

The intelligent people under the prevailing political and economic situation of the region apply their weird of inventing 'Religion". As the people can not go away with the fear, they are under the obligation to obey the Messengers of God to get mental peace. Let us think of the souls of every individual without looking in terms of particular religion or community being a part of humanity as we want pleasure and peace in the short span of life cycle declaring the religion "The Religion of Humanity". A research student of Hyderabad writes as:

Sistashankar Pbk<sistashankarpbk@yahoo. com

**All are children of the same God; hence everyone has the right to enter Heaven. That is why God says "Forget all the differences like, I am a Gujarati . . . I am a Christian . . . I am an American . . . etc and remember me, so that you get purified to enter Heaven."**

In view of the conquest of India by Muhammad bin Qasim, the Muslims faced with new religion like Buddhism and Hinduism, which was not known to them. The people addicted with these religions were idol worshippers and their doctrine was at the farthest to Islam. It is said that Muhammad Bin Qasim have been instructed by the caliph in Damascus (the religious Head) not to fight with idol worshippers as they did in the Arab land as long as Hindus and Buddhists did not fight with the Muslim Rulers, and as long as they paid the jizyah or tax due, they must be free to worship their gods as they please, to maintain their temple, and to live their life as they wish by the precepts of their faith. The same status was also given to those of Jews and Christians and paved the way for coexistence in tune with divine orders. The creatures of other religions or other animals are also the creatures of God (Allah), so God has also given them the right to live in their own way that was the doctrine of Islam. In the Middle East, the Muslim religion was established by the act of 'Jihad' which was wrongly interpreted by many. It was also seen in other religion as well. When Arjun preferred not to fight in the battle ground as his conscience was burdened with the prospect of killing of his own kith and kin, Lord Krishna advised Arjuna to fight for Dharma, to fight for justice, and such fight is what is called in the Quran as Jihad, which wrongly interpreted by many. This shows that the fundamental virtues do not differ in religion. Those who believe in the creation of God in the universe, the best creation being the humanity, can not live in enmity, as the God wishes his every creature must be kind to each others. Poverty, underdevelopment, discrimination and corruption manifested favoring a particular religious group, the enmity bound to grow. In pre-independent India, the whole country irrespective of religion was against colonialism. All rose to the occasion to fight against British for 'Swaraj' with different flags under the then tri-colour. If that historical feeling of oneness is nurtured to fight against the common enemy like poverty, discrimination or corruption, the unity among different religionists would make progress. As the true spirits of all religions call for egalitarianism and justice, the people of varied religion can jointly fight against all types of injustice, be it social, political or economic. Every country is busy to spent money for the purchase of weaponry; alternatively if the money is utilized for the good of mankind, then hunger could be eradicated from the earth easily. Although in India Hindus have to pay jizyah tax, Islam promotes peaceful coexistence among people following different faiths as the Hindus could go to temple and worship according to their faith as such people are taught to live in a pluralistic society.

The history looks to the fact is that there are different religion existed till to-day in the universe. To understand any religion in depth it requires devotion and dedication. Keeping the religious philosophy aside it is seen people are living with love and amity in the same country preaching the religion of their respective faith. And again, at the same time, unfortunately, religion in many part of the globe has contributed very often to the stimulation of conflicts and wars as found in human history. Parliament of the World's Religions in 1893 noted the following with regret:-"Time and again we see leaders and members of religions incite aggression, fanaticism, hate, and xenophobia—even inspire and legitimize violent and bloody conflicts. Religion often is misused for purely power-political goals, including war. We are filled with disgust". Brutal acts of individuals or violent group clashes of different religions or of same religion were also not uncommon in history. Wiseman of society only could handle this kind of dialectics carefully with the satisfaction of all. To defeat the destructive and divisive elements of religions, a strategic and effective ways of dialogue with a sense of love of cooperation among all Wiseman bringing the world of politics and ethics of religion together is necessary to foster the inspiring and peace-building elements among religions. However, in the words of Jimmy Carter (US President), "Religious representatives need to exercise their moral authority and mobilize the vast human resources of their communities in the service or peace making. The rest of us, in turn, must recognize the growing importance of religious factors for peace making and develop ways, both informal and formal, to cooperate with religious leaders and communities in promoting peace with justice."

It is also realized by wise man that cultural affinity through inter-religious festivity is necessary to develop a new civilization to build up the peace of humanity. President Muhammad Khatami of Iran, at UN said, 'The Islamic Revolution of the Iranian people . . . calls for a dialogue among civilizations and cultures instead of a clash between them'. At his suggestion, the assembly proclaimed the year 2001 as the United Nations Year of Dialogue among Civilizations. Hans Kung, the foremost authority on interfaith relation concluded-"There will be no peace among nations unless there is peace among religions. And there will be no peace among religions unless there is authentic dialogue among religions". No body can deny the existence of diverse religions all over the globe, that is an accepted fact and that fact demands tolerance and respect to one another.


## Terrorism & Religion:

A section of the people believes that "Islam a Religion is based on Terrorism". It is because, according to them, the impact of Islam on the way of life of Muslims is far greater than that found in the Western Culture since the middle Ages. In USA out of 1. 3 billion Muslims only 13 million are extremists; their understanding of Islam is some what different. A Muslim is the brother of another Muslim, who neither could oppress him nor condemn him for any act. All things of Muslims are inviolable for his brother in faith, and in his blood. He is forbidden to speak against the will of another Muslim.

> **"If a Muslim discards his relation, kill him"**—Muhammad, Prophet of Islam. According to Muslims Islam is a shinning beacon against the darkness of repression, segregation, intolerance and racism. The Arabic word "Islam" means submission and is taken to mean submission to God. In other words it means peace, purity and safety. In common understanding, a Muslim has surrendered his will to the grace of Allah. After 11 Sept. 2001, attacks, some politician

describe Islam as a "Religion of Peace" in order to differentiate between Islamic terrorists, Islamism and non-violent Muslims. Many Muslim political leaders condemned the attack of 11 September. The data suggests that 6. 5% Muslims world wide thinks that 9/11 attack was justified while 55. 4% think that the attack was unjustified. Control of peace or control of Islam is not the out come of Terrorism. Terrorism does not represent peace. Terrorism represents evil or war. The path of 'Rejection of Violence' finds the way of approach to 'Religion of Peace'.

But many believe that Islam does not permit the individual to enjoy the freedom of action and attachment with the characteristics of the Democracy that so many Western Country follows to-day. To the critics Islam is a totalitarian ideology that rejects democracy, personal freedom, and every other religion. Islamic law or Shariah Law is not compatible with Democracy where freedom of liberty is the fundamental basis of Democracy, where the policy, and the law of administration is decided by the opinion of the majority people while Shariah Law is the law of Quaran, which is fixed by the Almighty (Allah), and no one has the right to change it. Saudi Arabia, a country ruled by Islamic Law, hold a Religious Police to enforce all aspects of Shariah Law. Any kind of sorcery, witchcraft or blasphemy is considered crimes punishable by death. The Law permits beheading people convicted by these kinds of crimes. This is what Islamic Law advocates but the modern World thinks otherwise. There lies the contradiction of Islamic Law or Shariah Law with that of the Law of Democracy. In the Muslim world, it is belief that Islam is the only true religion, all other religion is false and an insult to Allah. It is the belief of most of the Muslims that with Islam, there is no Freedom of Religion, there is individual's Freedom, and there is only Islam and the Islamic way of life.

### "He who fights that Islam should be Superior fights in Allah's cause"

-Muhammad, Prophet of Islam.

America is superior in all aspects, superior in the accumulation of wealth, superior to give a better life to its citizens, while Bin Laden, the Chief of al-Qaida claim, the enjoyment of better life can not be an absolute right of America. According to his inner vision, the act of Terrorism is nothing but a process to achieve that goal, a goal of achieving a uniform better life for all its citizens extended over the globe.

America was a democratic country and it wanted to implement its democracy to the fullest extent right from the beginning. That is why America was very liberal to any religion to the freedom of the people. The period 1880-1914, showed a rapid rise of Muslim population in the land of America. During this period several thousand Muslims immigrated to America from Ottoman Empire and South Asia. Native born American Muslims are mainly Africa American who makes up a quarter of Muslim population. There were Muslim emigrated from Arab land too. In 1800, about 5 Lakhs Muslim slaves immigrated to America from Africa. America is now worried with the growth of terrorism conducted in most of the cases by the Muslim militants organized in secret under the patronage of few Muslim countries. The growth of Muslim population in the world is also a matter of concern. The statistics measure the average population growth rate of Global Muslim Community is 1. 8 % per year while that of the World population is 1. 12 % per year (recorded from internet). In 2011, it is predicted, World Muslim population will grow twice as fast as non-Muslim, over next 20 years, and the reasons are many. In India the Muslim population growth rate is abnormally high average 10% higher than Hindu population (recorded from internet) for many factors. If the religion is not mixed up with politics, the growth of the population of any faith is no problem with the life process. The freedom of liberty of the people would permit to take up or not to take up any faith of religion to the best of his or her self individuality. In the civilized world of 21$^{st}$ century, people must be above religion and live in the Globe in a bond of love and affection cherishing a better life free from poverty, hunger, and disease and must be in the attempt to be a party to the group of genius who are sacrificing their life in the constant search of finding another planet like Earth when the humanity could bring a revolution in the Universe.

**WHAT IS THE USE OF RELIGION?** Religion is a learning of ideals, supposed to be generated by the customs of ages that preaches love for mankind and are meant for transforming our hearts and taming our minds with a view to realize the divine spirit within us. But in practice, religion has generated hatred and anonymity towards the followers of other religions of other community. Thus religion is doing immense harm to every society and finally to mankind.

A society is nothing but a group or tribal collective grouped around a common identity such as religion being an identity, which can in turn come into collision, cooperation and conflict with other societies. Such common identity gets change with the change of time. To-day the world had seen the destruction of Buddhist's remnants of sculptures in Afghanistan in the regime of Taliban. It shows once upon a time Afghanistan was under the domain of Buddish religion and not a Muslim dominated region as prevailed today. With the change of time the common identity of religion is changed. Thus religion is in some sense indispensible for fostering the societies that spawn them. The religion Christianity has served Europeans pretty well, Judaism despite a pretty set-back as in history has served the Jews. Once the world had seen the Persians, the powerful Romans but to-day where are the Romans? There is no fixed religion or tribal identity that is good for immoral. It changes with time but humanity exists for all time. Many times a religion, or a particular manifestation can emerged out of circumstances to build up a society as had happened to a much to the Muslim world because religion is a powerful weapon for stability, growth and development. But miss-use of religion destroys the humanity. Everyday, it is heard—gruesome attacks, killings of hundreds of innocent lives in different parts of the globe. It is heard-a brutal and barbaric attack by terrorists in recent past that in a school of Chechnya in Russia where more than 200 innocent young children and teachers were killed. There was bomb blasts in Mumbai at five different places where several hundreds and thousands of innocent people were killed and injured. If the religion generates hatred towards the people of other religion, then "what is the use of religion?"

In view of the murderous attacks, bomb blasts and other nightmare incidents that are happening across the world almost every day under the guise of religious sentiments exploited by the few individuals can not be ignored at ease. The news of dying of about 200 people in Nigeria during prayer time is undoubtly shocking news to any human beings. Is it not a religious violence and is not an act of sin. These kinds of incidents have turned life into a miserable state and the suffering of the innocent people is ever increasing. Is religion a blessing or curse to mankind? A seen of religious violence that had happened in between Shiite & Sunni Muslims in Heart of Afghanistan under Hamid Karjai government was kept in record and religious groups were asked to find a solution of peace.

## WHAT ARE THE ETHICS OF RELIGION?

The human history tells us that religion brought solace and unity to people when science was not that advanced during the ancient times and progressed to enrich culture as well. People who are practicing religion, found to be sympathetic to human suffering. Is science a blessing or curse to mankind? All modern inventions that are beneficial to mankind sounds as the blessing of science but missiles and bomb those that are detrimental are referred to as curse. Governments or UN can bring restrictions in making arsenals which they think transforms the limits of morality. But in the case of religion no body can bring any kind of restrictions because religion is a belief of inner conscious and that is to be nurtured by self only self. The good and the evil approach a man attained at every stages of his life. It is he who is to select the good for the cause to be blessed and the bad for the cause to be cursed. Religion has no function in deciding good or bad. It is the virtue of ideals composed in religion that shows the path of life, functions towards community and mankind at large.

The goal of all religion is the same that is to serve the mankind although their founders who preached them lived in different parts of the world and spoke different languages and never met each other.

What is noticeable is that Hindus are going to temple for Puja, Muslims are going to mosque for Namaj, Christians are regularly attending Church on every Sunday—all are different in the sense of inner mind to find peace of mind but all approach to the same sense in the case of nature's call such as to public toilets. After all every one is a human being.

## EXPLOITATION OF RELIGION:

There are few people who are utilizing the religion for the benefit of self to establish himself as the leader and hence as the spoke person of the community at large. In the administration of State in the atmosphere of historical set up religion has been utilized by political leaders to acquire the center of power forgetting the ethics of religion. Thus the religious leaders in many cases turned to politics to acquire power even by indulging religion in criminal acts instead of good teachings of religion. Religions are being misused and religious sentiments are exploited by politicians to acquire power of administration. What is seen in India that the religious festivals which are meant for rejoicing and gaining spiritual strength have turned out to be a battle ground in the open street when the issue becomes a big headache for the police? The festival should be observed for spiritual advancement in accordance with the belief of own religion without killing people nearby.

In conclusion it can rightly be said that the human beings are in search of love, peace and brotherhood in the Universe but still they are in dark to find the right path of approach. If the priests of all religions make sincere efforts to practice its true teachings instead of using religion for political gains, then the welfare of mankind is not far off to achieve. Every people of all religious community should work together in that direction for peaceful co-existence and save the humanity from all the brutalities committed in the name of religion. If no religious principles guide the sentiments of mankind, the Earth might see a worst type of brutality where people will be unbounded under the obligation of any sense of morality. The present age is in the need of all peace loving religious leaders of the world to come together and do something to educate their followers that no such outrageous acts are committed in the name of religion and remove the fears of thousands of innocent people and save this world, an earthly paradise to live in.

Religions are like flowers of a garden. A garden is beautiful by the beauty of different flowers. Similar to that religions are the beauty of the Earth to make the Earth a heaven provided our mindset enlarges to accommodate all religion with equal respect. The service of all religion is the service to mankind. If so all religion leads to humanity. Hence there need not be violence with religion.

# [34]

## My Journey to Karimganj College:

Karimganj College is situated at the bank of river Kushiara at the junction of India-Bangladesh Border. It was the only sub-division of earlier District Sylhet of East Pakistan to remain in India because of the demarcation made by Redcliff making the river Kushira as the line of demarcation, and the Land of Karimganj being situated on the other side of the river, it is fortunate enough to remain with India. Karimganj College is memorable to me as it gave me the first hand knowledge of literature, art of science as beginners and above all the art of etiquette of culture through the performance of occasional cultural functions, debate, and events of farewell, and annual college functions as if I was one with all.

Karimganj, the Land of rising Sun, has got the tremendous importance just after partition of India. During partition, the State Bengal was divided and a part of Bengal named as East Bengal went to form East Pakistan but unfortunately the District Sylhet, a part of Assam also went to Pakistan due to political ground but the Land Karimganj by the blessings of God Kamakhya, the Goddess mother of Assam, was fortunate enough to remain with Assam and now serving as important entry of Gateway between India and Pakistan of two Nations. Before partition it was a thinly populated area but after partition it became a thickly populated area, the influx of refugee and riot victim people of East Bengal and particularly the people of other sub-divisions of the District Sylhet flooded the houses and even the surface land area of Karimganj taking shelter in the open space with make shift arrangement of tent. However, the situation had changed after the implementation of Liaquat-Nehru Pact (1950), the Muslim people who had left Karimganj have returned and the demography changed completely. Now it is a Muslim majority district. Few patriotic people took the initiative to establish few Schools and a College for the education of the children of these landless, moneyless refugee people who began to gather in the border town much before the demarcation the of the newly born state East Pakistan. The foot print of the College was established one year earlier of the declaration of Pakistan. The year was 1946. The birth of Karimganj College was came into being at the juncture of movement of partition of India in poor state of condition but to day it has risen to a higher status and giving service in the teaching of arts, science and other branches at per with other Colleges of Assam under Guwahati University and had contributed GU, however small, to keep a respectable position in the list of UGC(University Grants Commission) in the service of teaching to the students of North East, but however the Karimganj College is now brought under Assam University after Assam University came into being at Silchar. My experience in **Karimganj College** was horrible and recorded evidences are like a foolish typical village boy. To describe the fact, however humiliating, I must say the truth. One day I had been enrolled as a student of Karimganj College by the help of my guardian. Coming from the remote area of Silchar Road, about 5 Km away from Karimganj College, all on a sudden, I appeared alone to Karimganj College to attend classes without knowing the class room, teachers or students of the college, and entered the college premises. The very site appeared to me, as if a place of learning center or a place of fighting center. Students are rushing fast in groups to occupy the front seat in the change of room. In my fate there was no space in front. I was fortunate enough to occupy a seat almost at the last. Having being succeeded in fight in occupying a seat, in the first day of my college life, I felt a little joy of proud but very soon that joy turned into misery of despair when I realized that I entered into a wrong class, a second year English class instead of first year class. I have no alternative but blame myself and had to leave the class with head down. But I was not disheartened to fight ahead to keep my head up. Later on in the course of time I spent long four years in this college keeping my head high, in study, as well as, in college debate, and became very popular not only among students but also among professors. The love and affection of few professors are still fresh in my mind namely Gourish Dey, Prof. UL Das, Prof. Narayan Das, Prof. Haran Bhatt, Prof. Ashu Sen, Prof. Digan Das. It was the knowledge of my College by dint of which I was successful to occupy a seat in Chemistry in Guwahati University (GU) in the days of hard competition in 1963 and that knowledge helped me to go for research work at National Chemical Laboratory (NCL), Poona and later to University of Manchester Institute of Science and Technology (UMIST) under Manchester University to come out with a success of PhD to serve Cotton College till August 1999 to the last day of my service life.

**A Synopsis of Karimganj College:** College was established in 1946 at Karimganj, the sub-division town of the district Sylhet in undivided India, situated at the bank of river Kushiara. It is now one of the pioneering Colleges of Assam, imparting education in science, arts and commerce. It is a great pleasure to me to see that the college is offering courses in computer science such as B. Sc in computer science and BCA. The National Assessment and Accreditation

Council (NAAC) has recognized the college as B+ College, a great achievement for the eastern corner College of Assam. I had the opportunity to visit the college in the last year. Dr. Radhikaranjan Chakraborty, the Principal had shown me the Department of Computer Science. I was amused by seeing the intense activity of the student in the Computer Science course, a new and dynamic branch of science. Dr. Chakraborty said me the introduction of computer course has brought up a new life to college with enhanced excitement and competition among the student to peruse with the course. The College has opened up the scope for the student of Badarpur, Karimganj Town, Nilambazar, Patherkandi, Lowairpoa, Longai, Mohisashan, Sutarkandi and other adjoining area to study in the subject of their interest.

**An early History of the Region:** The early history of Karimganj is not very clear. But the record shows in the 6th century it was under

Kamrupa Kingdom for about a hundred years. In the 7th century it came under Eastern Bengal. There was a place called Panchakhanda (8 miles away from Karimganj town, now in Bangladesh) developed as the greatest centre of Hindu-learning in the entire Eastern India of the early period of 10th century. At that time the region was known as Srihatta. After that it was the period of expansion of Muslim religion. Hazarat Shah Jalal, a warrior Muslim Saint from Yemen, conquered Sylhet in 1328 A. D. A portion of Karimganj district comprising the present Thana area of Patherkandi (under Tripura King) forcefully merged with Sylhet and ruled under Sultans as Bengal. The forceful conversion of Hindus to Muslim took place in this period. The area was further extended under the rule of Mughal Empire in 1576 during the region of Akbar. The British established their authority in 1786. In November 1857, Sylhet became a center of Infantry because of Chittagong mutiny. The Sub-division Karimganj came into being in 1878. Karimganj played an important role in the freedom movement. The Chargola Valley tea-belt of Karimganj sub-division organized the famous Chargola exodus. At the end, my heart goes to wish "Let the college welcomes the new generation of student who enter this institution with shaky thought, should come out with sound knowledge and sound thought". I will say again "Let every student of this institution develop intellectual and moral power in a healthy environment and strengthen him/her physically, mentally and spiritually.

# [35]

**My Journey to India to find the Hidden Treasure**, a treasure that rested on the teachings of "GURUKUL" is beyond purchasable with any amount of wealth. The Ancient Education in India was based on religion that brings a control over body and mind. Knowledge was passed on orally from one generation to another in ancient India through three basic processes, which are (i) 'Sravana' (stage of acquiring knowledge of 'Shrutis' by listening), (ii) 'Manana' (meaning pupils to think, analyse themselves about what they heard, assimilate the lessons taught by their teacher and make their own inferences,) and (iii) 'Nidhyasana' (meaning comprehension of truth and apply it into real life). India has the world's largest population of illiterates; no nation can afford to have a large number of its population to remain illiterates. It is because of the method of education, the teaching of education remained confined within a very small section of the society. It is also restricted only to those, who possessed brilliant feats of memory and capability to keep its sanctity. It remains confine to Brahmins and high class society where Vedas, Smritis, Sutras and Upanishads were being learnt in Sanskrit. Masses in general remain busy in their hereditary or traditional occupations learning skills more on job and not on any other formal education. In order to complete the initial training of teaching, student had to take a place at the home of Brahman Teacher, who was called Guru. In daily practice the students seated on the ground in front of Guru, who would repeat verse after verse of the Vedas until they had mastered and memorized them. It was significant that the practice of learning was transmitted orally. In the later Vedic period, the learning was extended to other branches of education too.

**The Gradual Change of Teaching Pattern in India:** The research of history shows that even in the ancient days, sages and scholars imparted education orally, but after the development of letters, it took the form of writing. Temples and community centers served the role of schools. With the spread of Buddhism in India, education became available to everyone; the language adopted was being of Sanskrit.

There were many universities build up during that period in India. Few of most important universities of ancient India were Taxila (being the first university of world established in the Seventh century B. C.), Vikramshila University and Nalanda University came into existant in 4 A. D. The Nalanda and Vikramshila Universities were at par with the University of Taxila as found in the records of Huan Tsang. These institutions were considered to be the best Universities of its times in the subcontinent and that commands an honour to ancient Indian educational system. The historical research has discovered that a well organized system of education actually had been existed in India during the Rig Vedic Age.

The Temple existed adjacent to Nalanda University was also a part of Nalanda University where academic as well as religious teaching were performed. The visit of the ruins of Nalanda University clearly still now exposes a little of the activities of the University. Teaching that was imparted to every student by generation to generation by the Gurus or by elders in this country since ages is a record of history. This indicates that the Aryan realized the importance of education to build a disciplined life although teachings were based on the ethics of religion. In the history, it is found that Nalanda University, which flourished from the 5th to 13th century AD, was an academic center of excellence. Students coming from China, Sri Lanka, Korea and other distant places took part in learning education. In 11th century Muslims established few elementary and secondary schools in India which led to the establishment of few Universities at the cities like Delhi, Lucknow and Allahabad. In British India, English education came into being with the assistance of European missionaries. Since then, Western education has made a steady progress in the country.

**The Teachings of Guru was** to teach the student by the principle of precept and example, set by the virtues of good conduct, loyalty to truth, mental discipline and sense of duty. It was because; these qualities are virtues of happiness in the life process. In the educational system teacher and student look for (i) skills and information and (ii) one's inner urges, so that man can live in health and happiness along with the satisfaction of transcendent entity which is called the Aathma (the Over all soul or divine). According to Katha Upanishad, who is possessed of supreme knowledge, the person is he, who could have the concentration of mind in leading his senses under control like spirited steeds controlled by a charioteer.

As is said the teachings in India in ancient time was perceived through Guru (preceptor). The educational system that prevails bring both teacher and student together in the art of learning skills so that man can live in health, happiness and in the art of understanding one's inner urges and their sublimation to attain peace, equanimity and bliss. Man is not a machine but bounded by the body structure including head, heart, mind and matter. Above all these, there is an immanent transcendent entity which is called the Aathma (the divine or self). It is beyond the observation of physical eye but it can be sensed by our five senses in the midst of 'unseen' as 'the tree' is seen but the root that sustains it and bears it, is invisible. The building is seen, but the foundation structure on which the building stands is beyond sight. Thus Aathma is present in the self. It cannot be seen by physical eye, but it is sensed by five senses. The basis of self is nothing but Aathma-this was the great. Since Vedic age, knowledge is thought to be the third eye of a man, which gives him insight into all affairs and teaches him how to act. The basic principles of social, political and economic life were welded into a comprehensive theory of Hindu Religion. In ancient tradition the ideals and conduct are regarded as Dharma or Virtue of Religion. Thus ancient India becomes a country more of religious culture and less of a geographical and material entity, so to say a country of spirit. Thus India was the first country to rise to the conception of an extra-territorial nationality and hence forth the country became the happy home of different races, each with its own ethno customs. Thus the country of Spirit has expanded to Bharatvarsha or Suvarnabhumi and to a Greater India beyond its geographical boundaries. Learning in India was sought as the means of self-realization, as the means to the highest end of life, which is said to be Mukti or Emancipation. In the search of the values of life in Hindu philosophy it is evident that Death is the fact of life. Thus individual's supreme duty is to achieve his expansion into the Absolute, his self-fulfillment, for he is a potential God, a spark of the Divine. Hence education must be in the endeavor to achieve self-fulfillment and not in the acquisition of mere objective knowledge.

Modern education system was implanted by British rulers for the purpose to prepare Indian Clerks for running local administration. In 1835, Lord Macaulay introduced education in India by introducing English in the higher classes. The introduction of Wood's dispatch of 1854, known as Magna Carta of Indian education had actually laid the foundation of education system in India. Thus the British Ruler was successful to create a class of Indians who were Indians in blood and colour, but English in taste, in opinion, in morals and in intellect. The atmosphere was most favourable for Lord Macaulay to lay the foundation of modern education in India as the missionaries and their supporters as well as National leaders, intellectuals and Reformers all welcomed the changed and even exerted pressure on the company to encourage and promote western education in India. Missionaries welcomed education because they were in believes that the modern education would lead the people to adopt Christianity. Humanitarians, intellectuals and nationalist leaders welcomed education because they believed that education would bring light to Indians to understand the values of science and the significance of democracy that had prevailed in the west and above all education would remove the prejudices of social evils and better enlighten the people about the political and economic situation of the country. In view of the popularity of English, the British in 1844 through a declaration, the knowledge of English was made compulsory for all Government employment and thereby the government made all English medium schools became very popular. The British in 1837 created Universities at Calcutta, Bombay and Madras and thereafter higher education spread rapidly. In respect of technical education, three Medical Colleges one each at Calcutta, Bombay and Madras was established in 1857 and one engineering college was established at Roorkee.

English education not only produced a huge population of Indian to be fit for Clerical works to run the British administration but also had produced national leaders, intellectuals and reformers like Raja Ram Mohan Roy, Dadabhai Naoroji, Ferozeshah Mehta, Gokhale, Tilak, Lala Lajpat Rai, Moti Lal Nehru, Patel, Ambedkar, Gandhi, Jinnah, Jawaharlal Nehru, Subhash Chandra Bose, and any more. They thought of building a culturally rich, prosperous and powerful India out of poverty stricken, superstitious and inward looking society. The culture of Dharma had brought superstitious in disguise and bothered little for the economic betterment of life. They thought of English education would take out the Indians from the clutches of religious superstition.

They believed that (i) Western education would give Indians the understanding of scientific and democratic ideas that prevailed in Western World, (ii) Education would help to realize the real issues of backwardness of Indian society, (iii) Education would improve the life by the conquer of hunger, poverty, diseases and discard the evils of superstitions, (iv) English education would enlighten the people with the principles of democracy, the results of which would make the people courageous to raise their voice against imperialism and tyranny. However, initially education was remained limited to Brahmin and upper caste rich Hindus as the education was very much costly. The education on the other hand had brought a greater opportunity for the British to devise a unique method of distribution of power to prolong their rule over the land keeping the natives busy in their infighting.

The second half of the nineteenth century saw the impact of modern education in India in two fronts. On the one hand the Christian missionaries brainwashed many Indians especially the poor and converted them into Christianity. That is why to-day we find many Christian are present in India. On the other hand, Indian reformers got alarmed at the erosion of Indian culture. Organization such as Brahma Samaj founded by Raja Ram Mohan Roy (1828) in Bengal, Parthana Samaj in Maharashtra (1867), Arya Samaj (1875) founded by Swami Dayanand in Northern India and Rama Krishna Mission like society were built up for the protection of Hindu culture. These organization fight against social evils caused by ignorance, racial discrimination like untouchability, superstitions and inhuman treatment to women, Sati, Polygamy, child marriage etc. National leaders and intellectuals realized the impact of British Rule in the case of racial discrimination in the areas of education, jobs and their lordly superiority. In the later stage few of nationalist leaders encouraged the youths to fight against the British with bombs and bullets in secret and spoiled the academic atmosphere. The relation between Indians and British deteriorated day by day. The British tighten their administration in Calcutta in particular and shifted the Capital from Calcutta to Delhi although initially the British had thought of to make Calcutta the 2nd City of British Empire, the London was being the first. This was a loss to Bengal and draw back to the intellectuals of Bengal.

# [36]

The India's pre-independence era could be compared with that of Japan when Japan was under complete control of British and America after the fall of Atom bomb and the surrender of Japan to allied Force in1945. The superiority of nationalist leaders of Japan lies in their thinking of sending and encouraging the Japanese youths to go to United Kingdom to learn the basic science, where skill of science was first evolved in the United Kingdom to bring industrial revolution and later the technique of science was implemented in industries in Japan. But Indian leaders never encouraged the Indian youths to go to the British Land to know the engineering technique for the development of industries. Rather Indian leaders went there to appear in ICS examination as routine work because the success would bring for them an administrative post in India under British government. This might be one of the reasons why India remains backward while Japan moved ahead economically. United Kingdom a small island inhabited with small number of people but learnt the style of administration with devotion and sincerity. Their endeavoring attempt gave them the opportunity to bring industrial revolution first in UK in Europe and make the country of Small Island economically sound and a powerful nation in Europe. After independence such a big land of India was administered by only a few of ICS Officers who worked under British. These Officers who had the power in their hands and who controlled almost every walks of national life were working to deny justice to common men. It was for the superiority complex because of being seated in the power of center forgetting the value of morality and in effect its reflection was also found in the educational system as well. Common Indians accepted such kind of oppression and exploitation as a part of life. Even today, the people are tolerating the corruption, scams and criminal activities as developed in different sector under the cover of politics. This is how the Indians are living. A picture of exploitation and inefficiency since the ancient time till today is prevailing in India. Now at the present stage of population explosion, the development and better life for all irrespective of rich and poor is a distant dream to think of.

India achieved independence since sixty years but the people could not see or realize any kind development really had taken place in India for common men. Rather people are suffering with the pain of distress and discomfort and poverty. Now the student has taken the upper hand in the process of development. Indian IT engineers are bringing foreign exchange by the service of their works abroad and by the act of expertise in the IT sector industry. Few of them are also exploring IT industry in the country by their own afford or abroad as well. So to say the Youth of India are in the process of Nation Building. The method of modern teaching is completely different. India has adopted in most of the cases the Western method of teaching as its base was established by the British and in most of the cases, the British method of teaching is applied although teaching by local languages and few local industrial teachings are prevalent in some sort of modified pattern. Once India was very poor and illiterate because of the absence of learning institute except the learning of ethics of religion in the few Temples, but to day India is one of the learning centers of all kinds' literatures, science, medicine, sports and others. The percentage of literacy as well as the number of Indian youths in academic proficiency has increased. A Nation is developed by the activities of the youth as because the youth is the age of discovery, dreams and accomplishment. To-day the Indian youths has shown to the world that they have potential and energy. If their hidden energy of knowledge is cherished in right direction, something miraculous and unknown in the universe could be evolved for the betterment of mankind as had shown in the IT sector. But high intectuals are utilizing the growing potential energetic Indian youths for their benefit for making higher profit. The big companies of the world are in search of Indian youths as the source of talents at low cost. Having being India, the largest youth population of the world after China, the entire world is looking towards India as a source of technical manpower. If the Indian youths work in close unity with the people of working class, they could bring miracle, they could capture the power of development by the new designs of communication like that of Japan where people move easily in shortest time by the trip of small carrier of flight, or by the trip of bullet train making life easy and comfortable, and they could flourish economy bringing new concept of industry involving the large potential of youth in the progress of country to make India from developing nation to a developed nation.

**Hope for the Best:** The youth in general hopes for a world free from poverty, unemployment, inequality, discrimination, exploitation of man by man. The youth thinks for a world free of discrimination on the grounds of peace, caste, color, language, gender and above all religion. Youths are the backbone of a nation, who can make a nation, who can destroy a nation. Modern technology has reduced the dimension of the Earth and national integration becomes the new concept of global philosophy.

**My vist to a Don Bosco School, Imphal:** The school is situated at a very remote area called Chingmeirong, Imphal of India for the purpose spreading education in the interior area. It was established in 1957 and run by the Salesians of Don Bosco, starting with Lower Kindergarten (LKG) to 10th grade with such as efficiency that in no time it has been affiliated to the Board of Secondary Education, Manipur. The motto of the institution is to serve the God and serve the children of the country through education in building their character in the sphere of discipline, in developing intelligence and self dependence. It brings in mind the wide thinking of Don Bosco for the cause of mankind and the organized discipline system in the creation of Sister and Father for running the institution all over the world. It also brings thrill and surprise in the creation of Don Bosco in Imphal, one of the earliest centers in the North East of India. The school was established on 5th March 1957 by Father Peter Bianchiband and Father A Ravilico. By their untiring effort, a piece of land was bought in Chingmeinrong, the place where the church stand now, and the school was started by the name of Don Bosco Youth Centre. In 1958 a building was constructed for the school and classes were shifted there. In the course of time, the student number increases year after year compelling the school to raise the floors and now it is a big school extended to 4th floor in 1990. The school pioneered education in the English medium in the state. As the school catered exclusively to boys, soon after it was started a school for girls managed by the Salesian Sisters of Don Bosco. To day there are some 50 high schools and higher secondary schools run by the Catholic Church in Manipur and a Don Bosco College at Maram.

It is interesting to know that the mission of St. John Bosco was started with street boys through Oratory at the Rifugio. His devotion in the face of all difficulties led many to the conclusion that he was insane and an attempt was also made to confine him in an asylum. It was because of his association of the boys he befriended, who belonged to the community of nuisance character. He was ordained a priest in 1841. He was distressed, finding young people—unemployed, sad and roaming the streets. He decided mentally "At all costs, I must stop boys from ending up here." One December day in 1841, a street boy from a village entered the church to seek warmth from the biting cold. After three days, he had around him nine urchins, a month later twenty-five that grew to eighty. And by the end of summer of 1842 he had over 300 boys. However, in the later he was joined by his mother "Mama Margaret" as Don Bosco's mother came to be known in the creation of first Salesian home. She sacrificed what small means she had, even to parting with her home, its furnishings, and her jewelry, she brought all the solicitude and love of a mother to these children of the streets.

In 1859, he founded the Society of St Francis of Sales, the Salesians of Don Bosco in collaboration with many young people who had been inspired by his work. The mission of the Society was to respond to the needs of the young. He was successful to consecrate a church on 9th June, 1868 which was placed under the patronage of the Lady, Help of Christians. In the same year he was successful to form a society consisting of fifty priests and teachers bounded under a common rule which was Pius IX.

If we look to the life history we find, Don Bosco, the founder of the Salesian Society, was an Italian, and born of poor parents in a little cabin at Becchi, a hill-side hamlet near Turin of Italy, 16th August, 1815 and died 31st January 1888. He lost his father at the age of two and spent the early age as a shepherd. When he was young, he would put on shows of his skills as a juggler, magician and an acrobat. He received his first instruction at the hands of parish priest when his ready wit and retentive memory came into light. Owing to the poverty of the home, he was very often obliged to go to field works closing the study book. But he had never given up his desire of study and wish of serving the destitute. After leaving the seminary he went to Turin and got an opportunity to visits the prisons of the city where the deplorable condition of the children, who were confined in places, abandoned to the most evil influences, and with little before them but the gallows, made such a indelible impression upon his mind that he resolved to devote his life to the rescue of these unfortunate outcasts. According to Don Bosco knowledge never makes a man perfect because it does not directly touch the heart although it generates power in the exercise of good or evil. It requires frequent Confession, frequent Communication, and daily Mass. Besides these games as well as culture of music are also the nutrients of children heart.

**Salesian Family:**

The Daughters of Mary Help of Christians are the second biggest and living part of the great Salesian Family which relives the Spirit and Mission of St. John Bosco who founded the congregation in collaboration with Marry Domenica Mazzarello, as a Co-foundress. St. John Bosco achieved success in his mission of works with the assistance of Mary Help of Christians, whom he considered as his mother, teacher, inspirer and guide. According to Don Bosco, education to be a "matter of the heart" and he said the boys must not only be loved, but know that they are loved. The educative style of parting was based on three basic principles: **Reason, Religion and loving Kindness.**

To-day the mission concerns more over women empowerment through education and development activities as a response to the challenging situations of women in society. At the time of Don Bosco's death in 1888 there were 250 houses of the Salesian Society in all parts of the world, containing 130,000 children.

The congregation was born on 5th August, 1872 with 11 girls from a hamlet in Italy, making Mary Domenica Mazzarello as the Head of the organization. The organized group was committed to give their devotion to God for the service of the poor girls. It was surprising to see that a tiny group had grown into a gigantic organization and working in 81 provinces in 89 nations within 5 continents with in cooperation of locals numbering 1511 local communities. The followers of Don Bosco succeeded in establishing a network of centers to carry out the administration of such a big organization through out the Globe in spreading the love of God in the sphere of education to the children, young and youth in all front of their lives. In recognition of his work with disadvantaged youth, he was canonized by Pope Pius XI in 1934. The expedition was started in India, a country very ancient in age but very backward in education particularly in the rural area and poor for political, social and illiterate character of orthodox nature, by the arrival of six pioneers from Italy on 22nd November, 1922 at Tanjore, Tamilnadu. Today it has grown into six provinces—Chennai (1946), Shillong (1953), Mumbai (1982), Kolkata (1987), Guwahati (2000), and Bangalore (1993). The number of sisters has increased to 1154. Italians are not Indians but they are human beings and giving service for the cause of humanity which is not found to be seen in the customary education system that prevailed in India in the ancient time through the Gurukul system of education. It is only a bit of service was initiated by Swami Vivekanda, a man of vision but unfortunately he left the world at an early age of thirty nine only.

**Don Bosco & India:** Don Bosco's method of study knew nothing of punishment. The rule of discipline was obtained by instilling a true sense of duty, and carefully removing all occasions for disobedience. He said that the teacher should be father, adviser, and friend. In 1887 he wrote in his book "I do not remember to have used formal punishment and with God's grace I have always obtained, and from apparently hopeless children, not alone what duty exacted, but what my wish simply expressed." In Kolkata, the Don Bosco School Park Circus better known as DBPC was established in 1958 and run by the Salesians of the Kolkata Province. The motto of the school is Virtus et Scientia, meaning Virtue and Knowledge in Latin. The school is functioning since January, 1958 and has been in service to the people of Kolkata for more than 50 years. Don Bosco Schools in Tamilnadu are giving service in teachings to the children staying in the Refugee Camps in Tamilnadu, who these refugees were the victims of racial violence in SriLanka.

**Sisters and Refugees:** With the change of situation "The Daughters of Mary Help of Christians" gathered together to meet the challenging task of the problems of refugee at Tamilnadu migrated from SriLanka. It concerns not only the education but also a shared home for the diversity of the people, the young, children and immigrant women and also the illegal immigrants which challenges the Educating Community. Roughly more than 60. 000 refugees from Sri Lanka have been accommodated in 105 camps in Tamilnadu. Recently more than 19, 00 refugees have been arrived since January 2006 in Tamilnadu. The conflict between Sinhalese and Tamils in Sri Lanka started in 1956 when Sinhala was made the official language of the country and Tamils were down graded and discriminated in every affair in job, education and what not. Sisters were doing their job to help the refugee family in all fronts. In Kolkata also the service to the refugees of East Bengal is shown by Mother Tarrasa. The service of Italian Sisters is service to humanity irrespective of country, caste, religion or status of family.

**Thinking of Swami Vivekananda (SV):**

Vivekananda, an Indian monk, but a man of genius, who thought of present India hundred years before the Independence of India. He knows India is a country consisting of 530 princely States. The people of all the states are illiterate but they developed their own language for exchange of communication. They have own systems of rituals for the performance of their culture. Although they differ in language, in the performance of culture, the great saint Vivekananda knows they are all equal in their vision of thought, in the ethics of culture although they differ in the performance of rituals and that tempted him to think of one nation of one India hundred years before. He thought of religion in integration. He was well known in India and in America as well during the last decade of the nineteenth century. The unknown monk of India suddenly came in the lime light at the Parliament of Religion held in Chicago in 1893, at which he represented Hinduism. The Youths of India struggled with poverty, education, culture, and liberty for more than hundred years facing holocaust of mass killing among brothers in the event of division of the country but yet the intellectuals of youths remained firm to establish a country, a nation of Indian Union, a homeland for all irrespective of caste, language and religion. Vivekananda was not only a monk, a saint but a great statesman, a great philosopher, a great politician in the form of monk and a great servant of downtrodden. The vision of SV will be complete only when the youths of India will change the poor India to a developing India and developing India into a developed Nation where people of all community will live in peace and prosperity maintaining equality, fraternity and friendship of brotherhood.

**Early Mathematics in India:** It is a fact; the ancient India was a country of religion and a country of poverty and illiteracy. But it is also a fact that the concept of literacy began in India first by the establishment of University Taxila in the present state of Pakistan. The teachings were based on 'Shrutis' or listening where repetition of Verse of Vedas was continued till the sweet Verse of Vedas settled in the mind. The concept of repetition gives the idea of counts that was the beginning of the concept of numbers. Thus it is said that the knowledge of Mathematics started in ancient India. This concept of knowledge of Mathematics was emerged in the Indian subcontinent since 1200 BCE. The contribution of scholars like Aryabhata, Brahmagupta, and Bhaskara II was of immense importance in the development of the subject. The decimal number system in use today was first recorded in Indian mathematics. Similarly the binary number system, the root of computer tools, the concept of zero, the negative numbers, arithmetic, and algebra besides trigonometry were the contribution of mathematicians of India. In recent expansion of internet the language Java in computer science was originated in India. The earlier mathematical concepts were not only remained in India alone but even transmitted to the Middle East, China and Europe and henceforth further development in the field of number of Mathematics continued. Thus the foundation of many areas of mathematics used in the international arena was experimented and first studied in India. Hence India is called the center of the concept of Mathematics.

## My Journey to Belur Math:

It was my desire to see the Belur Math which was established by the Indian Monk Swami Vivekananda for the Service to Mankind. It brings in light that to know who was he and how he came to the conclusion that "Service to Mankind is the Service to God". He was Swami Vivekananda, who born on January 12, 1863 initially known as Narendranath Dutta, who was the chief disciple of the 19th century mystic Sri Ramakrishna Paramahamsa and who the founder of Rama Krishna Mission was. He was a person who introduced a doctrine by the spirit of Vedanta and Yoga in Europe and America. He was credited with raising interfaith awareness, bringing Hinduism to the status of world religion during the end of the 19th century. He is best known for his inspiring speech beginning with "Sisters and Brothers of America" through which he introduced Hinduism at the Parliament of the World's Religions at Chicago in 1893. From his childhood, Vivekananda showed inclination towards spirituality and God realization. He came in contact with Ramakrishna who taught him Adyaita Vedanta and that all religions are true and service to man was the most effective worship of God. In course of time Vivekananda became a wandering monk, touring the Indian subcontinent first and later sailed to Chicago to attend the Parliament of World Religions in the year 1893. As an eloquent speaker, he was invited to several forums in the United States. He successfully preached the teachings of Vedanta, Yoga and Hinduism in America, England and Europe. His teachings influenced the other national leaders like Mahatma Gandhi, Jawaharlal

Nehru, Subhas Chandra Bose, Aurobindo Ghosh, and Sarvepalli Radhakrinan. It was a point of discussion how a Monk Swami Vivekananda said the Service of Mankind is the service to God instead of observing the rituals of religion to show the devotion to the Almighty God. The wandering Monk went to South India at Emakulam and proceeded to Kanyakumari on foot during the Christmas Eve of 1892. There he meditated for three days on the "last bit of Indian rock", and that in later the rock became famous as the Vivekananda Rock Memorial. At Kanyakumari Vivekananda had the "Vision of one India", also commonly called "The Kanyakumari resolve of 1892". He wrote, "At Cape Camorin sitting in Mother Kumari's temple, sitting on the last bit of Indian rock—I hit upon a plan: We are so many sanyasis wandering about, and teaching the people metaphysics-it is all madness. Did not our Gurudevo used to say, 'An empty stomach is no good for religion?'. We as a nation have lot of our individuality and that is the cause of all mischief in India. We have to raise the masses'.

Vivekananda returned to India on 15th January 1897. According to his philosophy "Jiva is Shiva" (each individual is divinity itself). It was his 'Mantra', and he assimilated the concept of 'daridra narayana seva'—the service of God in and through (poor) human beings. He concluded that these distinctions vanish into nothingness in the light of oneness that the devotee experiences in MOKSHA. He founded the Sri Ramakrishna Math and Mission on the principle of one's own salvation and for the welfare of the world. He advised his followers to be holy, unselfish and faithful. Swami Vivekananda is believed to have inspired India's freedom struggle movement. His writings inspired a whole generation of freedom fighters including Aurobindo Ghosh and Bagha Jatin. He was the big brother of the extremist revolutionary, Bhupendranath Dutta and Subhash Chandra Bose who were the prominent figures in Indian independent movement.

**Ramakrishna Mission:**

The creation of Ramakrishna Mission to different places started with creation of Belur Math at Dakshnieswar at the opposite shore of River Ganga, 50 km away from the City of Kolkata in early 1888 and worked for relief works for the cause of sudden calamities apart from other activities.

He used to say "If God can be worshipped in an image, can He not be worshipped in a living person". Swami Vivekananda transformed relief and rehabilitation into an act of worship. The statistics shows to day the Math and Mission have 171 centers all over the world—128 in India, 13 in USA, 12 in Bangladesh, 2 in Russia, one each in Argentina, Australia, Brazil, Canada, Fiji, France, and UK. Besides, there are many sub-centers. After triumphant success in spreading India's message of Advaita Vedanta, which is nothing but Eternal Truth of Eternal Religion-Swami looks to other religious leaders as well as political leaders. The writ-up of other leaders are found to be seen such as: Mahatma Gandhi said, "Swami Vivekanada's writing needs no introduction from anybody. They make their own irresistible appeal." Further Gandhi said that his whole life was an effort to bring into actions the ideas of Vivekananda. Many years after Vivekananda's death, Rabindranath Tagore, a noble Poet Laureate had said, "If you want to know India, study Vivekananda. In him everything is positive and nothing negative." Mission made a service to flood Victim recently victimized. The eminent British historian A L Basham stated that "in centuries to come, he will be remembered as one of the main moulders of the modern world." One of the most significant contributions of Swami Vivekananda to the modern world is his interpretation of religion. It is a universal experience of transcendent Reality, common to all humanity. In addition to that Swamiji met the challenge of modern science by showing that religion is as scientific as science itself; religion is the 'Science of Consciousness'. As such, religion and science are not contradictory to each other but are completer to each other

## My Journey to see the Cottage Industry of India:

It is a kind of specialized form of small scale industry where the production of commodity takes place in the surroundings of homes and the workers, the so called labors are no body other than the family members of the family or sourrounding family only. In general the machineries commonly used at homes, are utilized for the production of commodities. Basically it is a home made product unorganized and produced at home by the tradition of generation. The commodities of these industries are basically consumable products and that are being produced through the utilization of the traditional techniques. In the atmosphere of prevailing unemployment, people have no alternative but to go for home made small scale industries for the survival of livelihood. Thus a huge section of labor of large population is absorbed to stabilize the rural economy.

**The Danger of Indian Cottage Industry:** Now medium and large industries are growing at random in almost every state of India and Gujarat in particular. These are capital intensive in nature. This is because the large industries utilize all sorts of cost effective technologies by dint of which the cost of production remain at lower rate. On the other hand, the Cottage Industry is fundamentally labor intensive and utilizes traditional techniques in the manufacturing process which are not cost effective at all and that makes the production at higher cost. Thus today Cottage Industry in India faces the risk of extinction if they are not protected by the government by giving enough financial or other form of support to sustain.

**Rise of Cottage Industry in England and Europe:** There was a time when Cottage Industry sprang up across the European continent and in England in domestic cotton processing. It was started by Farm households with raw cotton material. The raw materials were distributed throughout the countryside by the travelling merchants. These were then clean and spin into yarn or thread. Again the merchant returned with new bundles of raw cotton, picking up the processed yarn. These were taken to another home where weaving produced cloth. In this way every individual family of every home became a partner in growing an enterprise—the Cotton Industry. Even today the term is applied to any industry.

**Cottage Industry for Modern America:** At present there is severe economic crisis in the US bringing much big business to a skeleton, many banks to the verge of liquidation and in net result abolition of jobs and increase in the number of unemployment. The conditions that are destroying the giant corporations and large-scale manufacturing industries may be opening the ways to profitable home-based and family-run business—the so called Cottage Industry to an extent not seen ever before for nearly a century in this country. A family farm is an income of self employed family as well as an income of the nation. Modern technology in America, and around the world, often requires work-at-home. These were the works of writers, reporters, designers, and manufacturers. These were very much a part of Cottage Industry. The mechanical parts, automobiles, airplanes, accessories of computers and many other products are designed, developed and built at home. Toys, books, furniture of all kinds and thousands of other products are being produced either in basements or in garages, of any private residences. All these are part of Cottage Industry. At present it may be a test of time for US citizens to revive America's current economy by diverting attention to the home made product.

**Cottage Industry is Essential for India:** Cottage Industry preserves an enormous potential for employment generation. The person who is being employed feel proud of himself as he is basically regarded as a self-employed one. Cottage Industry has given economic independence to the women of India. India is a country of huge population. Most of the people are living in the villages. Cottage Industries support a large section of the population living in rural India. It is the traditional business of rural India that supports the rural economy. Cottage Industry is the Lifeline for Poor Villagers in India. Big cities with big industries only support sections of educated and skilled technicians. Indigenous goods reflect the cultural heritage of India. The product of good quality can fairly compete with the foreign goods. Manufacturing of quality products involves those traditional artisans and craftsman who have inherited the art of work from their previous generations. Goods like dress fabrics such as Khadi, leather, silk, cotton, wool, muslin, etc, and others like ornaments, statues, idols, stones, gems, etc besides edible items like spices, oils, honey etc have a huge demand in India and in foreign markets as well. Since ancient times in India, indigenous products have been attracting foreign traders and merchants and that helped India in establishing trade relations with the Greek, Chinese and Arab merchants. During the period of medieval India, Indian traditional business flourished well under the rule of the Turk, Afghan and Mughal dynasties. But the Cottage Industry suffered a set back in India during the British period. Industrial revolution in the west brought a disaster to home-made Industries in India. However, the 'Swadeshi' and the 'Boycott' movements led by Gandhi in the independence movement of India helped in the demand of khadi and other Indian fabrics to a little extent. The making of handicrafts and handlooms forms the core of the cottage industries. Indian cottage industry plays an important role as far as employment in India is concerned & the swing machine is used for making textile product.

**Cottage Industry in India after Independence:** India achieved her independence in 1947 and since then the leaders of India trying hard to improve the economic conditions of the country. It is most likely that the lack of administrative experience of a newly born country of large dimension that was formed by the union of smaller states after being left out by the British Emperor was the reason of failure of development till 1991. Untied Kingdom was a country of Industry unlike India. Most of the Indian leaders were influenced by the growth of the UK. As such their initial attempt was to improve the economy with the establishment of large industry. Many public sector steel industries have been established at the early stage of Independence neglecting the agriculture and cottage Industry. However, in the subsequent five year plan the rectification was incorporated. Since then, the small scale industries are run with a joint co-operation of the public and the private sectors. Now, almost in every state in India has its own set of cottage industries. The art and craft items of the region reflect the culture of that region. Many are self-employed in the manufacturing of cultural items and that have provided them with the means to earn their livelihood. On October2, 1993, the govt. of India has started the "Prime Minister's Rozgar Yojana Scheme" for the educated but unemployed youth for providing them with self-employed ventures in Industries. The youths are now provided with the facilities of getting training in the government-approved institutions where they could learn the techniques of services and business, etc. The trained persons were also provided financial assistance for the initial expense in setting up an industry. Under the Tenth Five-year Plan, the areas are selected-these are Leather and leather products, Textiles and Readymade Garments, Gems and Jeweler, Pharmaceuticals, Information Technology, Bio-Technology, Automobile component and Food Processing. To flourish cottage Industries training facilities are now provided to Handloom Weavers, Spinning Industry, Power loom Industry, Garments Industry and similar like other industries for the benefits of common people.

## China is a Competitor to India in Cottage Industry:

China is like India a highly populated country who flourishing her cottage Industry by the utilization of the mass population in large scale production of rural product. China is now one of the fastest budding economies of the world. China supplies her products to all markets, all over the world. The items of the cottage industries of India do not find any buyers in India and abroad as well because of their high prices or because of availability of better quality goods elsewhere. China is a country of tough competitor to India in regard to Cottage Industry. Once, home-made clothes were made by the "Charkha" of Gandhi. Those days have gone, now the people get inspiration from the dresses used by Bollywood or their favorite pop-stars. The future of Indian textiles carries a big question mark. People prefer to eat olive oil to ghee and avoid pickles. People use allopath instead of Indian Ayurveda. Thus the herbal medicines and indigenous food items draw a lesser number of buyers. In consideration of all these, the Cottage Industry of India had to fight a better battle a head for survival.

# [37]

## My visit to Dakha & Sylhet of Bangladesh:

Dakha is the capital of Bangladesh and located on the banks of the River Buriganga, the city has a population of about 7 million, making it one of the largest cities in the region. It has a colorful history and known as the **'City of Mosques.'** Modern Dhaka is the center of political, cultural and economic life of Bangladesh. Its industries include textiles (jute, muslin, cotton) and food processing, especially rice milling. A variety of other consumer goods are also manufactured here. The Muslim influence is reflected in the City more than 700 mosques and historic buildings found throughout the city. Dhaka is divided into an old city and the new city, and many residential and industrial communities. Its history can be traced from the 7th century. The city was ruled by the Buddhist kingdom of Kamarupa and the Pala Empire before passing to the control of the Hindu Sena dynasty in the 9th century. After the Sena dynasty, Dhaka was successively ruled by the Turkish and Afghan governors descending from the Delhi Sultanate before the arrival of the Mughals in 1608. It served as the Mogul capital of Bengal from 1608 to 1704 and was a trading center of interest for British, French, and Dutch before coming under British rule in 1765. Under Mughal rule in the 17th century, the city was also known as Jahangir Nagar, and was both a provincial capital and a centre of the worldwide muslin trade. The development of modern city was started under British rule in the 19th century, and soon became the second-largest city in Bengal after Calcutta (presently Kolkata). In 1905 it was named the Capital of Bengal, and in 1956 it became the capital of East Pakistan. After the partition of India in 1947,

Dhaka became the administrative Capital of East Pakistan, and later, in 1972, the Capital of an independent Bangladesh. The city suffered heavy damage during the Bangladesh war of independence (1971). The Romanized spelling of the Bengali name was changed from Dacca to Dhaka in 1982.

**The political history of Dakha** shows that the people living in Dakha are changing their religion time to time as the people desired. But the language and the culture never changes. In the 7th century Dakha was under Buddhist Kingdom, and under Buddha religion, in the 9th century Dakha was under Hindu Sena dynasty, and under Hindu religion and under Mughal Rule under Muslim religion. Thus it seems people change their religion when the people rest their belief in particular religion in search of peace of life. In Bangladesh what is seen now an open revolt against the minority Hindu people for no fault of them to face torture and attempt to burn their belongings, threaten as if all Hindus are enemy of the nation as because they belong to a community who belief in the faith of Hinduism. It was not seen before as there are no such records of history. In earlier time people's outlook was narrow as they were compelled to live in a limited region but now people are not living in limited region rather the world is their space to live in and the world is nearer to them, nearer to their bad through the gift of internet. In the days of 21st century such an open assault, killing, burning or torture over the minority Hindu community is below dignity, below humanity and it goes down by the dearth of civilization. Religious fanaticisms are no more in human civilization. The civilization lies in the uplifting of the economy and human status to get the pleasure of life. United States, a country of only three hundred years old has made the country an earthly heaven where people from different regions with different faith meet together. But we, the people of Bangladesh, one of the oldest civilizations in the human history are still lagging behind in education, human culture and above all in economy. On looking to Asia it is the country Japan, where from many things to be learnt. A country destroyed by Atom bomb but again had risen to the top of world economy and had increased the status of its country men, is something to be looked into and had set the lesson for the Mankind.

The country of Bangladesh is not up to expectation of economic progress as the Government frequently changes from civilian to military and again from military to civilian because of political unrest. The country is poor because its economy could not grow up with the growth of population that causes unrest as the life of common people is hard-pressed. Unless stability exists, no government could work peacefully giving concentration in economic front. Security, stability and economy are three vital fronts where the government is going to concentrate to boost up its economy. The city has historically attracted large number of migrant workers, who are Hawkers, peddlers, small shop owners, rickshaw-transport workers, roadside vendors and stalls employees. Urban developments have sparked a widespread construction boom, causing new high-rise buildings and skyscrapers to change the picture of the city, requiring a huge number of workers. Progressive attempt were made for the Growth of the country in the sector of finance, banking, manufacturing, telecommunications, while the business in the sector of hotels and restaurants were continued as an important elements of the progress of Dhaka's economy. Unless better facilities were provided by the widening of roads, cleaning the streets and roads, the number of tourists is less likely to improve. Although Dakha is well connected with all the districts through roads and bridges, yet it is not smooth and good for business. There are other avenues left unused for its economic growth. The vast wealth of river water is unutilized. The government failed to utilize the recently discovered gas & oil scientifically for the growth of country's economy. Besides these, further development of Chittagong Port is a point of importance for robust economic growth. Increase of population is a set back for growth but proper utilization of man power is an asset for the country. The population of Dhaka city that is about 6. 7 million including wider metropolitan area, calculated once, but the number now had increased to 12. 3 million as of the record of 2007. The population is growing by an estimated 4. 2 per cent per annum, one of the highest rates amongst Asian cities. In view of wider spectrum of unemployment a large section of rural people tends to migrate to Dhaka in search of employment threatening the already strained city. But the presence of sky-scraper in Dakha does not reflect a country of poor people rather a place of wealthy persons living with luxury. But the surrounding peoples are poor, who are no other than the floating people, the people of the street living at the cost of their labour, the labour might be a worker at the factory, a Rickshaw-puller, or may be a driver. The country might be poor but Dakha the capital city of Bangladesh is gorgeous to see with Office Buildings and Skyscraper but the streets are covered with Rickshaw-puller and poor peoples. In the past decades Dhaka has made significant improvement in respect of some quality hotel for decent accommodation for tourists. But even now there are few three to five star hotels with modern facilities brightening the greatness of the city.

The design and luxury of modern 'Lakeshore Hotel' indicates Dhaka city is not poor or less gorgeous than any other modern city. It has luxurious 'Hotel' business; Hotels are standing tall in the heart of the city at the center of commercial zone with clean spacious rooms, comfortable accommodation having with good services and services with conglomeration of food. In addition to these hotels, there are many Guest Houses with average of 8 to 10 rooms; those are operating mainly from Gulshan, Banani, Baridhara and Dhanmondi. About 10 of these guest houses have restaurant facilities too along with all other modern facilities. Famous global cuisine is also available in these restaurants. Chinese restaurants, along with Thai, Korean, Japanese, Vietnamese, Italian, or Mexican, restaurants are giving service to an aristocrat class of people local or foreigners and many such restaurants are scattered all around the city. The hotel Westin of Dhaka is one of the gorgeous hotels of the City that needs to be counted in design and construction.

The rapid rise of population has made the city densely populated. The poor people along with rich are also living in the city for the earning of bred and butter. Under the circumstances, Dhaka becomes a city of contrasts between old and new, rich and poor, industry and folk. It has beautiful National Parliament House and ultramodern Bashundhara City, the largest shopping mall in South Asia. Again it has the 17th Century Lalbagh Fort. The City is in need of large buildings for factory and industry. A class of people takes the advantage of the state of affair and constructs buildings at low cost without proper specification making the building insecure. The object is to earn money and not the security. Large industries were growing up in those insecure buildings where the work is going on in full swing with chief labour Force. Sometimes big building gets collapsed with the death of chief labours. Some times fire broke out with the loss life and property as the buildings were not safety proof for fire. This is the city experiencing with the cycles of life.

On Friday, an eight-story building collapsed killing more than thousand. One or two survives such as Begum's rescue from the debris of collapsed building brought a sense of happiness and hope as workers continue to pull out dozens of bodies every day. The garment worker rescued 13th May, Friday (accident occurred on 11th May, 2013), that showed the horror and aftermath of one of the deadliest factory accidents in Bangladesh's history. The latest estimate puts the death toll above 1,000.

These are the chief workers of Bangladesh. They are ordinary citizens of Bangladesh, not concern with the power politics which party is in the power to run the government. They are interested with the work because, the more they could produce in their work, the more is money for them. They are in urgent need of money to feed their little ones. In the distress of economic condition of the country, every thing is costly, their hard earned money with their maximum effort is even not sufficient to run the family. They have little time to think of safety precaution. They don't know which building is secured and which is insecure. The government has no control in the construction. They have surrendered their life to the mercy of their owners. It is because; the owner of the factory is their father-mother. Unless they are employed, they have no work and no money. Under this economic situation of the country, few rich people or few politically powerful people are utilizing these poor people at their advantage and exploiting them at their Will without any binding of responsibility or any decorum of safety. The people die by the collapse of building, matters little to them. New people will come to work under an identical arrangement and factory work will continue. The factory owner has no liability practically. By act of Law the Factory owners are liable for the cause of such death, but they have money, they have political power, they can turn the law to their advantage. They have no body to help them except the Al-mighty.

[It's as if they are saying "we are not a number—not only cheap labor and cheap lives; we are human beings like you. Our life is precious like yours, and our dreams are precious too"]

Long distant passengers use public buses-both air conditioned and non-air-conditioned being operated by the state-run Bangladesh Road Transport Corporation (BRTC). Auto rickshaw (three-wheel) are increasingly becoming popular in the city. Two-stroke engine taxis locally called CNG, being run on compressed natural gas are found to be very popular in Dakha. However, Dhaka is known as the rickshaw capital of the world. 400,000 cycle rickshaws run each day and cycle rickshaws and auto rickshaws are the main mode of transport for the inhabitants of the city. Relatively low-cost and non-polluting cycle rickshaws good for common people, nevertheless cause traffic congestion and have been banned to operate on a number of city streets. Dakha is also connected with India through Kolkata and Agartala by BRTC besides air via Zia International Airport. However our visit to ultramodern Bashundhara City was spectacular and unforgettable memory.

Uncle P. R. Roy Chowdhury & H. P. Roy Chowdhury @ Bashundhara city Dhaka—in Dhaka, Bangladesh, by Tultul Chowdhury in face book].

There are many boys of Sylhet are living in the United Kingdom where they are doing the catering business very successfully. They have brought lot of wealth to Bangladesh. That is why there are many big building; super market and health resort are growing up to the District

Town of Sylhet. One such resort is called Nazimgarh Resort recently built, very nicely situated outside the main city of Sylhet. Nazimgarh Resort at the suburb of Sylhet of Bangladesh is a testimony of the love of youths for their country, who are staying abroad particularly in the United Kingdom, earning a lot by dint of their service particularly in catering business but never forgets to send money to their relatives in Bangladesh, the growth of resort was the indirect investment and fruitful outcome.

**Indian Democracy is in danger:** It is true Pakistan was created on religious basis. But India is a democratic secular country and trying to maintain the secular character since birth. However, Indian political thinkers are disturbed due to the constant threat of torturing the Hindu community of the neighboring country. To keep the character of secularity, will it be unethical or unfair to direct the neighbor country to maintain peace while in the absence of which India will have no option but to interfere to bring peace and stability, India being a country of Hindu majority can not remain silent when Hindus in the neighbor country get tortured, burnt and butchered. There are many instances in the world where a country interferes for the sake of its own security. A letter published in a paper of Eastern India 'The Sentinel' is high lighted here to count:

**Inside Bangladesh:** Hindus again the scapegoats (The Sentinel) . . . . Silchar, March 5: Hindus are again made scapegoats in the ongoing violence across Bangladesh, triggered by the nationwide demand for death sentence to the 9 leaders of Jamaal-e-Islamic including the front-liner Dilwar Hussain Sayedee involved in heinous crimes, mass killings, atrocities against women and men in general. The death sentence was awarded by International Crime Tribunal which was supported by Awami League Government of Begum Sheikh Hasina. In fact, the patriotic and secular forces of Bangladesh have rallied against the radical elements led by Jamaat-e-Islami, its youth wing Shibir, Bangladesh Nationalist Party led by Begum Khaleda Zia. Millions of freedom lovers pitching their clamour for punishment to the war criminals of 1971 Liberation struggle have given call for "renaissance" in the country to make Bangladesh free from all extremist and fundamentalist forces. The clarion call was given from the historic Shahabad Square of Dhaka. The Jamaat-e-Islami flexing its muscle gave call for nationwide 48 hours bandh and BNP for 24 hours. It was during this volatile situation that the President of India, Pranab Mukherjee, landed at Bangladesh on Monday to make nostalgic journey to his in-laws' home and to address the 47th Convocation of Dhaka University. Even during his visit amidst tight security, violence continued and the Hindus have been its worst victims. Reports from various districts as flashed in the electronic and print media spoke of large scale attacks on Hindu houses, their properties, places of worships and atrocities by Jamaat-e-Islamic activists. The victims are also Christians and Buddhists. Till date, 1500 Hindu houses, more than 50 temples and places of worships have been either burnt or damaged. Expressing their serious concern at the atrocities, Hindu, Buddhist and Christian Aikya Parishad and Bangladesh Puja Udjapan Parishad put forward 4 point charter of demands before the Hasina Government.

The demands included immediate steps to stop all sorts of violence against Hindus, criminals involved in the crimes be arrested and put on trial, damaged and burnt houses, temples and business interests should be compensated and those displaced rehabilitated, besides implementation of the recommendations of Shahabuddin Commission for investigation into the atrocities on Hindus in the aftermath of 2001 elections which brought BNP Government and its coalition partner Jamaat-e-Islami to power.

The Hindus have been upset at the fact that Sheikh Hasina Government has also taken the intriguing stance of not adopting enough and adequate measures against violence on them which continues unabated. The leaders of the Hindu, Buddhist and Christian Aikya Parishad and Bangladesh Puja Udjapan Parishad expressing their anguish and anger before the media-persons on Monday said the violent situation of 1971 has been created in 2013 by Jamaat-e-Islami. One of them gave graphic details of violence against the Hindus in Chittagong, Dinajpur, Bagura, Noakhali, Cox Bazar, Lakhipur, Gaibanda, Sylhet, Moulvi Bazar, Thakurgram, Satkhira, Bagerhat,

Joypurhat, Comilla, Brahmanbaria, Rangpur and many other places. If Hindus cannot be safe even under Awami League regime, what will be their fate when Bangladesh Nationalist Party with Jamaat-e-Islami as its partner comes to power in 2014? This question is now making round among the panic-ridden minorities of the country. Begum Khaleda Zia has not kept her hobnobbing with Jamaat-e-Islam secret when she cancelled her scheduled meeting with the President of India, Pranab Mukherjee. The Hindus expected some words of assurance from the President about their safety and security. Instead, they felt disappointed to hear him repeat the stereotype diplomatic statement "India stands by Bangladesh".

It is not for the first time that the Hindus have been at the receiving end for no fault of their own. According to a media report, Jamaat-e-Islami and its Pakistani cohorts have taken up the mission for "driving out Hindus". There is every reason to believe it. The population of Hindus which was 33% in 1947 has now been reduced to 8% only and it continues to decrease. The Hindus, Buddhists and Christians have become irrefragable in the path of the extremist and fundamentalist forces. Their decimation will strengthen their hands to take back Bangladesh to the post liberation era. It is high time that both Bangladesh and India should join hands together to ensure the safe stay of Hindus instead of "cosmetic show of amity and friendship" between them.

**Tragic Life of Hindus in Bangladesh:** I have gone through the history of Bengal and India as well. Before coming to write anything of the region and the people I prefer to classify the period where it is possible to see the change that occurred under the lapse of time confronting with the change of behavior of the people in the atmosphere of social, politician and judicial atmosphere. It is better to see as (i) Hindus under British, (ii) Hindus under Pakistan, (iii) Hindus in East Bengal and (iv)Hindus under Bangladesh as the destiny decides the faddish fortune of any individuals.

**Hindus under British:** Knowing the British endeavor to establish British trade center at India since 1690 and also to supersede the French influence in India, Clive took it as a challenge to establish British dominance in Bengal as soon as he had been assigned with command of Bengal after being returned to Madras from London and asked to proceed to Bengal. It is in the history of record that the East India Company of British had increased its strength in Calcutta after capturing the Fort William and defeating the French force in Chandannagar under the leadership of Robert Clive, who did not stop from fighting until he could occupy the thrown of Bengal at Murshidabad. He designed the plan in secret after consulting with Mir Zafer, the commander in Chief of Nawab Siraj Daulah. He went ahead to capture Murshidabad and meet with the Nawab's force at Palasey. Clive defeated the Nawab of Murshidabad, Siraj Ud Daulah in the battle of Palasey and captured Bengal in 1757. After the fall of Murshidabad, the British devoted its major energy in rebuilding the new Capital. The Capital Calcutta was established by British by fastening the three villages namely Kalikata, Sutanuti and Gobindapur near the ninetieth period of 18th Century. British preferred the Hindus in British administration as the power was captured from a Muslim Ruler. Bengali Hindus of Bengal became the most powerful wings of British administration. Thus the Hindus of Bengal flourished in education, administration, knowledge, culture and even in sports. The administrative power not only made the Hindus Bengali powerful in the British administration but also made them powerful in society. The people of 24-Pargana of Bengal in particular were very much powerful, the impact of their power even spread to every activity of the society. The Bengal experienced a period when it was dangerous for anybody to move ahead of Bengali-British Executives in the streets of Calcutta. To save the society from the onslaught of tyranny Raja Ram Mohan Roy introduced Brahma Samaj, the ideals of which is to moderate the society from public exposure. The Brahma Samaj brought a social reform, including abolition of caste system, and of the dowry system, emancipation of women and improving the educational system. In 1866, Keshub Chunder Sen campaigned for the education of women and against child marriages. However, that was the glorious period of Hindus of Bengal particularly the Hindus of 24 Parganas of West Bengal.

The dominance of the Hindus of Bengal was spread over the area of Bongo, Bihar, and Orissa and even in distant Assam.

(ii) **The Hindus under Pakistan:** The Independence movement of India was started under Indian National Congress after the Congress being formed in 1885. The Bengali Hindus of Bengal took the most active part in the Independence movement right from the beginning. The Bengalese was both in front as the front runner of non violent movement and in back as a pioneer of Bomb blast in secret as the torch bearer of sabotage work against the British administration. The British administration was very much disturbed by the behavior of Hindu young leaders which they never expected as the Hindus were being favored by British after the fall of Murshidabad. In the atmosphere of volatile Bomb blast and that too in disguise, the British thought of otherwise. The policy was framed to punish the culprit under strict stricture of law and reduce the strength of Bengal in totality. So the order of bifurcation was experimented by imposing it over Bengal in 1905 instead of vehement protest. The agitation was continued against the division of Bengal which was also supported by the leaders of other states. Finally after seven years in 1912, the government withdrew the order of bifurcation of Bengal. The unity of Bengal was restored. But the administration never deterred from their policy of weakening Bengal. They did it in a clever way. To safe guard the British Empire, the British shifted the Capital from Bengal to Delhi in 1911 in disguise during the course of Bengal movement of unification and also reduced the new recruit of Hindu Bengali in the administration. Simultaneously, the clever British began to favor Muslims keeping the policy of 'Devide and Rule' alive. The relation between Muslim and British slowly and gradually get increased. Jinnah went to England in the mean time and became an important and reliable person of British government. The formation of separate home land for the Muslims of India became an important subject of discussion. Jinnah took the full advantage of the situation. During the course of time Jinnah could convince the British administration to take a part of Bengal to form East Pakistan. It was the reason for which the British came forward with the proposal of handing power to Indians with the formula of division of the country. Under the temptation of administering the

British India, the then Indian leader Pandit Jaharwarlal Nehru agreed in the general meeting of the congress in the proposal of the division of the country along with Petal in spite of the opposition of Mahatma Gandhi.

Pakistan was formed making Islam as its religion and thus the newly born State was formed only for the Muslims. As a right of birth place, Hindus can live there as a mercy of the State machinery. Thus the **born and bred by birth,** the Hindus of East Bengal became a second class citizen of his or her birth place. The rioting took the upper hand under the new administration of Pakistan. Lakhs of Hindus became refugee and fled to India for safety. It was the policy of the Pak administration to root out the Hindus from Bengal. The present Bangladesh Government is trying its best to expose that to the world that the people of Bangladesh believe in universal brotherhood and not in religious hatred culminating in rioting as had happened during the period of Pakistan. PM of Bangladesh never hesitate to visit Bhutan, a Buddhist religious state or to meet the Roman Pope Paul, the Religious Head of Christianity to bring back the love of humanity and the peace of the Nation. Prime Minister Sheikh Hasina of Bangladesh & Roman Pope Paul had made their conversion most cordially with each other for the cause of peace in the nation.

**Hindus in East Bengal:** There was a district in East Pakistan called Noakhali where Hindus were majority to the extent of 95%. The subsequent rioting has reduced the number to less than 10%. This was the result of the impact of administration of Islamic East Pakistan. While the district Murshedabad under India of West Bengal was a majority of Muslims to the extent of 70%. Today the Muslim population in the district had risen to 90%. This was the result of the impact of administration of Secular India. Hindus of Bengal who fought to the extreme for Independence of India have no place to live in with full right even in India. This was the most tragic part of Hindus of East Bengal. Many of the Hindus had left the country and taken asylum in Canada and in other western countries. Their plight is comparable with that of Israelis. A Hindu of East Bengal had to take permission for living inside of India. The sacrifice of their forefathers in the independence movement is forgotten and did not carry any moral value or right over the new Indian Union. The formation of Israel in 1948 by a resolution of UN, allowed all Yhudi people living in German, New York, London or French or in any other place to move to the new born state without any permission. But the same was not true for the Hindus of East Bengal. They had to face immense pressure in settlement in Easter, Western or in central India. The then PM Nehru had to send request to every state for the creation of refugee colony for these State-less victims. To day we could see how many states had implemented the Nehru's order in the creation of refugee colony? Every Wiseman could judge how well these people were treated in India although they know that the out burst of Independence movement was initiated in Chittagong Armoury? In India to-day Hindus are equally treated with the Muslims of Bangladesh as infiltrators. This is called the traverse of destiny.

**Hindus under Bangladesh:** Islamic religion has established the Muslim supremacy in Bangladesh but that was at the cost of the downfall of the economy of the country. Unless the economy of the State is strong and sound the standard of living condition of its citizen can not be improved. The economy of a country had risen only when every citizen sincerely devote themselves for the development of the country. India's economy had shown a rising trend because every citizen of India is a part and parcel of India by law, by constitution and by what not. America is a country of proud Nation because every citizen irrespective of black and white is a well wisher as well as a soldier of the nation. Bangladesh is realizing the economic plight and the present government's farsightedness had shown the reasons for the good relation with India which the administration had founded the best way to economic progress. Hindus of Bangladesh is also treated as an asset of Bangladesh even though constitutionally equal right is denied till now. It can not be denied that the opportunist party time to time takes the religious sentiment as the weapon for the fulfillment of their political desire making the Hindus as victims of torture.

Patriotic Political leaders are the best thinkers for the creation of destiny of a nation. Sheikh Muzibur Rohaman was the leader of that to create the destiny of Bangladesh. Sardar Petal was the leader for the creation of Indian Union of nation with Princely States; Lincoln was the leader for the creation secular Republic for the United States of America. Hazrat Muhammad, a leader as well as a prophet was the leader for the creation Islamic state in the Middle East. Since the creation of Islamic State, the fight for the expansion of Islamic State continued and expanded to Northern Africa and to the near territory of the different countries of Europe after under going several crusade in the last few centuries. Now under the presence of different atmosphere of science, the fight for the expansion of Islam had taken a different path. Few individuals dare to sacrifice their lives for the cause of Islam and for the territory of Islam. One world, one religion was the goal of Bin Laden, a milliner, but in the end he had to die. In the Middle East, there is Islam and the people are following the path of Islam but territorial fight, political fight and social fight is continuing to the extreme super seeding all records of history. People cherishing the same religion even then they have to face fighting due to difference in individual's opinion. There is difference of opinion among Christians in the United Kingdom residing as Protestant and Catholic. But there is no in-fighting or there is less fighting because they learn to leave under the atmosphere of understanding of tolerance. In the United States there was serious fighting once among Blacks and Whites. But to day they are living with lesser degree of fight and in the path of forming an ideal secular democracy, already achieved to the extent of 99% by placing a black in the seat of the Presidency of the United States of America. In Bangladesh also a section of political leaders are in favor of one Islamic nation of one religion but there are many more in favor of running an administration of multi-religious nation. The long cherish of a particular religion have found to have a hereditary effect over the genes in the history of the development of mankind. In India it is found in Persian People, where many of the Persian people are revolutionary in their thinking be it the industry, politics or set of business. The next is found in the intellectual mind set of Gujrati people in the advent of economic front. To day in London, the highest number of rich Indian people is Gujrati people. But now the situation is changed if you think of a country, it is essential to take into account the contributions of all sections of the society for the progress of the country. To develop a nation it is necessary the cooperation of people of all casts and all religion. The repeated onslaught over the Hindu community of Bangladesh will help in thriving out the Hindus (already had done since the formation of Pakistan) to establish an absolute majority of Muslim Country but that would not help to thrive in the progress of the Nation and the people at large. A nation is said to be proud of by the activity of its citizens. The world has seen many stages of development which was not due to the out come of the knowledge of one section of the people, or one community of the people or one religious section of the people. The recent development of IT industry in US is the brightest example. It was due to the pioneering effort of IBM Company when knowledgeable people of the world, Indians student in particular were sucked in USA for research to find out the mystery of IT. Indian students were working there with high salary where they were Indians by name but American by nature. This is what was known as 'Brain Drain'. Similarly the products of Samson company. Every product of Samson Company is a supreme product because it is formed by the research work of the talented youngsters of the Universe as the Company had established research centers at every developed country.

**The emergence of Bangladesh:** The leader Sheikh Mujibur Rahman of Awami League was instrumental in the creation of Bangladesh in the year 1971. He was successful to bring an uprising in East Pakistan which was exploited by the Islamabad administration of West Pakistan since its birth. The then Pak President Yahva Khan had launched a military assault on East Pakistan which caused about ten million refugees fleeing to neighboring India. India intervened and liberated Bangladesh. Thereby the influence of Pakistan was reduced to a great extend apart from the existence of religious bonding of affinity. The administration of Bangladesh changes time to time and as such the relation with India. The administration of present government appears to be different than the previous Rulers and hence a much of the development is expected in the region and a curtailment in the activity of terrorism in consonance with global situation. The PM of Bangladesh has made a visit to Bhutan to improve the good relation with the neighbor countries in difference to Pakistan. This is a good beginning in the development of economic progress.

**The present Economic plight of Bangladesh:** Bangladesh is one of the poorest of poor country in the world but the fallacy was that neither a single people of Bangladesh was starving nor dying out of starvation. It was probably due to the fertile land of Bangladesh where any kind of crop could be grown very easily. But on the other hand the lacking in the infrastructure of the growth of Industry and lacking in the implementation of family planning process in controlling over population have caused the development standstill besides the continuous unrest in the country in the process of administration. Two days after the landslide victory in the Bangladesh election in December last year, the Prime Minister Sheikh Hasina the Wajed declared "I want to make this point very clear; no one will be allowed to use this land to carry out terrorism in India". Before the year is out, Sheikh Hasina has begun to deliver on her promise. The handing over of Arabinda Rajkhowa, the Chairman of militant insurgent group ULFA to India was a major event to establish a good relation with India and set the green signal for economic cooperation. Hasina has been invited for Indira Gandhi Prize for peace, Disarmament and Development. Militant immigrants from Bangladesh to India are likely to be stopped for ever. The cricket match between India and Bangladesh has gained a ground for improved relationship between the two countries.

**The Cultural affinity brings Unity:** Since the formation of Capital by the British Emperor, the center of Indian culture and trade were shifted from Delhi to Calcutta. There is difference in the religion of the majority of two Bengal. The religion Islam is in Bengal of Bangladesh while the religion in West Bengal of India is Hinduism. Apart from the difference in religion there exists a strong affinity in the sphere of culture of two Bengals. A large number of celebrities of Bangladesh are regularly visiting the epical center of Bengali culture Calcutta now newly named as Kolkata. This has emerged a bond of unity between two Bengals shattered by the past events of sectarian interest and exploited by the politics of Indian subcontinent.

A Victim of Bangladeshi Citizen: She was Sangeeta Chakraborty, daughter of Late Ataul chandra Chakraborty who was born and brought up in the village Karimpur, who could not see the light of imparting education either in School or in any college of the Capital city of Dacca or any college of the district town of Commila. It was not because of her economic dearth but because of her insecurity of life, as she was leaving in the faith of Hinduism in the atmosphere of Islam. Her father did not deter her from education but taught her himself at home and sent her to set in the examination and finally qualified her to be a graduate. But alas! She had been married with a boy, Kamal Chakraborty, an Engineer of the same village who had flown to USA and living there since long. It was the destiny of her life that who has not even seen a town till graduation but all on sudden had flown to a distant place US, so to say a heaven of Nation. It is the Hindus in general release a sigh of relief to see their siblings leaving in western counties to get free from the regular irritating torture of second class citizen of the country of birth even though they could not see and share their affection at ease because of distance and expense of long journey. She is now an American Citizen living in Chicago maintaining the Hindu traditions. She was living there with a bond of affinity of love of her sons and daughter with peace of mind.

**Subtract from yahoo. com net:** Do you know why the Hindu Bengali of Pakistan currently of Bangladesh has no State in true sense?

People of Israel were state less once but UN has given them a State in September 1948. The Hindu Bengali of undivided Bengal fought for Indian independence the most but after Independence of India these people were rewarded with nothing but agony and despair although Padit Jaharlal Nehru declared at mid night of Independence that door of India will remain open for these people but practically stopped. Now they are happy in Bangladesh by dint of the mercy of the Muslim citizens but without any right of class one citizen like others. They have no state but the world is their state.

Answers given by different persons in yahoo. com: Answers: (4)

<u>SD</u> Such people are usually provided amnesty and could move to any Commonwealth countries. Perhaps, many have already moved.

Thereby Hindu population of Bangladesh has reduced significantly in last few decades. There is no point in discussing past follies. India needs to accept them as our citizens, should they want to come back.

Bruno fighter buzz, poor India, weak India, leaderless India, policy less India, timid India, not only in Bangladesh, Pakistan, Afghanistan, Arab, African countries, but every where Hindus are suffering. Suffering in Pak or in Bangladesh is coming in light, but in Arab or in African countries' it rarely comes up. buzz India is not for Hindus, it is for Congress, BJP, Muslims, Christians but not for Hindus, hi Nehru hi Gandhi-what you did to this nice country.

The best option, they have is that, the Hindu Bengali need to separate all ties with India and join Bangladesh, right now, they have nothing more then an unimportant state of India (west Bengal), and on the other hand, Bangladesh is a proud independent country. Assam also should follow the step for their self good.

Shan Barani: The Hindu Bengali were fools, they were 60% in 1760, but they did not breed adequately and Muslims became majority in Bengal only in 1881 they were fools because they fought against the far enemy the British instead of the near enemy, the Muslim. They were fools that once they were inside India; they did not drive out the Indian Bengali Muslims like that of the Sikhs did to Indian Punjabi Muslims.

## War Criminal & Judgment: (Bangladesh):

In the end of January 2013, in view of war criminal, the judgment was pronounced by the highest court of judiciary in Bangladesh. But the Jamayat Party was dead against the implementation of the punishment given by the highest court. To show the protest of grievances they choose the soft target of torturing the Hindus by burning their houses and belongings and destroying temples and Puja Mandals of Hindus. The miscreants throw away the Hindu ideals of Temples to jungles or in water. This is heartening to Hindus because they live with Hindu faiths and they get peace by the worship of Hindu Gods. This is inhuman and against the love of humanity. A religious Muslims would never do such inhuman activity and hurt the sentiment of a mind who believed in a different faith. The writings of Quran never said that the people of other religion can not live in the globe. It is stated in the Holy Quran that all animals including the human beings of diverse religious faiths are also the creatures of God (Allah). All creatures have the equal right to live in the globe. The value of love and feeling of brotherhood could be carried only by a human being at the time of death and nothing else.

# [38]

**Modern Kolkata:** After a long suffering, after 1991, the growth of economy appears to be hopeful. People have to learn to live a better. The daily commuters are now fortunate enough to go in Metro running under Ac. Of course the scene of the modernity is limited to under ground only. There are new areas like Rajar hat is coming up very soon but all over surface area is far below in standard in compare to any city of developed country.

There is heavy rush in traffic Bus, traffic congestion because of worst road condition, and not to speak of the pedestrians, where every footpath of street is occupied by the small shop owners, who are mostly no other than the ill-fated people of East Pakistan came here as refugee and maintaining the hard pressed family with daily income of the shop in the absence any scope for a better employment for earning. Thus the city does not look like a city but a city of tent house. If the other city like Bangkok highly populated can make the city a place for all standards providing all facility, why does Kolkata could not? Is it for short of money or excess of corruption or lacking of planning of administration?

Culture of Theater: Once Calcutta was very much well known for its theoretical performance. Once theater like Star, Biswaroopa were attracting a large crowd by their wonderful performances in doing theater in the cover of a close Hall where people could get a pleasure of satisfaction at the evening roaming the whole day in the strain of sufferings. But a new trend is now noticed in the players in the performance of their college festivals where they are showing their ability in doing open show of theater. In Jadavpur University Campus open theater were performed to bring in front the pleasure of life and bond of unity in disguise. My Journey was to enjoy the feature of Unity in the Festival of India, where people in general enjoy a couple of days once in a year such as in Mumbai in the festival of Ganesh Puja and such as in Kolkata in the festival of Durga Puja and so on in other places. Belief of the people is that divine power in man is awakened by the worship of Gananayak Ganapati in the festival of Ganesh Puja.

## Ganapati Bappa in Mumbai and Druga Ma in Kolkata:

It is the favorite cry in loud voice coming out from every mouth shivering the heart and makes the atmosphere a festive one. The atmosphere tempted the every individuals to get free from all walks of life and get ready to participate in the celebration which are observed in every corner of the city by creating temporary sheds for the festival of God (Ganapati Bappa in Mumbai and Druga Ma in Kolkata) decorated with colors, erecting designs of special character, exhibiting the beauty of artistry where the people male or female, old or young, boys or girls everybody enjoyed the festival through the performance of rituals bringing a sense love & affection of humanity and a devotion of sacrifice forgetting hatred and annoyance. The night of the City exhibits the beauty of lightening in every street leading to the center of Puja Mandap, the temporary shed where the sacred replica of Ganesh in Mumbai and Durga Ma in Kolkata were placed for worship for fixed days.

The Goddess Durge, a form of Shakti (the Goddess) were worshiped in groups in the Kolkata mostly in the streets by building temporary arrangements under intense pomp and pleasure and worshiping with the performance of rituals under devotion.

**Indian Unity in the festival of enjoyment** is a sign of love and satisfaction beyond boundary. During the performance of Puja week, every working people takes leave off their works and goes to the center of festivals with the whole of family and exchange greetings with known or unknown fellows as if all are very dear to each other. Many centers of events of enjoyment were created taking the little boys or girls in the acts of vents, bringing the celebrity of sweet songs in front and finish the night at the end with pleasure and excitement through the performance of a play of theater full with suspense and pleasure of excitement in every mind. Everybody comes out of the house in the search of looking the sites of attractive centers making the streets filled with streams of people converting the whole city into a city of festival forgetting the difference of rich and poor, high or low. In the City people of different states use to live with different culture, and speaking different languages. But in the day of festival all are equally taking part, making the events of festival in every corner a success. This is what is found in Indian Unity wherein every Indian is proud of its Nation.

**The divine power:** It is a belief in the minds of men that all works can not be completed unless the force behind comes in for rescue in disguise. The source of unknown force is no other than the God, Ganasha where it is said God in man is awakened. Gananayak Ganapati (the God-Ganash) has bestowed on each creature different power in a lesser or higher degree. By worshipping the deity of Ganapati the divine power in man gets awakened and this power helps a man or woman to fulfill all the worldly desires. For achieving a divine life for the cause of blessings of God one has to discard the beastly passions of human life.

**Mystery behind the performance of festival** is the attraction of unknown love and affection of the fellow country men known or unknown as the feeling of oneness, all is being the children of God. Ganapati is regarded as the goddess of wealth and is rightly worshiped in the commercial City Mumbai for a period of ten days. Durga Ma, the goddess of strength is worshipped in Kolkata for a period of three days to get the blessing of Durga Ma to fight with the devils of humanity. Calcutta was a City of India, where Lord Clive established the British Rule, what is now transformed into Kolkata, a home land for every citizen of every States, where the British Rulers were being sent back far away to London. The city was over burden with population but the construction of Metro has brought a new life to the commuters. In the festival time, the lightening of the City changes the picture of Kolkata. People forget themselves in the midst of mass people and moves on and on in streams of unknown destination. The festival of three nights ends with the exchange of love of affection & blessings. A seen of Ichhamati River of Indo-Bangla Border vanishes the line of demarcation of the boundary because the flow of water and so the boat full of people along with idols moves with the waves of water and never follows the order not to cross the boundary. It was always a moment of joy and a moment of unity.

It is interesting to see the happenings of Ichhamati River, where people are watching the immersion of the idols of Durga Ma from boat, the boat is reaching to a point where it is difficult to identify, the boat belongs to which side of India or Bangladesh making it a point of non existence of boundary between Indo-Bangla Border when the authority of the two nations forget to bring any rule of law to impose over these people dipped in love of humanity who tends to sacrifice themselves along with idols of immersion. There are other areas of Ichhamati River, where immersion of the idols of Durga Ma were carried out displaying many beautiful scenery of immersion. The common people are less concern with the belief of God or the unknown power of the strength of Durga Ma but more concern with the performance of festival and with the thrust of happiness in the midst of songs and drums. Recreation is a part of life to bring strength and energy in future works which is very much present in all the developed Western countries in the form of the activity of club but in India it is in the form of Pujas like activity making arrangements for songs and dances.

"Durga **is a form of Shakti of Al-mighty**" is the belief of Bengalis particularly to the woman folk of the Bengali. According to them Durga is one of the many forms of Shakti (the goddess). Bengali people is very much keen in doing Durga Puja once in a year as the practice of customary rituals to acquire energy (Shakti) for the whole year in doing the activity in the process of life with satisfaction. The Puja is held in the month of September-October as per record of dates for three days. As every individuals takes part in the performance of the festival, the office of the government, the office of the private company, all declare holiday for those three days and all non official staff, the workers, all remain absent in their routine works without obligation to take part in Puja festival. In the days of Globalization, this festival is not remain limited in India or in Kolkata but it had spread crossing boundary and now Durga Puja is celebrated in London, NY, Canada and other places and the interested NRI people are importing the images of Goddess made with shoa (light material) from West Bengal.

**"Goddess Durga was the divine power against all evils"**-is a fact of belief to Bengalese which is impinged in their mind through a story depicted as legend in the epic of religion. The legend explained that Rama went to Lanka to rescue his abducted wife Sita from the grip of Ravana, the King of demons. Rama worshiped for divine power. The Goddess Durga, who was the Goddess of divine power against all evils fought against Ravana and rescued Sita. Since then Durga Puja is celebrated as a victory of joy against evils in Bengal. After the performance of three days of Puja, in Dashami, in the last day, a tearful farewell is offered to the Goddess. The images are carried in processions and finally immersed in nearby river or lake. Vijaya Dashami is an event celebrated all over the country.

# [39]

**My Journey to Kaziranga** of Forest of Assam, a place where the wild animals are living in Forest Area of Kaziranga under the protection of the Govt. of Assam and the place is being turned into a National Park and become an International Tourist Center. India is full of Nature & Natural Beauty which we could see only when we open our eye with a spirit of undertaking the strain of journey to the planes, hills and rivers or lakes. The Forest Areas of Kaziranga and Manas are the areas of wild life animals and considered as the world Heritage sites. Let us go for a little history of Assam before going to the forest area of Kaziranga.

**A little of Assam history:** Assam was ruled by Ahom kings for the period 1228-1826, about 600 years. So to say, the Ahom dynasty and the people of Assam were the descendants of ethnic Tai people and that was established by Tai prince Sukaphaa, who was a Shan prince of Mong Mao, in present day Yunnan Province, of China. The Prince came to Assam after crossing the Patkai Mountains. It appears in the history that there was sever infighting and killing among the descendents of the Kings for the power in the later part of the kingdom. Even then there seems to be some sort of discipline where the Tai priests can decide who should be ascending the throne. The king could be appointed only with the concurrence of the council of ministers. During the 17th century, the power struggle for thrown was very much acute. There was quick succession of Kings. The new King never hesitates to carry out the execution of rival kings. The ruling of Ahom dynasty was ended with the Burmese invasion of Assam and later annexation by the British East India following the Treaty of Yandabo in 1826. The kings of the dynasty were called as Asam Raja, or Chaopha or Swargadeo (ruler of heaven) at different time.

It is noticeable that the King gave the due respect to their queens where the coins contain King's name in front but queen's on the reverse unlike even the developed nation like UK, Greece where ladies were not given due respect as because ladies were not counted as voters in that period of time. It is also found Ahom queens (Kowaris) played important roles sometimes in the matter of state where some queens maintained office even after the death or removal of the kings as happened with Pakhori Gabhoru and Kuranganayani who were queens to multiple kings.

Subsequently, religious Dharma also played an important role in Ahom Kingdom. Sutamla (1648-1663) was the first Ahom king to be initiated into the Mahapuruxiva Dharma and kings continued to be disciples of one Sattra or the other. The succession of power to the throne and the religious faith had brought down the dignity of Ahom king and depleted the Ahom kingdom.

In the ruling of 600-years, 39 Swargadeo, who were the descendants of kings regarded as Sukaphaa. These kings gradually established the kingdom by territorial and political expansion of the kingdom what is now called Assam. It was the kingdom in the Brahmaputra valley in Assam that maintained its sovereignty for a long period of time and successfully resisted Mughal expansion in North East India. It was able to establish its suzerainty over the Brahmaputra valley which had developed a new political and social life in the region. In spite of the fight for succession of power, the king's ruling had established a sense of unity among different tribal groups and that unity had made the king powerful among his Forces to resist the expansion of powerful Mughal Empire in North East of India. The modern Ahom people and their culture are a syncretic blend of the original Tai culture, the indigenous Tibeto-Burman and Hinduism. Many of the Tai followers of Sukaphaa married local girls and slowly assimilated with the Ahom communities. There are many ethnic groups, including Tibeto-Burman people become the part of Ahom communities. The 1901 census of India enumerated only about 179,000 people as Ahom later the number was increased to eight million including the Tai-Ahom settlers. Sukaphaa finally established his capital at Charaideo near present-day Sivasagar in 1253 and since than the function of the state was conducted from Sivasagar.

The then Ahom kingdom had consolidated its power, built their kingdom for the next 600 years. The first major expansion was at the cost of the Sutiya Kingdom, which was annexed in 1522 under King Suhungmung. The expansion's success was due to Ahom military prowess, and a love for cultural unity apart from political outlook. Suhungmung was the first Ahom king to adopt a Hindu name, Swarga Narayan and since than the custom of Hinduism became prevalent in the society. Thus by bringing the various tribal groups and regions under one social custom and under one governing polity, the Ahoms are considered the architects of modern Assam. Ahom power declined in the latter half of the 18<sup>th</sup> century when the Moamoris rebellion took over the capital city and brought an administrative chaos in the capital. Taking the advantage of the chaotic situation, the Burmese army invaded the kingdom, and uprooted the capital. After the total destruction of the kingdom, the Burmese installed Jogeswar Singha as a puppet king. Me-Dam-Me-Phi is a traditional religious ceremony of the Tai-Ahoms. In this ceremony the Chao Phi or the natural forefathers (presiding gods) and Dam Chao are worshipped.

One of its greatest achievements was the stemming of Mughal expansionism which could not be stopped in Northern India but stopped in North East Assam. In the celebrated battle of Saraighat, the Ahom general Lachit Borphukan defeated the Mughal forces on the outskirts of present day Guwahati in 1671 not by fighting against the mighty Mughal force but by the act of skill of General Lachit Borphukan in guiding the Force in the fight against the Mughals.

What we have to day, Forest Area of Kaziranga turned into a National Park, the whole valley of Assam being turned into a series of gardens, miles after miles beautifully managed by thousands and thousands of tea garden laborers, making the whole range of tea garden a scene of sea of beauty, further laborers being provided a disciplined and enjoyable life in their own territory, giving the opportunity of marry making at the taste they desired, Shillong, a place of deep jungle is now turned into a beautiful city, the city being turned into a beautiful capital, is for British. India is a country known for its ancient culture where in through the teachings of 'Gurukul' the students have learnt the ideals of life, how to be faithful, disciplined and tolerant. Did we observe these ideals in the posterity of generation of India? Yes, Indians can say we set the example of maximum tolerance in the independence movement of India. Indians also showed their tolerance towards the behavior of his neighbors. In regard to discipline Indians would be failed to point out a single sphere where Indians could say boldly that Indians were disciplined, be it administration in office work, military in the purchase of weapons, or function of ministry with sincerity. In regard to the ideals of faithfulness, it had vanished from minds of all most of all Indians if not Indians could not heard the allegation and counter allegation in Parliament almost in every day. Indians public in generals blame themselves being illiterate, backward but got the pleasure of happiness for sending the learned persons in their parliament, as the world could say a country of great democracy.

Kaziranga is a National park, a place rested in the district of Golaghat and Nagaon of the State Assam. It is one of the World Heritage Site as the park hosts two-thirds of the world's 'Great One-horned Rhinoceroses, the highest number of tigers making the place the highest of tigers among the protected areas of the world, a park standing as a home to a large breeding population of elephants, wild water buffalo, and swam deer. The history recorded that on 1 June 1905 Kaziranga was proposed to be a 'Reserve Forest' after the visit of Mary Victoria Leiter Curzon, the wife of Viceroy of India, Lord Curzon. Lady Leiter Curzon persuaded her husband to take urgent measure to protect the dwindling species of single horned Rhinoceros. Since then the forest area was preserved and protected under different circular. In 1985, Kaziranga was declared a 'World Heritage Site' by UNSCO for its unique natural environment.

So to say, it was the gift of Queen of Lord Curzon to the people of Assam in the year 1904, when she, the Mary Victoria Leiter Curzon, the wife of the then Viceroy of India Lord Curzon paid a visit to Assam and went to see the Kaziranga Forest Area. She was overwhelmed by the surrounding beauty of nature and the variety of animals. She expressed her desire for a better arrangement for the Forest Area. However that was the beginning of the development of Kaziranga Forest Area. Since then Kaziranga Forest Area was beginning to improve year after year and now it is transformed into Kaziranga National park. A series of beautiful tourist resorts is also being built up for international tourists. Animals are better cared with open shelter and food. Every year hundreds of thousands of visitors local and abroad are visiting the Kaziranga Forest Area.

Roaming inside the jungles seating at the back of elephants under protection is an enjoyable journey for every tourists. No body prefers to miss one hour Safari rides to have a look to one horn rhinoceros by chance. The rapid running of deer and often bathing of Rhinos and elephants in pond and rivers is a seen of excitement to enjoy life with nature.

Visiting the big Cities like Delhi or Calcutta people are enjoying the city life, enjoying the nights in a big hotel in dances and pleasure, looking the beautiful streets of Capital but visit of Assam will lead a visitor to a land of Nature decorated not by the artificial means but decorated by the beauty of Nature, a Nature situated at the extreme North-East of India. The earlier history named it "The Land of Pragjyotisha" as is found in Mahabharata. The epic Religious Book describes the battle of Mahabharata where Lord Krishna played the important role in initiation a battle between the two king families of same blood for the cause of prevailing justice and for the cause of creating Gita, the religious book of Hinduism, which a Hindu should follow to get the answers for any eventuality of human life. The beautiful girls of Assam enjoy their festivity by the performance of dances offering prayers to Lord Krishna. The visitor can enjoy the beauty of dances and pleasure in extreme satisfaction by understanding the meaning of the song and dance.

At the beginning of the British Rule in India, Assam was not included in the territory of British India. But later in course of time in 1826, the British Government extended its territory and Assam was brought under British Rule. It was British Rule who brought the plantation of tea in the Assam Valley. Today tea gardens throughout the range of Assam valley is a natural beauty site where lacks of labors, who were once brought here from different parts of India are working here together forming a different class of community even though their ancestors lived in different places of India and nurtured under different language. Girls of Tea garden workers are enjoying their days through songs and dances free from all worry and anxiety, how much poor they might be, giving the pleasure to all the onlookers.

**Assam Black Tea is a Breakfast Tea:** The British people are habituated with alcoholic drink. But in the greatness of British people, the drink that they had created here was a new kind of drink, not alcoholic but a soft drink looking better than alcoholic drink. In addition it is found the drink has a good health effect too. It is a known anti-oxidant. Southern China is a place for plantation of tea for a long time. Assam crossing over Arunachal makes a boarder with Southern China. Under the patronage of British officials during the rule of British period, the plantation of tea was started in Assam with the expertise of the workers of China. The initial study for the plantation of tea was researched in Southern China. The successful tea plantation in Assam resulted in the production of a good variety of tea to generate very strong, bright attractive coloring liquor by boiling tea leaves with water. The new drink has brought a new excitement to the residents who are living there. This has brought a rapid change in the habit of drinking liquid in Assam. It became a means of friendship to offer with honour. The production of tea in Assam had revolutionized the cultural habit of the people of Assam. The tea plantation has given a new beauty to Assam Valley, which lies adjacent to the Brahmaputra River. A traveler going through Assam valley by road get lost by the beautiful visions of Tea garden spreading miles after miles with the picture of Tea leaves of same height carrying trees of umbrella, who are being used as living Umbrella to provide shade under hot Sun to the young leaves of Tea-tree, after an interval of certain distance. To day Assam Valley is one of the largest tea growing areas of the world. Assam is producing more than 1500,000 pounds of a high quality tea yearly. When Assam tea is mixing with Darjeeling tea, the mixture produces a different flavor enjoyable to drink in a tip of little soup.

**Assam** is a place, situated at the foothills of Himalaya's inhabitated with the population of diverse tribes, each of which has its own traditional customs and culture. During festive period the different diverse groups come together to exhibit their traditional culture through song and dances making a center of merrymaking with the exchange of love and affection. The major festival of Assam is Bihu which is celebrated three times in a year with three different objectives. The festivals are named as Bohag Bihu or Rangali Bihu in April, Magh Bihu or Bhogali Bihu in January and Kati Bihu in October-November. Rangali Bihu (festival of Merriment) is observed with colorful dances and songs. The young boys and girls take part in the festival cutting across the bar of class and caste. Words fail to describe some of the wonderful events of performance exhibiting some extraordinary customs. The festival describes their artistic sense. Their brilliant choreography brings in front their customs of province. The beautiful dance performance increases the beauty of the festival and above all it brings an atmosphere of unity of love and affection among all sections of people. The festival of merriment keeps away the daily distress of life process.

The mighty Brahmaputra is the Father as well as the mother of Wild Animals: Assam is the homeland of hundreds and thousands of the endangered one horned rhinoceros. The river Brahmaputra is flowing on the northern boundary of the Kaziranga Park making the area very fertile. The fertile soil had grown up thick jungles making the area a safe homeland for hundreds and thousands of wild animals. Some times the animals such as Rhinos, elephants and deer come over the national high way endangering the life of visitors as well as the local residents. But in the area people does not remain away from the joys of merry making. The display of any kind of dance would be a show of showing the activity of Lord Krishna, the God.

Lord Krishna is very popular in this region. In any activity, the performance of songs and dances are always remaining attached with the activity of Krishna. Here it is very common to see, the children are performing a dance drama depicting them with the color of Krishna and creating a center of amusement even in the remote area of Assam surrounded by jungles and tea-gardens.

**Ahom Kingdom and Sivasagar:** The Palace of Ahom Kingdom, in the ancient Talatal Ghar is a witness of the greatness of Assam, a place of rich cultural heritage, protected by trained personals. The pomp and pleasure of the Palace is in no way less than any other places of kingdom of India as that was prevailed in the autocratic rule of Indian sub-continent during that period.

The Talatal Ghar is one of the grandest examples of Ahom architecture in the ancient time. It was Swargadeo Rudra Singha, who shifted the capital of Ahom Kingdom from Gargaon to Rangpur (Western part of Sivasagar) in Ad 1702-03. Rangpur was not only the Capital of Ahom Kingdom but also served as its military base. So to say, the Rangpur Palace is a seven-storied structure, four above ground (the Kareng Ghar) and the remaining three below ground (the Talatal Ghar) and that was constructed and completed by Swargadeo Rajeswar Singha and his successors, during AD 1751-1769. The Palace (The Talatal Ghar) houses two secret tunnels, and three floors below ground level which were used as exit routes for any eventuality during the Ahom wars. After the death of Swargadeo Rudra Singh, the Talatal Ghar together with Kareng Ghar (the above-ground floor) constitute the Rangpur Palace and since that time onwards, the Palace went through many architectural alterations to its structure making it an irregular shape. At that time there was no cement as is available now but it was made by an indigenous type of cement (a mixture of Bora chaul-a sticky variety of rice grain-eggs of hens, etc.). It was surprising to see that the Palace had two secret underground tunnels as we heard of to-day that the small nation like North Koreia has made under ground military base to store nuclear weapons and missile and dare to threaten the super-power United States. One tunnel of Talatal Ghar was about 3 kilometres in length, linked to Dikhow River, while the other was 16 kilometres long, leading to Garhgaon Palace and was used as an escape route in case of an enemy attack. Visitors are now restricted to go through under ground tunnels. But people can take a view of a staircase inside the Talatal Ghar palace from distance. Charaideo (A Tai word meaning a Town at the Foot-Hill) was the first capital of Ahom Kingdom established in 1228, which about 30 km away from Sibsagar town is of present Assam, although the capital of the Ahom Kingdom moved away many times but yet Charaideo remained as a symbolic center. People can visit the Mausoleum of Ahom Royals of Assam located at Charaideo, still in existence in Sivasagar district. The tombs (Maidams) of Ahom Kings and Queens at Charaideo reveal the excellent architecture and skill of the sculptors and masons of Assam of the medieval days. These tombs are comparable with those of Pyramids of Egypt and that brings the object of wonder of the medieval days.

Sivasagar or Sibsagar (the ocean of Lord Shiva): It was a beautiful place at the foot-hills of Himalaya Mountain surrounded by the natural beauty and covered by big water body and consisting of so many water tanks what was a befitting place to be a Capital of Ahom Kingdom, even to-day there are many existent capital in different states of India including Guwahati, (the capital of Assam) appears to be inferior in scenic beauty compare to Sibsagar. It is expected very soon it would be a very attractive place for tourists by the patronage of the government. The Sivadol at Sivsagar is a historic temple, a place of worship by the people of Hindu religion. Visitors get pleasure by the visit of temple as the site of the temple embraces the body and mind with an urge of devotion. The beauty of the town is not only for its existence at the foot-hills of Himalayas but also for its large water body. The town has a 257-acre water tank, also known as the Borpukhuri. Its bank is decorated with three temples (Dols in Assamese). These are Sivadol (104 feet tall), Vishnudol and Devidol. It is in the record of history that these temples were built by Kuwori Ambika, wife of Swargadeo Siba Singha, in 1734. Another attraction of the place was for the existence of Large Tanks. (i) Joysagar (Loysagar Pukhuri)-It is said to be the biggest man-made lake in the country and it is spread over 318 acres of water on the edge of the town in an area called Rangpur,

5 kilometres away from the present town of Sivasagar. This lake was built by Swargadeo Rudra Singh in honour of his mother Joymoti. (ii) Gaurisagar-It is spread over 150 acres of water, where the three famous temples, namely the Vishundol, Devidol and Sivadol were constructed on its banks. (iii) Rudrasagar-A Shiva Temple was also constructed on the its bank, which looks like a beautifully constructed tank, a place only 8 kilometres away from the town of Sivasagar.

# [40]

**My Journey to Shillong, a place of beauty and Comfort:** It is compared with the Scotland of United Kingdom. Once no body knows how beautiful a place could be in the midst of a deep jungle. The great British had ruled India for a long two hundred years or more and extracted hidden wealth of Virtuous India but somewhere, sometime they explored hidden treasure which no one can think of. The place "Shillong" was once thought to be a place of animals but the British had made it a wonderful living place by surprise, of course, as it was being liked by the queens of British Officials, who were those ladies living in comfort of cold weather of British Land.

**Shillong is situated at a high altitude,** covered with nature, having a climate of cold, smooth, and cloudy ever enjoyable but trilling and adventurous to take up trip to higher regions of the hill. Shilling, a place in the north-eastern India, is a hilly strip and once the place was the capital of Assam in British Raj and the best choice able place for the British families who were residing in India during British administration. The place "Shillong" was beautiful by the presence of beautiful Pine Tree, carrying a-his sound, the beautiful lake, and by the thunder of constant flow of water in fall. The place is a gift of nature as the cleanliness of the roads is made by the nature itself. The nature has provided a most comfortable climate for the place through out all seasons of the year. Of course, in the course of time men has enhanced its beauty by making the Shillong peak, a place at the top of Hills from where the visitors can enjoy the real beauty of vision of the whole city of Shillong that was being built up in the course of time since the foundation given by the British, and also by the time the necessity of human living encourages to build Schools of children of high standard, Colleges for higher studies and clubs for recreation, where the presence of Shillong club since British Period is a place to enjoy a night with pleasure and drink.

Today it is the capital city of newly formed state Meghalaya (Jan. 21, 1972). During British Raj, the place was the Summer Capital of Eastern Bengal and Assam. The state Meghalaya is one of the smallest states in India, situated at an average altitude of 4,908ft (1,496 m) above sea level with about 22 lakh people. It was once a small village in the forest region at such a height. But it attracted the sight of British Rulers in 1864, and the place was made as the Summer Capital of Eastern Bengal and Assam for many years. After the formation of Assam, in 1874, it was made the head quarter of new administration because of its convenient location between the Brahmaputra and Summa Valley and more so because of the climate which was much cooler than tropical India. The clouds in the sky of Shillong are a charming beauty making the pedestrians afraid of getting wet by the storm of rain. The ups and downs on the way of road are a pleasure in the strain of every day journey.

**Shillong,** now become a place of Tourist attraction and the place "Police Bazar" become the point of evening gathering center and center for walking stroll, where tourists coming from India and abroad get the chance to see each other. Here a visitor can find number of hotels big or small of course with high cost as it is the focal point of attraction. Shillong has no rail connection but the place is well connected with the surroundings with motor able roads. It is about 3hrs journey from Guwahati to Shillong by road. There is no dearth of Buses, Taxies and Vans. There is air connection with a small airport at Umroi, 30 km away from Shillong. One can prefer a journey via Guwahati which is well connected by major air-port at Borjar and railway station at Guwahati.

It is a wonder place of heaven as it receives heavy rainfall from sky as the blessings of God particularly to make the place clean and cold during Monsoon. It must be known to the visitors that an Umbrella is a must in the rainy season. It is a place of Fashion. All kinds of dresses including the top quality brands from India and abroad are available in all standard shops. Traditional tribal dresses are available there with colourful decoration rarely found in other places. The Garo girls are found very much in their traditional dresses in the streets of Shillong.

The resting at Shillong itself is a comfort of pleasure. The fresh air and smoothing climate make a person bright and fresh. A beautiful fall was created by broken rocks in Upper Shillong; the British named it Elephant Falls as because the broken rocks resemble an elephant. One should see the Elephant Falls in the upper Shillong although outing is hardy due to climbing of 250 steps to reach the top apart from the smooth stroll in the Police Bazaar area and Shillong Lake area. Pubs and Clubs are there for recreation but the night life of Friday and Saturday is a special days of weekend to enjoy with drinks as the place is known for drinker's paradise because the cost of drink is lowest here due to tax structure of alcohol in this state. A person of academic interest can make a visit to State Central Library, located near Dhankheti, a library established at the time of British Raj that holds many rare books and almanacs.

The Legacy of **British Raj** is still visible in hilly Land. The house architecture and food habit of people is still comparable with that of British people. The Assam style houses with wooden floors was a typical comfortable art of house used by British in Shillong what is still used by the majority people in Shillong having being accustomed with religious faith of Christianity though a significant number of Bengali, Nepali, Assamese, Biharis and Marwaris are a part of the residents living there making it a fairly cosmopolitan City. It is likely that at the very outset local tribal people were charmed by the service of British people under the patronage of Church, people in general opted for Christianity instead of Hinduism. Besides these all other North-East Indian tribes are also present in the city. An interesting aspect of the khasis is that they are matrilineal society-the mother is the head of the family, youngest daughter owns the whole property and mother's surname is passed on to children.

A village situated at the top of the hill gradually has taken a shape first a hill resort, then a small town and now a big town rose to the importance to become the capital of the state. The scenery is natural but the utility of life here is artificial. As the people of high standard is living here the restaurant, the resting place such as standard Hotel, Town Club as well as Night club and play ground for Golf Course has grown up here to attract people of aristocracy from distance. Its Golf Course is the oldest Golf Course in India and its unique location has made it so beautiful that it is compared with the "Glen Eagle Course" of the United States. Shillong Lake is a place of beauty of Shillong. Every time people gather there to take the view of lake, the view of the coloured fish of the lake as preserved by the care taker. Again young groups of boys and girls take the courage of exploring boating in the lake. The spectacular activity makes the place ever enjoyable.

A Visit to **Cherrapunjee** itself is an adventure journey. Cherrapunjee is 56 km away from Shillong. It is known as the world's wettest place. A visitor can get cloud face to face in the journey towards Cherrapunji. The journey is full of thrill and excitement as the motor car passes through a road by the side of a canal that goes down below 200ft. running parallel to jig jug road, sometimes remained covered with snow but the efficiency of the driver discovered the road and runs the motor car in the cover of snow, a thrill not to be described but to enjoy only. Here the author remembers a journey to Cherrapunjee which he had to under take at his early service life with Professor Kopila Chatterjee, a distant descendants of the Noble lowrate Robindra Nath Tagore residing in Shillong in the old house of Tagore while he was in service of a College to carry out a picnic along with a batch of 100 students of boys and girls. The picnic was completed with pomp and pleasure but on return journey it was impossible to move as the whole area was covered with such a heavy snow that there is no sign of road or sign of canal as if everything was covered with snow, it was snow and nothing but snow. Professor Chatterjee was a respectable man, he tackles the situation and finally we took shelter in the bed room of Maharaja of Ramakrishna Sevashram of Cherrapunjee for the whole night, a memorable picnic party that came in way of my service is not to be forgotten

# [41]

## My Journey to Darjeeling which looks like Switzerland:

Tiger Hill is situated at an altitude of 2590 (8482 ft) is a spectacular space to visit; the space has already earned the reputation as a space of important spot, a space from where the magnificent view of Sunrise is visualized. A visit of rising sun gets a pectoral view of the movement of Earth. A cloudy sky covers the sun with cloud and nothing gets visible. Here the view of "Kanchenjunga" is wonderful; no one can forget the view of beauty of "Kanchenjunga" once visited. The great eastern Himalayan Mountain is standing in front holding the Mount Everest at the top, the World's highest peak. It is also visible from here if the luck is in favour. It is possible to see if the day is bright. The beauty spectra of "Kanchenjunga" and the beauty of "Rising Sun at Tiger Hills" are unparallel scene of beauty. It is only a matter of time that "Kanchenjunga" or "Rising Sun at Tiger Hills" will top the list of attraction for tourist. Indians may not know yet the importance of the character of these places but in other places these are already in the market. In UK there are many restaurants that are doing business in the name of "Kanchenjunga". The rising Sun is a unique feature, a feature no where available in the World.

Darjeeling is a flavourful district, internationally known for beauty and beautiful climate, as this hill town is resting on the lower range of Himalaya and allowing the residents and visitors to enjoy the smooth climate of cold weather, good for refreshment particularly in summer time, in the atmosphere of hot air. It may not be developed artificially but its natural beauty is there which is in no way less inferior to any scenic beauty of any other hills anywhere in the world.

In Darjeeing, every morning lots of visitors come together here to have a glimpse of the rising Sun. Those who are lucky for a sunny day, they could see the wonder of rising Sun when every one will realize how fast our Earth is moving while apparently we do not realize at all the movement of Earth. But those who are unlucky for a cloudy day miss the opportunity to see the wonder of Tiger Hills.

In Darjeeling the important Road is the Mall Road. A walk along the road will makes the mind fresh and pleasant as you will come across with lots of visitors, foreigners and philosophers who were doing something or thinking something of new you don't know. Here shops were in line and restaurants are ready to serve the customers local or abroad. Chowrasta is the central place of Mall Road and the place is the attraction of the town. Here people get together to chat, spent time basking in the sun or just to spend few moments to have the pleasure of life. The Brabourne Park is not far away where people prefer to spend their time in open space; the space is being free from Vehicular movement, the space from where one can watch the Scenic Beauty of the mountain.

**Darjeeling & Rangit Valley Cable Car:** But unlike the Geneva of Switzerland the place is located at the eastern corner of India without any infrastructure of developed system of communication although journey by taxi or by toy train is enjoyable. The place has not yet acquired any international reputation like that of Geneva. Yet the oldest Ropeway journey is remarkable and progressive work is undertaken to make it internationally famous. It is one of my striking features of memorable experience, the travelling of Darjeeling Hills by Darjeeling-Rangit Valley Cable Car. It is popularly known as Ropeway Travelling. It is about 3Km away of the town in the North and as such it is known as North Point. The Ropeway is extended from hill top to the bottom of the valley up to Singla Bazaar. Its historical importance lies as the Ropeway is the India's oldest passenger ropeway but at present it has been extensively modernized and visitors can now safely travel over the clouds to witness the Arial view of the lush green tea garden extended at the lower surface area of the valley. Moving through small cabin in space crossing over dip jungle from bottom surface to the top surface of the Hills with the help of rope is quite a thrilling journey. No doubt it is enjoyable but the journey is full of excitement and a thrust of danger.

**The plantations of Tea:** The plantations are continuing here dating back to the mid 19th century as the demand of Darjeeling tea is increasing day by day; the cultivation of tea plantations is also extending in greater area making the creation of several tea estates around the town. The cause of excellent weather conditions has made the cultivation of tea a great success. The vision of green scenery in large open space of land is a beauty of Tea garden in the slops of Darjeeling.

### Geneva Switzerland:

The city Geneva is situated along the banks of Lake Geneva at the foot of the Alps and sparkling as one of Europe's most beautiful cities. Today, the city of Geneva is a cultural center and second to none. It provides world class entertainment having top rated restaurants and huge opportunities for recreation. It is a global city, a financial centre, and a worldwide centre for diplomacy having the office of numerous international organizations.

**Bastion Promenade**-It is a name bestowed by the Genovese that is a gated park with a wide walking boulevard and that is used as a hub of local activity and enjoyment.

The picture shows the scenic beauty of Geneva is some extent similar to 'Kanchenjanga. The record of history describes the historical development of Geneva such as John Brink, a government Surveyor, laid claim over water fall power and over adjacent land of the Lake in 1835. He named the area as Geneva Lake in accordance with the name of his home town Geneva in New York. But in the next year 1836,

Christopher Payne, a pioneer settler from Belvidere, Illinois, extended a rival claim for the water power. He developed the lake in many fronts including development in flouring and wool carding. Farmers brought grains to the Lake Geneva. As the beauty of the area began to increase, people started to settle in the area increasing the cost of the land day by day. Immigrant settlers from New England and New York had flooded the area for settling into the Geneva town. At the beginning there was civil war between the tribal and the immigrants. After the civil war the town became a resort for the wealthy Chicago families. The family began to construct many mansions on the Lake. Lake Geneva became known as the Newport of the West. There was a heavy fire in Chicago in 1871. After that many of the Chicago family moved to their summer home on the Lake and rebuild the Geneva town to a beautiful City. The employee of the construction work and maintenance officials of these mansions together with the house hold employee founded a separate industry for the function of the over all activity of the Geneva Lake. After the arrival of the railroad, thousands of tons of Lake Geneva ice were shipped each year to the Chicago market. The people living there developed a high sense of humanity. In several occasion it is observed that the Will of the people is 'Supreme', be it to bring development or be it the sense of living in community. The opinion of the people of Lake Geneva acts as catalyst to tackle any problem, local or international to bring peace. Hence it is rightly said Geneva is the Capital of Peace of the World.

**Darjeeling of Bengal:** It is true that Darjeeling is like that of Geneva of Switzerland that is situated at the foothills of Himalayas like that of Alps and surrounded by the scenic beauty of nature. Darjeeling might not have big malls like the Geneva of Switzerland but it has its own natural beauty that it has beautiful mountain ranges. It is in the note book of development of West Bengal Government to make rail tracks like that of Switzerland to attract the tourists from all corners of the world. There are few artificial features that are found in the hilly land for amusement.

It was the opportunity of many Indians to see Singapore where they have seen a Hill called "Sentosa", it was designed as such where boys, girls, young or olds, mostly every one could relaxed, enjoyed by the site of vision by seating or by taking part in the activity, a unique center created for amusement and merry making. On entering the site one can see few gates named as (i) Holly wood, (ii) Madagascar, (iii) Far Away, (iv) The lost World, (v) Ancient Egypt, (vi) Sci-Fi City, (vii) New York, etc. Entering in any one, a person could see wonderful things, one could get the pleasure by the site of vision or by taking part in the game and going on driving the car just by holding the stirring, one could go to a lost world, where he or she would face with fear, danger, and what not but at last the pleasure lies in the secrets of excitement. It was the credit of the designer and the engineers who were to be called the master of creator of amusement with thrill and excitement. It is the wish of public like me to see something like the Hills of "Sentosa" will come out in course of time in the Hills of Darjeeling making it a place of attraction for merrymaking.

# [42]

**My Short Journey to Chunchali of Guwahati:**

The City of Guwahati is a place where stands a college since the time of British, where Prof. F. W. Sudmerson (1901-1926) was the founder Principal of the college namely called Cotton College. It was his untiring effort and non stop dedicated service for a long twenty five years that had shaped the structure of this college into an academic Institute in the remote eastern corner of India where the Author also spent thirty three years of his service carrier.

[Prof. F. W. Sudmerson (1901-1926)]

27th May 1901 was the day of emergence of Cotton College under the newly appointed principal F. M Sudmerson, who landed here from

Berelli of Northern India undertaking a tedious journey by ship continuing for three days as at that time there was no question of coming here by plane or even by train as the communication by rail-track was under construction in this remote area of India. Although initially he was liked by the smooth pleasant weather of the place as he thought that he could be freed from the hot weather of Berelli but immediately after reaching the cottage of residence, he thought to return. Officially, it was designed as Dak-Banglow (a place for high officials), but practically it was a place for no man's cottage, a cottage without the minimum facilities for living. But he was survived by his reliable Chaprashi (domestic servant), a Gurkha fellow. However, in this moment of uncertainty, he was consoled by few British citizens who were living in this region as Manager of Tea-garden to enhance the Tea plantation and encouraging its market abroad.

The day began here in Cotton College with a festive mood as if the whole Guwahati was excited with the news of stating an academic center at Guwahati. The Ben-Party was called for to make the sound of joy and happiness, the decorators were called for to make the venue descent and beautiful, the local singers were called for to be ready to make the day memorable and beautiful. Arrangements were made for the accommodation of personalities like Henry Cotton, the then chief Commissioner of Assam, Prabhat Chandra Borua, the Zaminder of Gouripur, Manik Chandra Boruah, the pioneer of Cotton College and many other dignitaries such as Raghu Nath Chowdhury, Nabin Chandra Bordoloi and many others. The Kingdom of Gourpur sent his Sangeeth Party to make the day, a day of special. The function began with the observance of rituals and festivity started without end but the audience was charmed by the sweet tune of flute played by the Gurkha fellow, the Chaprashi of the Principal Sudmerson. The young Principal Sudmerson was charmed by the feelings of the people of the region and astonished to see the thrust of acquiring knowledge by the people of this remote area and that had made a striking effect in the heart of this 31 years old British young fellow, when his mind was thinking how to serve the people of this region to the best of his capacity to give light of education. The feeling of service and the joy of devotion undermined all obstacles, obstacles in the cottage of everyday living, obstacles in the college in the guidance of teaching, learning, accommodation, and administration. He devoted himself completely to build up the college in all front and to do this he devoted the best part of his life, the long twenty six years till 1926 in the establishment of this college and imparting education to the young children of this region with a feelings of love in no way different than the love to his own children. Thus Cotton College is Sudmerson and Sudmerson is Cotton College.

Cotton College came into being and the academic Institution took its position as one of the best colleges of India and that was due to the untiring efforts of this great British Soul, the Soul of Sudmerson. He administered the Institute like a Tiger but cared it like a devoted Father cum Mother. He was an English man accustomed with the English etiquette and so he wanted to see the same kind of etiquette prevailed to his students. As soon as he met a student anywhere other than the college premises he compelled him to say 'Good Morning Sir' and next he would say 'Yes Good Morning'. The Indians of that period had no training to go to urinal for Nature's call. He made arrangements in the college premises for urinals. If any time, he found any student is violating the custom and going here and there for urinal, he never hesitated to pick him up and compelled him to say not to do so in future. Thus was his affection and dearness with every student.

Once, a student lost his life by accidental drowning in the river Brahmaputra. He was shocked and perturbed so much that he began to say that 'you boys could not pull him from water, had my daughter been here she could save the life of this boy'. It was during his time 'The Cotton College Magazine' first came into light on 9th Dec. 1922. He started the college with 57 students and when he left (27th Dec. 1926), the number raised to 527.

During the time of Silver Joyanti of Cotton College, in the year 1951, he sent a goodwill message so beautiful and meaningful that the college could never forget him.

Good Will Message . . . .

The principle which guided the past must guide its future. Avoiding of all narrowness of thought or class or creed, with charity towards all, let students and staff remember that education is only of value as it leads to greater service to mankind that narrowly pursued it but Dead Sea fruit of disappointment and embitterment.

What will be the centenary judgement upon the Cotton College? Will the students have served the province or will they have strewn only to serve themselves. The people of the province, down to the poorest, will give the judgement; see to it, each one of you, that you can wait that judgment with calm and confidence.

**Vale, F. W. SUDMERSON**

WORDWICK FARM,

Nutley, Sussex,

May 26, 1951.

**It was the occasion of Picnic by Sr. Teachers at Chunchali**, a place full of nature of Hills at the up and a scenery of ocean like water at down, down to the river Brahamputra in the periphery of Guwahati of Assam, very adjacent to the Guwahati Oil Refinery. As the place is in between hill and river, it carries a scenic natural beauty. A group of retired Professors of Cotton College went there to have a glimpse of the scenery all together and to have a gathering to meet together to enjoy the pleasure of eating in picnic. Once all were active and gave service in teaching young boys and girls coming here from far away places of Assam, who were greatly known and a better counted among the millions and millions of humanity living in large India, but today they are in their retired life still want to meet together to make a gathering and exchange heart in this uncertain world. They counted their pleasure by the academic performance of their students who could earn a honor of respect by dint of their merit some times in big cities like Delhi, Bangalore or some times in London, Europe, US, Canada or Australia. It was 21$^{st}$ December, 2009; here all of the senior citizens enjoyed the day by remembering the past events of incidents and their past-out days. The place of Picnic was beautiful by the scenic beauty of **Chunchali.**

This **Cotton College** was a gift of British to North East India. The British established the administration at Calcutta after the capture of Bengal in the period of eighteenth century making Calcutta as the Capital of India. However in the course of time the Eastern India including Guwahati was brought under British administration. To impart education for the demand of British administration, the British Emperor thought of expanding education beyond Calcutta. With this intension a College at Guwahati was talked about. Ultimately, a college was established in the year 1901, by Henry John Stedman Cotton, a British, and the then Chief Commissioner of Assam and since then the College was known as the Cotton College of Assam. Thus a gift to North East India was given by the British in the form of an Institute for academic teachings. Thus in the course of time this Cotton College became a center of learning in the North East of India.

During the British period it was the only Institute in the whole of North East of India where students from all corners of Assam used to come here for academic study. Gradually it became an important learning center. At the beginning the teachers were brought from England. Gradually Indian teachers replaced the British teachers. After Independence the College maintained an academic link with UK by sending teachers to different Institute of United Kingdom such as Imperial College of London, Manchester University & UMIST and many other centers, to remain at per in the academic atmosphere. Even in that period, apart from arts, the teaching of science was introduced in Cotton College. Now every year a good number of students were passed out and out of them many were going abroad in the quest of further knowledge and service.

**A day of relaxing in open Air:**

The day was great in the sense, that there were teachers above seventy and seventy five, no matter, they participated to make the day, a day of enjoyment and gather to meet others although some of them even lost their strength to walk but happy to move by Car & Bus to mingle with the family of Cotton College Institute. With all care and precisions the food was prepared in the open air; of course necessary things were brought along with the journey. This is how the Indians are enjoying in their short outing along with very senior persons. Indians were familiar with living in joint family. But with the trend of global change, in the field of communication and in the art of internet, the distance is no longer a distance, the culture is an open secret and all of these have a slow intrusion in the Indian culture. In the present atmosphere, the Indian culture is no longer an Indian culture but a Global culture. There is a change in dress, a change of taste of food and even a change of mind where living of Indians in the culture of joint family is reduced to the culture of living in single family. In most of the cases of educated family, the parents or the elderly persons has to pass their life lonely in the absence of their children working far away sometimes in the country and sometimes far away abroad. This is what the people are realizing the impact of globalization

**Teachings:** In those days teaching was imparted through lectures, showing visual charts and pictures and if necessary by writings on black board with chalk pencil. But now lectures are in modified form along with the exposure of audio visual screen. The information is better searched in computer in the screen than in the Journal of Library as is done in those days.

[Here the senior teachers of Cotton College are relaxing in the picnic spot, at the foothills keeping affront of mighty Brahmaputra]

How does the **communication** changed with the change of population density? The Guwahati was a small town at the time of British administration but it was a place of attraction since the beginning of its development because it was the gate way of going to Shillong, a hilly place full of nature and cool soothing temperature through out the year discovered by the British Queens where they prefer to stay with family as British citizen always like to live in the cold regions of India. Now Guwahati became the Capital of Assam instead of Shillong, the area of Guwahati is expanded many times leaving no area of land left off for further expansion. This has resulted in the growth of multistoried buildings making the small town into a big city of North East India. Of course development of the City is yet to go a long way to make it a center of tourists as it has many natural things to explore. It has beautiful hills surrounding the city, river banks of Brahamputra, island, development of each one might be a center of attraction for tourists. The increase of car in the narrow streets had slowed down the speed and increased the tension for Car parking due to the absence of Parking space. Air port is changed into international air-port making an everyday flight to Bangkok to enhance the communication link with South East Asian countries. At one time teachers used to come to the Institute by cycle but now teachers are coming by scooters or cars. The change of economic policy has changed the system. The teachers of Cotton College now attended their duty coming by car as they are living far away from the place of work because of the expansion of the city area. This is how the old senior teachers recapitulate their memories. I also use to come by cycles and later by car in Cotton College in my service life. Why did I prefer Cotton College as the place of my service, while I studied at the remote corner of boarder district of Karimganj? It is some thing to be talked about. I admitted in Karimganj College in 1957 as I heard a lot about Karimganj College to the senior persons of Karimganj Town. Karimganj College was came into being in the year 1946, just before partition of India under the leadership of Mr. Yaha Khan, SDO, of Karimganj, while Karimganj was the only subdivision in pre-Independence Sylhet without a college. And Pramesh Chandra Bhattacharyya (hereafter PCB) was the Founder Principal of Karimganj College. The establishment of Karimganj College in 1946 was undoubtedly a remarkable event in the history of

Southern Assam, particularly in the region which is now commonly called Barak Valley. At that time the head-quarter of the Subdivision was at Karimganj of district Sylhet which was the major constituent of Surma Valley. Needless to say that the other district of Surma Valley, which was Cachar, is now divided into Cachar, Hailakandi and North Cachar Hills District. The major portion of Sylhet district now forms the Sylhet Division of Bangladesh comprising Sylhet, Maulavi Bazar, Habiganj and Sunamganj districts. Immediately after the formation of the College, independence came to India with partition. The SDO, Yaha Khan left for East Pakistan and PCB was in complete responsibility in the growth of the college along with Assam MLA Rabindra Nath Adiya, a pleader and a social worker. PCB was a brilliant product of Calcutta University, who secured first class in Philosophy in M. A, where he was a direct student of Dr Sarvepalli Radhakrishnan, the world famous Philosopher and the second President of the Republic of India. Partition brought the influx of rootless millions where a small town like Karimganj at the border bore the first brunt of millions' displacement. The influx brought more students from beyond the borders but it also brought teachers, even teachers from M. C College, which was established in 1892.

M. C. College (Murari Chand College) like Cotton College was an important college of Assam before pre-partition. It was initially established by Raja Girish Chandra Roy, a local noble man, in the name of his grand father. Raja himself maintained the expenditure for the period 1892-1908, the next 4 yrs the College was run with some Govt. aid and the College was fully taken up by the British Government since 1912. However the College was functioning in the City center till 1925, when the college was shifted to Titagarh Hills. There was lot of professors in Cotton College who were transferred from M. C. College in those days. After partition the College went to East Pakistan and the link with Cotton College was snatched away for ever. The partition had changed the scenario of the district of Sylhet, which brought misery for the Hindus who had to leave their home and hearths and move towards India for shelter in despair in the event of rioting and blood bath of human holocaust.

While the State extended help grudgingly for the new displaced students, the University would not exempt them from paying entry fees. PCB got coupons printed and engages students and teachers to raise funds for the new entrants. PCB said the college came into being because of the people, in the event of sudden emergency; the people's help would save everything. Since then Karimganj College is making good result under G. U. (Guwahati University). Dr. K. D. Krori, the retired Professor of Physics and the ex Principal of Cotton College was the science student of Karimganj College at the outset. His parents left Sylhet just after partition. The student Krori took the first position in the annual examination and in the final came out as 6th in order of merit (1949) while he appeared in exam under sick bed suffering with jaundice. Dr Krori after passing M. Sc from Kolkata joined Karimganj College and later in 1955 he joined Cotton College as a lecturer. The Author also did his B. Sc (Hons) from Karimganj College and M. Sc from G. U. He went to Shillong and there he immediately joined St. Anthony College due to the request of the renowned Professor S. N. Paul of St Anthony College in the cause of dearth of Science Professor. However, Author's urge for research took him to NCL (National Chemical Laboratory) Puna, while the Author was passing his days there. One day Author could see information in news paper for a vacancy in Chemistry in Cotton College; it tempted him to apply reminding Krori, who was a student like him of Karimganj College. When he got appointment he went to Physics Department and join Cotton College in Chemistry after the consent of Professor Korori. This is how the Author came to Cotton College and became very attached with a bond of love and affection of few Professors of Cotton College in disguise and spent long thirty three years except a gap of six years for studying abroad. After living more than fifty years, Guwahati now become an inseparable part of his of living space as the climate and environment of any other place does not suits him. Although the place of picnic was very near to the City, there was little travelling track by vehicle but gathering was unique for eating and humorous talking.

# [43]

My Journey to Hyderabad, a beautiful City of Modern India, the beauty was once designed by Nizam under the Mughal Emperor, and subsequently by other administrator, making it a city of political importance during the tenor of British Rule, the Nizam of the City being a faithful ally of British remained attached with the city till a final decision had arrived. The city at last came under Indian Union a marvelous city roaring the Modern India in the 21st Century. Hyderabad is now a symbol of one of the best IT City of India. It is considered as the second IT Sector in South India with hundreds of IT Companies in its IT Zones and IT PARK.

**Historical Background:** The record of the history says it belonged to Asaf Jah dynasty since 1719. Originally the dynasty family migrated to India from Baghdad in the late 17th century. It is also recorded that they were the direct descendants of the first Khalifa of Islam, Hazrat Abu Baker Al-Siddiq. The dynasty was founded by Mir Qamar-ud-Din Siddiqi, who was a viceroy of the Deccan under the Mughal emperor (1713-`1721). In 1707, the Mughal Empire crumbled after the death of the powerful Mughal Emperor Aurangzeb. The young Asaf Jah, declared himself the Nizam (an Urdu word, in short of Nizam-ul-Mulk meaning Administrator of the Realm) of Sovereign Hyderabad State. In 1798 it became one of the princely states of British India and the honour Nizam was bestowed upon the Ruler of Hyderabad. Nizam was young in age but wise in thinking. He did not wanted unrest in his state by going against the British like the Bengali people of Bengal. Nizam did not participated in Sepoy Mutiny of 1857 against British Rule in India. Thus in course of time Nizam became a faithful ally of British India and ruled over Hyderabad State until 17 September 1948 when the State integrated into the Indian Union. Nizam's wise decision helped to increase the economy of the state to such an extent that the State becomes one of the rich state in British Empire. Chowmohalla Palace-once the official residence of Nizam of Hyderabad is preserved for tourists.

**Modern Hyderabad:** A modern city will never find a building with old design. To day, the technology is changed; the interest of the people is also changed. People have learned to live in multistoried building having with all electronic facility. This is what we find in all big cities. Hyderabad also is not an exception. The position of Hyderabad was good in communication and other activity in the region that makes to declare that Hyderabad is the capital of the State. There was record of administrative success in the period of Nizam. In his period numerous institutions were grown up and he named all the institutions in the name of dynasty to keep the image of dynasty alive for ever. His efficient management of economy made him one of the world's richest men in the 1930. Nizam established a number of industries in Hyderabad in an area named it Sanathnagar as an industrial park to enhance the economy. He was not only a Nizam (administrator) but also an economist. The International Air-Port of Hyderabad has increased further international importance of the city.

**Hyderabad:** In 1947, the British left India and permitted the princely states either to remain independent or join India-Pakistan at their choice. Nizam wished to remain independent at first. But soon some Muslim nobles under Nizam made a plan to join Pakistan as because Hyderabad is a Muslim-governed state. As the state is situated in the middle of the Indian Union, its joining with Pakistan will make India insecure. Under the prevailing situation, the Viceroy Lord Mountbatten over ruled the decision. Finally India was compelled to enclose Hyderabad by military force for the sake of India's security. Thus the rule of Nizam came to an end. But in the long run Hyderabad lost its image as the most powerful state by the split of the state in 1956, based on the principle of the Reorganization of the Indian States on the basis of language. The units were Andhra Pradesh, Bombay, and Karnataka.

There are many things to see in Hyderabad so to say, the place is no less than a tourist's heaven. Here tourists can find many historical monuments—Charminar, Makka Masjid, Goloconda Fort, Falaknuma Palace, Qutub Shahi Tombs, and Birla Mandir.

**Charminar-**It means "Mosque of the Four Minarets" and "Four Towers". It enshrines the beauty of mosque; the historical record shows that the Mosque was built by Sultan Muhammad Quli Qutb Shah, the 5th ruler of the Qutb Shahi dynasty in 1591, shortly after shifting his capital from Golkonda to the place what is now known as Hyderabad. He built it as Islamic mosque for praying to God (Allah) to save the people from plague epidemic as the place was ravaging with plague heavily at that time.

Hyderabad is well known for its pharma and IT exports. It has been struggling to portray itself as a business hub. The power cuts and political disturbances have destroyed its images to a great extent when the state has already lost many external investment business opportunities. The recent twin blasts in Dilsukhnagar have come as surprise shock to business community who are now thinking in shutting their business unit here and looking to states like Gujarat to start-up new business opportunities. To bring the lost glory, the place Hyderabad including the State Andhra Pradesh as a whole, a place of peace and discipline in harnessing the tax as one of the highest tax earning states in the country, the state needs to beef up its security and investigating procedures by increasing spending in safety and security. To stop further attacks, awareness must be created among the public in office, in street or in crowded places. Further Cameras must be installed in any crowded business center. Intelligence secret agencies must be engaged in search of terrorists' moves. In December 1953, the States Reorganization Commission was entrusted with the responsibility of preparing the region for the creation of states on linguistic lines. Accordingly, merging the Telugu speaking regions, government established Andhra Pradesh on November 1, 1956. People were satisfied by the formation of the state and the Indian National Congress party remained in power since 1953 till 1983. In the mean time the influx of people from coastal region to the City of Hyderabad continued for better facility and better life. The Northwest region of the state including the capital City of Hyderabad is called Telangana. The unemployed youth of the region felt that they were exploited by the people of the Andhra region. The discontent spread among the people of the Telangana to such an extent that they started movement first for the protection of their rights and later the agitation has turned to the demand of a separate state. The agitated atmosphere has spoiled the economic growth of the state to a great extent.

# [44]

**My Journey to Taj Mahal**, of Shah Jahan, who was dipped into the sea of grief after the loss of his beloved third wife Mumtaz Mahal in 1631, who started to construct a monument after one year in 1632, keeping in mind to keep a symbol of memory of love, not seen in Earth ever before for the inspiration of eternal love. Emperor Shah Jahan himself described the Taj in words as:

["Should guilty seek asylum here, Like one pardoned, he becomes free from sin. Should a sinner make his way to this mansion, all his past sins are to be washed away, The sight of this mansion creates sorrowing sights; And the sun and the moon shed tears from their eyes. In this world this edifice has been made, to display thereby the creator's glory."]

**Taj Mahal:** The more you write the more would be less to describe the Taj, the one of Seven Wonders of the World. The Taj of Taj Mahal is located in Agra which is considered as the finest examples of Mughal architecture consisting of elements derived from Persian, Turkish, Indian and Islamic architectural styles. The attraction of Taj Mahal is its marble tomb. The dome is fifty-eight feet in diameter and rises to a height of 215 feet. It took about 12 years to complete the plinth and the tomb and another 10 years to complete the remaining parts of the complex. A labour force of 20,000 workers was recruited to carry out the work as found in the record. The Taj is a wonder to Indians and also to foreigners. Travelers always wish to have a Glimpse of the Wonder Taj at bright moon light. The picture of Taj in front along with the beautiful Garden at day time is a visit of pleasure.

I visited Taj Mahal many times. This time also I came to Delhi on 23rd December, 2009 for some other works but I could not stop my temptation to go to Agra for a day to visit the Taj. It does not matter how many times you visit the Taj, you will feel to see it again and again. The city is Agra and that becomes well-known world wide because of Taj Mahal. The city is about 205 Km away from Capital, Delhi. Taj Mahal tour is one of the most popular tour in India. It is a symbol of love and all the tourists find it stunning. A tour to Taj Mahal is an unforgettable experience to be remembered forever as the historical monuments leave the travelers spellbound. The best time to visit Taj Mahal is October to March.

The visiting of Taj never ends as it ravels different images at different times. No body gets tired to see Taj in different angle. The record says-the Taj Mahal was visited annually by 2 to 4 million people and overseas visitors were more than 200,000 people. Most of the visitors prefer to visit in the month of October to November extending up to the month of February because of cooling atmosphere otherwise the temperature is hot and not good for strolling. It was open from time immoral but the situation of the world is changing with the change of outlook. The thrust of Atom bomb is reduced by the rise of human skill between the super powers but a new threat has immersed in the world, the threat of terrorist act, no body knows in what way it would immerse because it is all in secret and every attack is an attack of new invention. The government of India is bound to impose restrictions for the cause of security and bringing hurdles for visitors. The complex including the Garden remains open from 6am to 7pm weekdays, except Friday when the complex remained open for prayers at the mosque. It is open for night viewing on the day of the full moon and two days before and after excluding Friday and the month of Ramzan. And only few items are permitted to take inside such as: Water in transparent bottles, mobile phones, ladies' purses, Cameras, and small video cameras. It is enjoyable and worthy to visit Taj along with the most beloved one. The view of Taj in front as well as from behind standing on the bank of the river side is also equally enjoyable.

The history says-Aurangzeb became the successor of Shah Jahan soon after the completion of Taj Mahal. There occurred battle among brothers. Aurange killed one of his brother and occupied the thrown by force and kept Shah Jahan under house arrest at nearby Agra Fort till his death. As Shah Jahan was kept under house arrest he used to see Taj Mahal from the distant Agra Fort through a powerful lense installed in the concealed room. His love for his beloved died only at the last breath of his soul.

It is the most beautiful monument ever constructed by the Mughals, the Muslim rulers of India that its architectural beauty has never been surpassed. In all, twenty eight types of precious and semi-precious stones were inlaid into the white marble. Its glow of beauty is beyond description, particularly at dawn and sunset. The Taj seems to glow in the light of the full moon as it is built entirely of white marble. Valadimir Putin, the Russian President made a visit to Taj in the moon light along with his wife Lyudvnila in 2000. Valadimir Putin and his wife Lyudvnila, the high profile couple made a personal visit for the realization of the spirit of love. They seated there in front of Taj, without any official decorum, relaxed and refreshed with the dept of love of the two souls.

**Shah Jahan buried:** Upon Shah Jahan's death, Aurangzeb buried him in the mausoleum next to his wife Mumtaz as he left his life with the memory of Taj Mahal. To day even after four hundred years, the symbol of his love has been remembering by the tourist of the globe paying a visit to Taj Mahal. In 1983, the Taj Mahal became one of heritage of UNESCO world Heritage Site and as such it was recognized as the "The Jewel of Muslim Art in India" and also universally recognized and admired as one of the masterpiece of the world's heritage.

# [45]

**My Visit to New Delhi:**

**New Delhi the Capital of India**, what is now transformed into a modern City being designed with the elegance and dignity of the Republic of Modern India, which would discover the difference with that of British Capital. In 1911 during the time to transfer the capital of British India from Calcutta to Delhi, a planning committee was formed, and a site 5km south of the existing city of Delhi, around Raisina Hill, was chosen for the new administrative center. It was a well-drained, healthy area between the Delhi Ridge and the Yamuna River; the area provided ample room for expansion. The land was acquired under "1894 Land Acquisition Act" after the removal of at least few families from local villages. Delhi has been continuously inhabited since the 6th century BC. According to the historic record, Delhi has served as a capital of various kingdom and empires. It has been captured, sacked and rebuilt several times, particularly during the medieval period, and therefore modern conurbation is a cluster of a number of cities spread across the metropolitan region. Delhi is believed to have been the site of Indraprastha, the legendary capital of the Pandavas during the times of the Mahabharata. In AD 1639, the Mughal emperor Shahjahan built a new walled city in Delhi which served as the capital of the Mughal Emperior from 1649 to 1857. The Government of British India felt that the administration of India would be easier making Delhi its capital. The new Parliament House is a beauty and pride of Delhi.

**The Parliament House:** At the beginning Parliament house was planned as a part of Rashtrapati Bhawan, but later on in 1919 Montague-Chelmsford reform committee changed the plan and designed it afresh as the Indian Parliament. The Parliament consists of Lok Sabha, Rajya Sabha and the President of India. Any legislative business is passed by the concurrence of the three. Lok Sabha is made up of 552 members. It is also known as the "House of the People" or the "Lower House". The Rajya Sabha is known as the "Council of States" or the "Upper House". Its members are elected by the members of legislative bodies of the States.

**The Red Fort:** During the reins of Shah Jahan, Agra was the capital of India. In 1639, Shah Jahan expressed his desire to shift the capital from Agra to Delhi. To fulfill his desire the construction works started and within eight years, Shajahanbad was completed with the completion of Red Fort in all its magnificence to receive Emperor. During the period of British occupation, although the Fort has changed its glamour to a great extent with the large-scale demolitions, even then its important structures have survived. PM of India in every year deliver his speech on 15th August, the day of Independence of India addressing the citizens of India from the historic Red Fort. **Delhi** spreads over the site of seven ancient cities and includes many historic monuments like Jantar Mantar, Lodhi Gardens besides Lotus Temple, umanyun'sTomb, Connaught Place, Akshardham Temple, and India Gate.

**Qutub Minar:** (i). Delhi bears many Islamic sculptures as it was under Muslim Rules for an about seven centuries, Qutub Minar or Qutub Tower is one such sculpture, the tallest minaret in India, originally an ancient Islamic Monument, inscribed with Arabic inscriptions, though there were few historic tomb in the Hindu period too such as the iron pillar with some Brahmi inscriptions located in Delhi. The Iron Pillar in the courtyard bears an inscription in Sanskrit in Brahmi script of the 4th century AD. According to this inscription, the pillar was set up as a Vishnudhvaja (standard of Lord Vishnu) on the hill known as Krishnapada in memory of a mighty king named Chandra. A deep socket on the top of the ornate of capital indicates that an image of Garuda was probably affixed to it.

Qutub Minar is the world's tallest free-standing brick minaret

Photo From http://en. wikipedia. org/wiki/File:Qutab. jpg by w: Qutb Minar in Delhi, India, originally uploaded from Flickr user Thovie333

(ii). The Qutub Tower has 379 stairs, 72. 5 meters high and the base diameter starts with 14. 3 meters, narrows down to 2. 7 meters at the top. Its construction was started in 1192 by Qutub-ud-din Aibak and was completed by Iltutmish. The Qutub Minar is made of fluted red sandstone covered with intricate carvings and verses from the Quran. Numerous inscriptions in Parso-Arabic and Nagari characters in different sections of the Qutub Minar reveal the history of its construction. According to the inscriptions on its surface it was repaired by Firoz Shah Tughluq (AD 1351-88) and Sikandar Lodi (AD 1489-1517).

(iii). Before 1981, the general public could climb to the top of Qutub Minar by climbing up the narrow stair case leading to the top of seven-storey. But, however, on 4 December 1981 an accident occurred whereby the supply line of electricity was cut off plunging the tower's staircase into darkness. Around 45 people were killed in the stampede that followed the electricity failure. Most of the victims were children because, before 1981, school children were allowed free access to historical monuments on Fridays, and many school groups were taking advantage of this. After that tragic accident public access has been forbidden. There were many stories; incidents were related with Qutub Minar. Bollywood actor and director Dev Anand has once desired to shoot a song related to his movie "Tere Ghar Ke Samne" inside the Qutub Minar, however, that could not be performed, the cameras used at that period being of bigger seize could not be accommodated inside the tower's narrow passage and the song was shot inside a replica of the tower instead.

**Jantar Montar:** The jantar mantar, ('calculation instrument') is located in the modern city of New Delhi. It ravels how the people could thinks of in finding the timings of the day in absence of modern scientific facilities. It is the witness of the presence of intelligence of the ancient people of India which have not been utilized in the British period in right perspective. Instead of diverting the intelligence and skill in the gathering of scientific knowledge from the British and British kingdom like that of the people of the other countries of Europe or Japan, our political thinkers concentrated their attention in sphere of occupying the chair of power of administration and not on the economy to remove the sufferings of the people. Nizam of Hyderabad had made 'Hyderabad' one of the wealthiest states in the British Empire by dint of his economic maturity. Indians fought against British to prevent British from taking of our wealth to England but they forget to earn the wealth from the British. The British were rich in wealth in the efficiency of the art of administering a country and in inventing technology in the process of manufacturing in large quantity the essential items of life process to sustain a better, prosperous and superior in strength and champion in the etiquette of civilization. Material wealth is perishable but the knowledge of wealth is non perishable. The intelligent Japanese youths earned the non perishable wealth from the intelligent people of British in British land without giving the importance to the destruction of material wealth of Japan by Atom Bomb in Japan. The knowledge of wealth is their inherent property, non perishable; no body can destroy or steel their wealth by any way. This knowledge of self dignity had made them superior in the field of technology and unparallel in the world. Their economy had risen from bottom to top and now Japanese are champion in the world in many respects. While Indians are at the mercy of others to up grade the economy. In the midst of poor economy, Indians are fighting with local issues, issues of religion, issues of caste, and issues of greater economic stage. There is nothing fault in that because human nature is the nature to fight to the last for success, Success for power, success for wealth and success for enjoyment for a better life.

Jantar Mantar is an astronomical observatory, built in 1734. Jantar mantar consists of 13 architectural astronomy instruments. The site is one of five built by Maharaja Jai Singh II of Jaipur. He was very successful in installing a Jantar Montar in his own state at Jaipur. Looking to the success of the observatory, Mughal emperor requested him to install such an instrument at Delhi because he was amused by his skill of architectural astronomy and he placed him in high esteem for his astronomical skills and cosmological concepts of heavenly bodies. As the task of revising the calendar and astronomical tables was given to him by Mughal emperor Muhammad Shah, he was doing the work with efficiency since 1724 onwards. The purpose of the observatory like Jantar Mantor was to compile astronomical tables and to predict the timings of day and night by the movement of sun, moon and planets. There are distinct instruments within the observatory of Jantar Mantor by dint of which hours, minutes, and seconds were ascertained. The materials used in building Jantar Montar are not derived from any foreign land rather the India itself and the stones are nothing but local stone and local marble, each instrument carries an astronomical scale, generally marked on the marble inner lining. Besides these, Bronze tablets, all extraordinarily accurate, were also employed in right place to get the accurate data. In 1901, the Jantar Mantar as good as calculating machine was declared a national monument in 1948.

# [46]

## My Journey to Saraswati Puja:

**It is in the search of the virtue of Brotherhood and Tolerance** that begins at the budding stage in India in performing Saraswati Puja. It is time immoral that the Goddess Saraswati is worshiped at School once in a year in a particular month with utmost devotion. It was the belief in the minds of the young children being imposed right from the date of birth of the School that wisdom of knowledge would not explore without the blessings of Goddess Saraswati. So on that particular day School Children gather in front of their learning God of respective School and perform the rituals of offering flowers and sacred leaves at the feet of God with great devotion and do the prayer for the blessings of Saraswati of learning and acquiring knowledge of wisdoms. The customary Puja is not important but it sets the seeds of fellow feelings and love of Unity. Hinduism believes the Goddess Saraswati is the goddess of knowledge and wisdom. The so called saying is that Goddess Saraswati is the daughter of Durga and wife of Brahma, the creator of Universe. Hindus worship her not only for "secular knowledge" but also for divine knowledge. Veda's etymology explains the compound word Saraswati as "Saaram vaati iti saraswati"—"She who flows towards the absolute is saraswati". Saraswati is worshiped every year in the month of January or February depending upon the day of moon. Of course it is observed under different customs in different parts of India but every where the prayer is for the blessings of learning to acquire knowledge and wisdom. The festival of goddess of learning is known as Saraswati puja or Vasanti Panchami as the session is called 'Vasanta Kaal', the season of spring. This festival of learning is celebrated by students in groups bringing a sense of brotherhood to fulfill every activity of puja celebration with devotion and sincerity. The puja process keep on injecting in the young mind a sense of devotion and fellow feeling keeping arrogance, and misbehavior far away and embraces only with the virtue of tolerance to bring everyone closer in front of the deity for knowledge of learning.

**Goddess Saraswati:** She is depicted as a gracefully seated or standing goddess, holding a veena, a musical instrument, a rosary and the scripture. The veena, a musical instrument is the symbol of knowledge of arts held in high esteem in Vedic tradition. The rosary points to the meditative qualities necessary to acquire knowledge. And the scripture is knowledge in itself. It is believed that Goddess Saraswati helps in the evolution of creation in the individuals by the union of power and intelligence. She is wisdom, fortune, intelligence brilliance, contentment, splendor and devotion. Brahma has the creative intelligence and so he was recognized as the creator of the Universe. As Saraswati is the wife of Brahma, she acquired the power to execute what Brahma has conceived. So she is the goddess of creative arts particularly of music, learning and science according to Hindu Vedic philosophy.

The children dressed in bright clean garments particularly with in bright yellow dress gather together before the idol of Saraswati and pray for the blessings of knowledge. Flowers are offered to the goddess and students place their books before the deity. Puja is performed with sandalwood, ghee, joss sticks, and with sounds of drums. On this day, people eat vegetarian food and initiate children into the world of the written word. Puja is performed by a Pandit (pujari) and after puja, Prasad is distributed among all the people present. As the night approaches, Schools and colleges were decorated with colored lights and other illuminating articles and the festival was celebrated with great enthusiasm and devotion. Hinduism is a way of life rather than a religion. The Hindus have firm faith on Gods and Goddesses whom they worshipped on various occasions by performing Puja and rituals. It becomes a customary thing to perform Saraswati Puja in every school where particularly the little children were beginning their learning right from three years and that continues till to sixteen years when they qualified for matriculation examination and become ready for higher study of his or her choice or take the challenge of facing the adventure of life for any eventuality. These categories of schools are very dearly to the society and Saraswati Puja is important to them because here a child takes the blessings of the God of Learning, through the occasion of Puja before beginning the learning. A child is child who is above religion, caste and community, every child attracts the greatest love of every parent, every guardian, every human being good or bad, honest or dishonest where lies a sense of humanity, God has given to every soul a vast ocean of humanity. Here it is a little sense of humanity that makes every child a dear one to every individual.

**The Puja-Special:** This year Saraswati Puja was performed on 21 ist January. I have the opportunity to attend a puja celebration adjacent to my residence. It was in a small children School named Vivekananda Mission School. Puja was performed by a young bright Brahmin boy who had been trained earlier and who performed daily the rituals of Brahmin in a routine work to keep himself devotional for performing Godly works. I have taken few photographs of school teachers, photographs of little children as displaced here.

The word Saraswati is historically connected with the Saraswati River. Water is the source of life. That is why the growth of population and subsequently the civilization has been built up on the bank of the river. According to Hinduism, the Rigvedic hymns dedicated to Saraswati assigning as a mighty river with creative, purifying, and nourishing properties. The Vedic theory states that the River Saraswati was formed by the present headwaters of the Yamuna River. It is recorded in the text that after leaving the Himalayan foothills, the waters of the Yamuna turned west and flowed southwest across the Punjab and Haryana regions. Along the course of the Indus and Saraswati Rivers, the Harappan Civilization had developed in the ancient time. The archaeologist discovered the old civilization from the remnants of ruins. The earliest known examples of writing in India have been found in the ruined cities that is now the dry riverbed of the ancient waterway. It is believed that the goddess Saraswati gained her role as personified communication and a gospel of knowledge due to the role of the Saraswati River in the development of written language in ancient India.

**Different Views:** Hindus celebrate Saraswati Puja across India and express their mental views in different ways: (i) some one considers Saraswati Puja (or Basant Panchami) is the most auspicious days in the year for initiation of children into learning. (ii) The day is auspicious because Saraswati Puja is observed on the 5th day after the no moon night in the Hindu month of Magh. (iii) The day is auspicious because it is believed that Goddess Saraswati was born on this day and Saraswati was identified with the Vedic Saraswati River. (iv) In Patna, the former Railway Minister Lalu Prasad Yadav celebrated the event with students of his alma mater. (v) In Kolkata, Monika, a local student said "we have come here for the Saraswati Pooja as Saraswati is the goddess of knowledge and education so that we get good results". There is tradition still prevailing in India that adults should not help children into learning, until the initiation ceremony is performed before the Goddess Saraswati. It is for this reason seen that a large number of children are initiated into learning at temples or at home in front of the idol of Goddess Saraswati.

**Rig-Veda & Demon:** According to Rig-Veda, there were some powerful Asura (Demon), who hoarded all of the Earth's water causing wide spread drought, darkness and chaos. Saraswati was credited for her intelligence for killing some of such powerful demons in association with Indra, the King of Heaven. She (Saraswati) is the symbol of intelligence, consciousness, cosmic knowledge, creativity, education, music, the arts, and power. Hindus worship her for divine knowledge and for absolute peace of mind. In some Puranas, she is associated with Shiva and in some Tantras, she is attached with Ganesha. Again according to Brahma Purana, Vishnu had three wives, who kept only Lakshmi with him and gave Ganga to Shiva and Saraswati to Brahma. However, the spiritual forms of Devas including Saraswati lie in the deities of fire. This is why the worship is completed with fire and with the sound of "OM", the lovely soul purifying word of the divine power.

**Arya Samaj & Dayananda Saraswati:** The Indian religious leader Dayananda Saraswati (1824-1883) founded the AryaSamaj (or Society of Nobles). He was born into a Brahmin family of Gujarat in western India, who left his family at the age 19 and undertook a long period of rigorous, ascetic study of the ancient Vedas—the oldest core of the Hindu religion and finally raised voices against the orthodox Hindu tradition and against idol worship. According to his view the existing religious beliefs and social institutions were hopelessly corrupt. With this conviction he began a campaign for a doctrine of reform urging a return to the pristine Vedic tradition. His reforms voiced for abolition of:

Idol worship, (ii) Child marriages (iii) Inequality of women, (iv) Cast wise hereditary privileges. He praised the Europeans for education, active lives and for their contribution in trade. In his religious teaching he accepted the old doctrine of karma but he advocated for a monistic philosophy which stressed ideals of self perfection and ethical universalism. He said "I believe in the service to others".

He favoured a religion based on universal and all-embracing principles which have always been accepted as true by mankind—the primeval eternal religion, which means that it is above the hostility of all human creeds whatsoever.

In 1875 Dayananda founded the Arya Samaj in Bombay to propagate his doctrine of philosophy. His followers perused the teachings of Vedas in minute detail, and injecting there the benefits of Western science and technology, including electricity, microbiology, and other modern inventions. His outspoken criticism of Hindu tradition and doctrine of reforms created hatred against orthodox and conservative circles. Unsuccessful attempts were made several times on his life, but finally he was poisoned in 1883. The Arya Samaj was one of the most influential movements of the early modern period in India. This movement has earned him the epithet "the Luther of India.

# [47]

**My Visit to Calcutta to celebrate Holi:**

A place called Calcutta is a City developed by the British as well as destroyed by the British. At the beginning by defeating the Nawab Siraj Ud Ulla when the British captured Bengal, they favored the Hindus as they acquired power from Muslim hand, they loved the locals and developed the three villages to a City and named it Calcutta. But again they were fad up with the Hindus by their activity of bombs and strikes; they reduced the power of Bengal by shifting the Capital from Calcutta to Delhi and finally destroy the Bengali Hindus by the division of Bengal. But still Calcutta and now it is Kolkata remain a center of Hindus to make celebrations with Hindu culture.

After celebration, the people like to relax, sat together and exchange the feelings of love by the exchange of sweets to remember the day of joy as is done by the Lord Krishna with the Guppies as described in the Hindu epics. Here is a picture where the residents of 37D, Paike Para of Kolkata are celebrating the Holi festival.

**Celebration at Nandagrame:**

Origin of Holi festival in India is centered round "Hiranyakashipu". In Vaishnava Theology, Hiranyakashipu was the king of Demons who was worried for his safety and the safety of all demons on the Earth as because the Kings of heaven were very powerful by the boon of Brahma, the creator of the Universe. To attract the attention of

Brahma, he began to penance remembering Brahma in heart and soul. He continued the penance for years together. At last Brahma decided to satisfy him so as to stop the act of penance. He asked him to ask for a boon. Hiranyakashipu took the advantage of the opportune moment and demanded that he should not be killed "during day and night, inside the house or outside, not on Earth or on sky, neither by a man nor an animal, neither by Astra nor satrap". This made him the most powerful and that had infused in him in disguise an infinite power of arrogance. He now no longer had been afraid of attacking the Heaven and the Earth. He had announced that now onwards people should stop worshipping Gods and start praying to him. There is reason of joy behind the story of killing Hiranyakashipu.

Holi is celebrated in a village in Nandagaon in Uttar Pradesh in a different way amidst of colorful sights of sound and dances. In the village all the ladies dance keeping sticks in hand which they use to beat up the men in a dense. Holi is a festival of color that is celebrated in the happiness of bringing a new harvest and goodwill among the local community and is celebrated all over India.

The State Nepal is said to be a Hindu state as because most of the people are in the belief of Hindu faith. Thus the festival Holi is a virtuous festival in Napel. People performed the festival with great devotion and pray to Lord Krishna to remove their sufferings and keep them in joy with the bond of affection and love through the celebration of Holi.

Similarly, Holi is celebrated in Uttarpradesh. The legend says the end of Hiranyakashipu occurred in a mysterious way without destroying the promise as offered to him in the form of boon by Vishnu. It was that later Lord Vishnu came in the form of a Narasimha (half-man and half-lion) and killed Hiranyakashipu at dusk, a time which was neither day nor night. Further the killing was on the steps of the porch of his house which was neither inside the house nor outside and by restraining him on his lap which was neither in the sky nor on the earth and mauling him with his claws which were neither astral nor avatar. There is reason of joy in the celebration of Holi behind a story.

Celebration of Holi in holy is carried out in Uttar Pradesh with Red Powder along with coloured water.

The popularity of the festival is as such that it did not remain in India or Nepal alone, it spreads beyond boundary. In foreign country people are celebrating the Hloi festival with pomp and pleasure bringing the love of friendship by exchange of color forgetting the identity of self in the midst of variety of color. This is what is called, the festival of color, the festival of Holi. Celebration of Holy is also performed in foreign land. Holy is celebrated in every city of India because there is a joy behind a story.

**Prahlad** was the son of Hiranyakashipu, the King of Demons but he was very holy and devotional to God. The nature of young Prahlad, the young Prince infuriated his father. One day, the King ordered his sister, the demon Holika, to kill his son. He assured his brother to do so. One day, the demon Holika, who was immune to fire captured little Prince Prahlad and entered inside a fire of furnace to burn him to death. But the mystery was that she herself had been burnt to ashes and nothing was happened to young Prahlad. It was in the legend that the demon aunt before her death prayed to young Prince for forgiveness and the Prince forgave her and announced that now on her name would be remembered once in a year. Since then every year the festival Holi was celebrated. Thus we find Holi is born from Holika. Men, women and Elephants, all together celebrate Holi at Joypur.

Here is a picture where men, women and animal Elephant are celebrating Holi. Besides India Nepal, it is also celebrated in Srilanka, and in other countries where large Hindu population are residing such as Sumatra, Guyana, South Africa, Trinidad, UK, USA, Maruitius and Fiji. In West Bengal of India and in Bangdesh it is known as Doul Jatra or Basanta-Utsav. Holi is mostly celebrated in the Braj region (Mathura), the region where God Krishna observed Holi along with thousands of Gopies (devoted ladies).

**Varieties of Holi:** The people of New Delhi, the Capital of India celebrate the festival of colors with traditional fervor and gaiety.

This is traditionally a Hindu festival but people of all other religions also take active part in it. People relish enjoyment by applying 'Gulal' (color powder) and sprinkled colored water on each other on the occasion, which heralds the beginning of spring. In Himachal Pradesh, the people in Kullu celebrate the occasion by sprinkling colored water prepared by mixing snow with colors. The people in Banaras remain in high excitement taking the traditional Indian intoxicant drink called 'Bhang'. India's oldest and holiest city Uttar Pradesh rich in Hindu rituals celebrate the holi festivity with color and merriment. It was a vision to be seen that people getting drenched in colors sitting on the steps leading to the Ganga River, were seen grinding 'bhang' along with milk and other various dry fruits to enhance the taste. Holi in Banaras is incomplete without bhang. Dharamdev, a priest said: "Since this is the place of Lord Shiva, bhang forms an integral part of this place but on Holi it has a special significance. People enjoy drinking it with milk. We all sit together and enjoy this drink". The people of different ages enjoy holi in different way. Elders celebrate Holi by exchanging greeting and distributing sweets. Young boys enjoy by dance to the tunes of popular Hindi songs in the streets. Sometimes even foreign tourists were seen to participate in the festival. A foreign tourist said in Calcutta "I am enjoying a lot. It is good. Some people are good and I am enjoying a lot". The new arrival of Chinese pichkaries (water spray guns), known by fancy name AK-47, was another novelty of the festival. In order to check law and order problems on the streets police personnel in thousands were on duties.

Indian community celebrated Holi in America too. On 7th March, 2009, the First Lady of America, Michelle Obama, served food to the homeless in Washington, at Miriam's Kitchen, a touch of compassion and good karma on the occasion of Holi.

The foundation of universal Responsibility of His Holiness the Dalai Lama in collaboration with the Department of Information and International Relation, Central Tibetan Administration had organized a Tibetan Film festival in Dharmshala, at Himachal to commemorate 50th year in Exile along with the occasion of Indian Holi.

**Janmashtami** (a) Janmashtami is celebrated as the birth day of Lord Krishna. It is observed on the 8th day of Shrav month (Aug/Sept) as per Hindu calendar. Lord Krishna is considered as the 8th Avatar, or incarnation of Lord Vishnu on the Earth. It was in the legend that Krishna was born to Devaki and Vasudev who were imprisoned by Devaki's cruel brother Kangsa. It was because of the fact that Kangsa heard in dream that the 8th child of his sister would kill him. He decided to kill all the baby of his sister as soon as a baby would be born. It was so happened that just after his birth, he was replaced by another baby and thus Krishna, the 8th baby, was survived at the cost of death of another baby. In the course of time Krishna thwarted all attempts tried by Kangsa to kill him. At last Kangsa was killed by Krishna himself. The victory of Krishna was celebrated by Radha and the Gopis accompanied with song, dance, and music and playing with red powder and red water. In Vrindavan and Mathura, where Lord Krishna grew up, the festivity of Holi continued for 16 days there till Rangapanchmi. People celebrate the divine love of Radha and Krishna in the form of Holi.

(b) The festival of North India called Lohri, the history of which is as old as that of the story of Indus Valley Civilization itself. This festival marks the end of winter and the beginning of spring and the New Year. The features of this festival lie in the lilting of Fire at night and atomized the community coming together in the midst of song and dance. The Lohri of North coincides with Pongal in Tamil Nandu, Makar Sankranti in Bengal, Magha Bihu in Assam, Tai Pongal in Kerala—all occasions are the celebrations on the auspicious day of Makar Sankranti.

**Krishna-Radha & Prahlad**: It is the usual practice to be seen that foreign devotees thronged the famous ISKCON temple on the day of Holi since early morning to offer their prayer. What was seen, the Priest had chanted and danced in groups to mark the occasion in the temple. Locals were seen to apply color to each other on the streets amidst cheering and shouting. Everyone had the same excuse "Bura Na mano, Holi Hoi—(Don't mind, it's Holi)". The exuberant festival of

Holi is associated with the love of Hindu Lord Krishna and his devotee Radha.

Holi is also celebrated for the survival of Prince Prahlad, whose devotion to the God, kept him safe even when he was forcefully taken to fire furnace to burn to death. In memory of happiness of Holi, community feast are very often arranged to make the day memorable.

**Dhulheti:** In Andhra Pradesh, Holi is known as Dhulheti, Dhulandi or Dhulendi and the day is celebrated by the people throwing color powder and colored water at each other. Bonfires lit the day before, which is also known as Holika Dahan (burning of Holika). The bonfires are lit in the memory of the miraculous escape of young Prahlad. It was in the legend, the young Prahlad, a staunch devotee of God Vishnu, escaped without any injuries due to his unshakable devotion. Holi is celebrated at the end of winter season on the last full moon day of the lunar month Phalguna (Feb/March). And Rangapanchami occurs on the 5th day of the full moon marking the end of the festival including men and animal that was being also found to be seen in Kerela where it is called "Pooram festival of Thrissur".

# [48]

**My Journey to Puri-Beach, a violent as well as a lively Beach:**

Any one who wishes to see the non stop flow of waves, he can do so without break because every wave is different in its flow of speed, height and in the magnitude of its cracking sound in the Sea of Puri-Beach. As the continuity of wave remains constant, the vision also tends to remain so with the flow of waves after waves, less it misses the moment of beauty. Thus it can be said Puri-Beach is a Sea of constant Vision. A new visitor generally forgets to sleep if he had the opportunity of looking to Sea-waves from his resting resort at night. Such a vibrant Sea beach is rare in the Earth.

It is believed that the place Puri is a Land of Lord Krishna, the Almighty: In Orissa Lord Jagannath (=Lord Krishna) is regarded as the most Sacred to all. The Ratha Jatra Festival is one of auspicious celebration held in Puri once in a year when hundred of thousands of people gather here to observe the celebration. There is a historical significance for observing the festival. However many of them prefer to go to Puri Beach to have a holy deep in the Sea. The devotion generated from the lively nature of the sea in which high waves from distance with loud noise is rushing towards sea shore making a large cracking sound as if to crush everything of the earth is no where to be seen. Its violence commands the power of Almighty and the devotional visitors get purified by the blessings of Jagannath having taken a deep in high wave. Every day visitors are coming to see the Beach. But until and unless a visitor touches the water and feels the cracking waves with the body of self, he never gets satisfied although it is known to all that to welcome a wave with full strength of body is most dangerous. However Nolias, the Sea guards are there to help and protect every visitor. There are some who dare to go on their own and enjoy the real thrust of waves.

Accidental death in Puri-Beach is a common Phenomenon:

The nature of Puri-Beach is very much attractive to any visitor. Its water, wave and intermittent sound is welcoming the visitors as if the beach is talking with the visitor to move forward to water and makes a ever ending friendship. There are people who could not stop the temptation of attraction dare to venture and move forward desperately into a little deep, they forget to return alive but they return after about two hours giving their living soul to the midst of sea. Even then the temptation of going into deep water is never gone down. This kind of scene is very common in rough weather when the roaring sea don't want anybody to be spared. The high waves with strong tidal current pull the swimmer inside the Sea. Thus the wonderful enjoyment sometimes leads to an unforgettable memory of tragedy. Although in Puri-Beach Holy deep is safe but Swimming is dangerous:

Puri Jagannath Temple is the place of attraction. From historical point of view the name of the place is the kingdom of Kalinga, which was invaded by the Maurvan Emperor Ashoka in 261 BCE. The state Orissa was the creation of British and it is named as such on 1 April 1936. However there was further change after the independence of India. The capital Cuttack was shifted to Bhubaneswar on 13 April 1948. Jagannath has been referred to as Udisanatha derived from Tantric literature, in Mahabharata it is found referred as Gajapati Kapileswaradeva (1435-1467 CE) and the territory is called Orissa Rajya or Orissa Rastra. Hence forth it is called Orissa. Most of the tribal people of this have been influenced by Hindus and have adopted Hindu manners, customs and rituals. The teachings of non violence in India were actually originated in this land of Orissa or ancient Odisha in 261 BCE in the battle of Kalinga when the mighty King Ashoka campaigned against the weak Kalingas. It was one of the bloodiest Wars in Mauryan history on account of the fearless and heroic resistance offered by the Kalingas to the mighty armies of the

Mauryan Empire. He was astonished by their unexpected bravery and sacrifice. The scene of killings and bloodshed brought a change in Kings' mind, when Ashoka completely surrendered himself and his kingdom to the philosophy of Buddhuya, a philosophy of non violence.

Konark is a small town in Puri district in the state of Orissa, being situated on the Bay of Bengal. It is the site of the 13th-century Sun Temple, which was being built by the King Narasimhadeva-I of the Eastern Ganga Dynasty. The temple is recognized as a mark of wonder of ancient works and recognized as a World Heritage Site. It takes the form of the chariot of Surya, the Sun God.

It is easy to reach Puri. Kolkata is the initial destination for the visitor, the City can be reached either by train from any corner of India or by plane via well developed international Air-Port of Kolkata. The next is a train journey of 14 hours from Howrah to Puri Station. There are plenty of Hotels and Resorts with reasonable rate comparatively chief where visitors can safely rest and enjoy the holydays at his pleasure. A stroll in the Swargaddwar (Meaning gate to heaven) Road will refresh a visitor by cool and pleasant breeze on the bank of the Puri beach.

Puri Beach Festival: It is held on the bank of Beach namely Sea Beach, Swargadwara at Puri and comes as a celebration of the beauteous and splendid Oriya spirit. It is conducted by the Hotel and Restaurant Association of Oriya, co-sponsored by the Ministry of Tourism for the pleasure of visitors. It is a festival of classical and folk dances and gives an opportunity to visitors local and foreigners to have a sight of hand crafts, handloom and sand Arts, followed by fashion show and rock dance.

**The Rath Jatra Festival of Puri:**

The Rath Jatra Festival, a festival of Chariots of Lord Jagannath is celebrated once in a year in Puri, the temple town of Orissa, on the East Coast of India. The Sri Mandir, the main temple at the center of the town, is most significant where the most popular Deities of

Jagannath (Lord Krishna), Lord Balarama (Krishna's brother) and Lady Subhadra (lord Krishna's sister) reside. In the festival of Rat Jatra, the Deities allowed to come out of the temples and carried by made-up Carts to a different destination. In the day of festival, many thousand people begin to gather on the main street near the Carts. It is not unusual for 75,000 to over one million people to attend the festival. In front of the Carts, the devotional chanting along with singing of the chanting groups makes the atmosphere a sea of emotion of heaven. The feeling of love of brotherhood is Universal that is realized only when a visitor makes a stroll on the Sea Beach starting from morning when thousands of people of different color of different countries could be coming across signifying a place of peace where every body comes here in search of.

To spread the love of brotherhood across the Glove, the Maharajas of Puri undertakes few restricted programme time to time. In 1990, Srila Puri Maharaj began his tours of communicating Gandiya Vaishnava Theology to the world. Annual tour began to Europe in 1997 and to the European Union, the United States of America, Mexico, Australia and Thailand in 2001. One of the most memorable event of the 2001 world tour occurred on Saturday August 25, 2001. On that day, Sri Maharaja visited the top floor of the World Trade Centre along with a dozen devotees and conducted a short nagar-Sankirtan event to spread the love of brotherhood. Just after about a month later attack on world trade center occurred. Had it not been done at that time, Maharaji could not visit the place with his devotees.

# [49]

**My Journey to Goa and its Beaches:**

Goa was a Portuguese colony in the 16th century and remains there as the smallest State of India in terms of area, the Land area being located on the West coast of India although originally it is known as Konkan. The Arabian Sea forms its Western coast and created innumerable beautiful beaches. Panaji is the capital of Goa and Vasco dagama is its largest city. Since 16th century Portuguese ruled over the State for 450 years until it was annexed by India in 1961. It is renowned for its beaches, places of worships and world heritage architecture. The importance of Goa is visualized by a visitor only when he looks to Goa from the following points of importance. (i) Millions of foreign tourists visit Goa each year. (ii) Goa's Soil is reddish in colour. (iii) Goa is a beautiful laid-back beach state. (iv) Christianity and Hinduism existed side by side in Goa. (v) Thousands of foreigners come to lay hours and hours on the beach of Goa and soak in the sun.

There is also found to be some ancient history as 300 hundred ancient tanks and a hundred medicinal springs had been built during Kadamba dynasty for the well fare of the society, that being found visible even today. Portuguese like the place very much as is evident from the point of their looking to the administration of the place where it is seen that their attempt was to set up a beautiful administrative system in Goa to bring discipline in every aspects of the life of Goa which is a prior necessity to make a place beautiful. Goa is divided into two distinct units such as North Goa and South Goa making Panaji the Head quarter of North-Goa while Margo the Head quarter South-Goa. Western Ghats (most of eastern Goa) is originated as one of the biodiversity of hotspots of the world.

**Thousands of foreigners come to lay hours and hours on the beach of Goa and soak in the sun:** Numerous clean beaches as well as Sunshine most part of the year makes this a natural vacations, holiday and partying place for Indians as well as Sun seeking Europeans and Americans. November to March is the best time when thousands of foreigners come to lay hours and hours on the beach and soak in the sun. Having being ruled by the colonial Portuguese for over 450 years, there is still a distinctive European flavor that has permeated all aspects of Goa's life including food, religion, language, festivals, dances and music. Goa is best known for its beaches and luxurious hotels. The important beaches of Goa can be named as: Palolem, Anjuna, Arambol and Candolim for sunset where Tourists visit these places each year: The River Zuari and Mandovi are the life lines of Goa. Mormugao harbor on the mouth of the river Zuari is one of the best natural harbors in South Asia. There are 40 estuarine, 8 marine and 90 riverine islands in the Goa.

Goa's soil is a special attraction for tourists as the soil is reddish in colour apart from the chemical reasons being of the presence of excess of ferric Aluminum oxides or anything else.

**The saying "Christianity and Hinduism exist side by side in Goa" is found to be true when the visitor finds** temples and Churches are existing side by side making the place, a religious place of importance too. Portuguese were there for long 450 years. They have their own life style in the preparation of food as well as in eating of food. The local were Indians but they were acclimatized by looking to the every day life style of the Portuguese. So to say they were Indians by physical appearance but they become Portuguese by nature. There was a complete change in the display of dance and music. There tune of songs and the art of display of songs are no longer Indian in nature. Thus a distinctive European flavor has been permeated in all aspects of Goa's life. Portuguese have left Goa but they have left here their rich cultural art. The people of Goa like their cultural art in the display of dance and song in particular so much that even after forty years they could not forget that cultural art. In any Indian cultural occasion they prefer to display a song with like that of Portuguese art.

The state of Goa, of India is famous for its beaches and the each and every beach is beautiful by its own individual's character. The tourists of India and abroad find a pleasure of happiness in these beaches and prefer to come here repeatedly making the long track of beach, a place of tourism. It is noticeable to see that the taste of tourists differs in their outlook. Foreign tourists, mostly who are coming from Europe or US, arrive in Goa in winter while Indian tourists prefer to visit Goa in summer or in monsoon seasons. Having being Goa under Portuguese rule for long 450 years and prevailing Latin culture, presents a somewhat different representation of the country to foreign visitors. The area of Goa's beaches is sufficiently lengthy covering about 125 Km of its coastline making a division of North and South Goa. The luxury is mostly found in the beaches of South where big hotels are standing for entertaining the foreign tourists.

**Palolem Beach:** It is a beach in the South Goa at a distance of 43 km from Marago or 76 km from Panaji but covered with shady palm trees and having with soft sand. Since its discovery, it attracted large crowed with each passing season where the crowed stay under the shadow of coco huts. The additional comforts one can find easily at the hotels or resorts situated nearby at a short distance from the beach.

**Baga & Calangute:** These beaches are existed side by side in North Goa, 16km away from Panaji. Here foreigners are found in large numbers busy in tanning themselves on the endless rows of side by side sun lounges. There are many good restaurants where the travelers can enjoy the taste of fine food and wine. Baga beach is well known for its activity in nightlife.

**Anjuna Beach:** It is a beach of North Goa situated 18km away from Panaji. Once it was home to the hippies, who prefer to live in unconventional appearance rejecting the traditional values. Although hippies has left the place but the legacy remains. The Wednesday Anjuna Beach flea market is always a bigger market where after the end of the day, the crowds descend on the shacks along Anjuna beach to listen to psychedelic trance after the sunsets.

**Colva Beach:** It belongs to South Goa to a distant 40 km away from Panaji and 8 km from Marago. It is one of favorite beach of Indian tourists as in the weekend the crowd arrives here by bus loads and explodes with locals as well. The area is well developed and good for merry making and pleasure as the place decorates with high or low prizes of hotels, beach shakes, food stall, small restaurants and bars but of course little of nightlife as such foreigners are less here compared to other beaches in Goa.

**Salvador & Goa:** The candela's beach is a wide spread beach of Goa, 15 Km away from Panjim, the Goan Capital situated in the North of Goa. It is one of the largest beaches but still it preserves its goodwill of maintaining its calm and peace. The Main Road that is the Condoling Calanguti Road is running with shops and restaurants after a gap of certain distance. The wide area is resort free but inns are there for the entertainment of the public. It is here found to be seen the dirt of roads clean by a woman, lays out a mat, not for sunbathing like foreigners, but to practice yoga. Further along the beach, another couple, who have arrived here for enjoying vacation, appears to be doing something of Sun-worshipping rituals to gather pleasure of their journey in the beach which can not be seen anywhere in Europe or America. The Indian people who had been associated with the British for long two hundred years certainly acclimatized to a certain extent with British culture. Here in Goa, 450 years of Portugal settlement followed a different pattern of life and made local Indians completely different. This was happened to be the Portugal's first colony in Asia as the state gained independence only in 1961. The residents of Goon are to somewhat different from the residents of other places of India as they are acclimatized with Portuguese culture more than the British culture like the places of other Indians. It would be surprised to know that the names of villagers of Goa are like those of Portugal such as like 'Salvador' Del Mundo (Saviour of the World), unlike Indians. The Portuguese culture is injected here so much that people like to expose themselves by the name of Portuguese. In India most of the people are Hindus but here in Goa 40% of Goon population is Christian. In old Goa, the States' former capital, the glimpse of gloomy baroque Churches indicates why the city was once known as Asia's Rome. The striking feature here is that despite India's stringent property laws, foreigners have the pleasure of right to buy here. It is not only Indians but many British have been enticed by Goon's laid-back lifestyle where English is widely spoken and political climate is peaceful and crime rates are fairly low. The other attraction is the cost of living which is comparatively very low. Having being the owner of a property, a couple can live comfortably in Goa in less expenditure in compare to any metro city of India.

Covering a length of 60 miles of the West coast, Goa is India's smallest state undergoing a number of change incarnations to attract foreigners to visit Goa. The lively days of Goa of late 1960 are now changed in many places into a spiritual menu of yoga and meditation whereby there exists a climate of plenum to keep everyone mellowed. In late 1980, there were places where strumming guitars were drowned out by blasting techno-trace and all night rave parties. Still sex, still drugs but not correctly rock 'n' roll found to be seen. But changes again, with recent ban on late night music, beach parting has become more restrained and Goa has shaped itself to the Indian traditional cultural amusement. It is a place to enjoy where more and more Sun-starved Europeans arrive on winter Charter flights to spend money to have the pleasure of merrymaking. Foreign visitors, shaven headed Neanderthals from Britain, Germany and Scandinavia insatiable thirst for bear wondering where the rave is.

Goa beach is someway compatible to Pattaya beach of Bangkok of Thailand as the Thailand has developed very much in creating some of the best beaches in the world. Each one has its own distinct characteristics; it is the person who is to find the right one. Bangkok is developed to such as extent that it becomes a country of Asian Investment boon. In 1990, many multinational corporations came here to set up office to start business with Bangkok. The city is now a major regional zone for financial business transaction. It has grown into an international hub for fashion and entertainment making Bangkok as one of the world's top tourist destination. To high light the development, only the Pattaya Park Tower is taken into account. Here it is breathtaking views having with sumptuous meals, the first and the highest seaside tower with a revolving restaurant. Any one could gaze at the beauty of the coastline and Pattaya City by standing on the Tower.

Anyone can stand and gaze at the beach of Jomtien Bay and Pattaya City or enjoy the view by looking through the Tower of observatory and taste the thrill of Speed shuttle and Sky shuttle. The Goa beach has the beauty no way less than the beauty of beaches of Bangkok but it requires further attention to make it more attractive as that of the beaches of Bangkok.

# [50]

**My Journey to Kerala:** After landing at Kochin airport I along with my friend took a taxi and went straight to the City of Thrissur, the cultural capital of the state and moved to a Hotel. There was a cultural program going on at the Lulu Convention Centre. We were lucky to attend the cultural show. It was a well organized center of attraction where the evening was illuminated with designed display of colored light making a festive atmosphere. The occasion started with Kathakali, Mohiniattyam, Kalarippayatta, Oppana and Thiravathira performances that kept everybody spellbound for one and half hour. After the event when we came out of the auditorium, we find well decorated elephants offering warm welcome to all which followed with a dazzling fireworks display, a show that delighted everybody.

**Kanyakumari Temple:** The center of attraction was the Temple of Kanyakumari that existed at Southern most end of mainland India. It is also the meeting place of three water regions, the Arabian Sea, the Bay of Bengal and the Indian Ocean. Kanyakumari has been a witness of ancient Indian culture, civilization and pilgrimage. The temple was made with virgin goddess Kanyakumari once in ancient time and the place was named as such Kanyakum. The legends say that Kanya Devi, an incarnation (avatar) of Goddess Parvati, was to wed Lord Shiva but the marriage did not take place as the Lord Shiva never turned up. According to legends, there was a huge arrangement for marriage and preparation was made for dinner where the rice and cereals remained there uncooked. The mystery of the place is that the stones present their look exactly like rice and cereals. There the people belief that these stones were the leftovers of the legendary marriage, which could not be solemnized. As the marriage did not take place at that time and even later, Kanya Devi remained a virgin goddess.

**The Description of the Kanyakumari Temple:** It may be started by saying that the temple was dedicated to Kanya Devi. The deity in the temple is placed as such that the face looks towards east leading to the main gate on the East but the eastern gate is kept closed except for some special occasions. The entrance to the Kenyakumari temple for general public is kept open through the Northern gate. There are three corridors that surrounded the sanctum. We walked around the outer corridor to see the 'Navarathiri mandapam' and proceeded to the second corridor, which encircles the shrine. The public can see here the Goddess very clearly. Every year the main festivals are held in the month of Vaikasi or May/June and Navarathri in September/October at the Kanyakumari temple. The custom that is prevailing there is that the male worshippers are required to remove their shirts before entering the temple.

**Way to Kanyakumari Temple:** The easy way to reach Kanyakumari Temple is by Air. The nearest airport is 80-km away—Thiruvananthapuram which is well connected with national International flights. Taxis and buses are available for movement to Kanyakumari from Air-Port. Of course Kanyakumari is also well connected by train services with all the places in India in the north to Delhi till to Kashmir. Kanyakumari is also connected by Buses with the big cities of South India such as with Chennai, Pondicherry, Trichy, Bangalore, Madurai, Nagercoil, Mandapam (Rameshwaram) etc. The temple of Kanyakumari is a reflection of Shakti of Mother Goddess as the power of energy standing at the junction of extreme end of the land and at the point of entering the seashore, the town situated at the point of junction is also known as Kanyakreferredumari and that the place was referred to by the British as Cape Commorin.

**Beauty of Kerala:** Its beauty is dues to its Land and the Sea extended to endless water. At the juncture of Land and Sea the beauty of Kerala had taken a turn of unique feature of nature making it a place of God, beyond written description. Its beauty has to be gathered by the sense of realization as it is a land of many enchantments. Kerala is at the extreme end of south-western part of India fringed with coconut palms. Its green backwaters in every pockets of this leafy land, sunny golden sands sprawling on the vast areas of Kerala beaches, dark, deep forest reserves carrying spicy aroma houses containing exotic species in their sleeves and above all, the magnetic attraction of pleasing breeze, that refreshes the tourists in solitary silence and reminds the tourists to take once again the exhilarating journey in this part of the land. The visit of Thiruvananthapuram, the political capital of Kerala itself can bring a unique pleasure in the minds of tourists. One can move to Kochi, Queen of Arabian Sea, once an obscure fishing hamlet, the first European township in India and one of the most glorious cities in its history and enjoy the beauty of land and sea. On the other hand one can enjoy the picturesque locations of Munnar and the serenity of hills. The joy of watching the parade of well decorated groups of elephants, each escorted with three efficient priests during Thrissur Pooram is unforgettable.

**The Beaches of Kerala:** The western border of Kerala is charming with palm fringed beaches as it is shared with Arabian Sea. The charm is there in going for adventuring on surfboards, and returning to shore for a snack of shrimp, or sleep for a little while in the sun at Kovalam, or just go out for a drive towards the state capital Thiruvananthapuram. The visit of Kappad Beach in Kozhikode, where Vasco da Gama, the Portuguese explorer landed in 1498 is worth seeing. Many foreign tourists visit Goa for relaxing in the sunny Sea-Beach.

**The Backwaters of Kerala:**

The backwaters of Kerala are its lifeblood. It includes networks of lakes, canals, estuaries and deltas of forty-four rivers that drain into the

Arabian Sea. The backwaters are the places of young aquatic life and sustain a self-supporting eco-system. The Vembanad Lake is the largest and store-house of backwater. The water from this lake flows through three districts and opens out into the sea at the Kochi Port. The second largest Astamudi Lake is recognized as the gateway of backwaters. The passing of holiday in the traditional houseboat (Kettuvallom) is the most exciting experience on the backwaters of Kerala. A traveler has to go through Kerala's backwater canals to discover the unique experience of rural Kerala. By undergoing a cruise through Kollam for eight hours a tourist will reach Alappuzha which offers sspectacular sights of snake boat races and lush paddy fields.

Kerala is now a major place of attraction for tourists in India. The extreme southernmost State Kerala of India is famous for its Backwaters, beaches, Ayurveda health holidays, hill stations, wildlife, festivals, world famous boat race, monuments and vibrant art forms.

# [51]

**Journey to Neighbour Country:**

Just as the life of an Indian in the United Kingdom or in the United States is affected to some extent by the social as well as cultural activity of those countries, similarly the life of Indians are to some extend is influenced by the social and cultural activities of the neighbouring countries. The position of India is almost at the middle of Asia based at the South end starting from Middle East after Europe in the west along with Pakistan, Japan in the East including the other countries such as Bangladesh, Singapore, Malaysia, Indonesia, Honkong, Taiwan and many other small countries, and China in the North. Asian country of India, China, Iraq are the countries of rich ancient culture but remain backward compare to newly born State like US. However, the newly born State Australia of Asia is developed by the patronage of British Kingdom. The countries of Europe are developed to day because of industrial revolution. In spite of all advantage and disadvantage few of Asian countries are developed, among them Japan is at top followed by Singapore, Honkong, Bankong, South Korea, etc. However the trend of development is there in China and India as well. To compare the life of India with those of other Asian nations my journey proceeded to few of the Asian countries where the life of those countries is narrated in nut shell.

**My Journey to Bangkok:**

**Bangkok a beautiful City, is now a Global City.** Bangkok is the capital and the prominent city of Thailand although it is a small port at the mouth of Chao Phraya River. It has now acquired the status of one of the Global Cities in Asia in the 21ˢᵗ century. In the legend it is believed that the city was given by the God Indra and built by Vishnukarm. The city is encircled by the river Chao Phraya by its innumerable cannels. Boats were once used for communication across the Cannels. But now Cannels are connected and converted into streets. That is why it is also called the Venice of the East.

**Bangkok is a cosmopolitan City:** The development work in Bangkok had been started after the second half of the twentieth century and continued in the 21ˢᵗ century to make it a global city. By the time it had been turned into a city of international trade. The people from neighboring country such as Laos, Myanmar, Cambodia and other Asian countries are regularly immigrating to the city. Besides Thais, Chinese, Indians, Europeans, and Americans are also living in the city making it a cosmopolitan

**The growth rate of Bangkok was the highest in the World in the period of 1985-1996:** The newly built Bangkok and the natural beauty of its surroundings have converted the city into a place of attraction for tourists. In the period of 1985 to 1996, the economy of Bangkok was flourished so much so that the national growth rate has been increased year after year to reach to the highest in the world. Its area such as Silom and Asok became the busiest business center. Because of the cultural and historical heritage the district Phra Nakhan and Dusit turned to be the sight for tourists. The venues like Grand Palace, Wat Pho, the Giant Swing, and Sanam Luang are located here. The beauty of Siam Square was similar to that of Shinjuku in Tokyo or Piccadilly Circus in London. Very recently Siam Digital Gateway shopping complex is going to be open in the Siam Square which will enhance its importance and beauty a step further

**Suvarnabhumi Air Port is a standard International Air Port:**

A newly built International AirPort 30 Km to Bangkok has increased the city's global status a step further. So long Bangkok has Don

Mucang International Airport which was one of the oldest airports in the world. With the ever increasing Air Flight Bangkok has been developing a new Air Port against all local and political opposition since 1970 with vast space of land and with all modern amenities. The new International Air Port named as Suvarnabhumi Air Port was opened on 28th September 2008 and the older Air Port was utilized for domestic flight.

**Bangkok is a vibrant, colorful city of 21st century in Asia:**

Bangkok is a City of 21st century. The commuters' problem due to huge concentration of people in the city of Bangkok making the movement nearly standstill had been solved by undertaking the programme of MRT (Mass Rapid Transit) underground Train and BTS (Bangkok Mass Transit System) Sky-train, one of the safest, most comfortable, quick and convenient way to get around Bangkok. Since December 5th 1999, it has transformed the face of Public Transport system in the Thai Capital. This has relieved off the commuters from the sufferings of chronic congestion, noise and pollution and had given a comfortable, air-conditioned and reliable ride through central Bangkok. The one rail line is running from North to South in the form of L and the other is in the form of a loop from National stadium (north) to Taksin Bridge at the end of the Sathorn Road. The two lines meet at Siam center when passengers can switch from one line to another. The impossible became a reality in April 2004 by opening metropolitan electric train (rot fai fah) by the construction of 21KM long bored tunnels consisting of 18 stations some of which even gone down to 30 meter deep under the city's major roads. These are the spectacular achievement in the city of Bangkok making it a vibrant, colorful city of 21st century in Asia.

**Bangkok maintained the natural greenery:** Bangkok is two meter below the Sea level. Naturally rising of water level tends to submerge many areas easily requiring adequate measures but simultaneously makes the soil very fertile for growing greenery. Lumphini Park appears as an oasis of greenery among Bangkok's skyscrapers. The administration has already designed a massive plan for growing green Zones as is done in the case of Bangkok's central Park.

**Bangkok is a place of Sacred Buddha:** Bangkok is a lively city both in day and night. Contact on communication has no problem. Pay Phones are present in Air-Port, at most of the hotels along with internet access. Even though the Thai is the local language, English is understood everywhere. The Road signs are written both in Thai as well as in English. But there are certain things which are strictly followed, such as smoking is prohibited in many public places, malls and air-ports. To win the hearts of locals one should avoid kissing and instead follow the custom of 'Wai', a system of wishing a person by placing the palms of two hands together and never by a handshake. Everywhere the image of Buddha is regarded as sacred. Visiting any Buddha Temple one should keep away the shoes. There are other things to avoid. (i) avoid touts to get rid off hefty commission, (ii) avoid dropping a litter big or small in the street to get devoid of the payment of large fines, (iii) avoid shouting to preserve the decency of the city.

**The Journey by Chao Phraya River Tourist Boat is a journey of entertainment:** It takes visitors on a cruise circuit of nine piers for a sightseeing tour of old Bangkok along with Chao Phraya River Tour from Sathar just below the Bangkok Sky-train Station at Taksin Bridge. The night life of Bangkok is also enjoyable. There are variety of entertainment venues and disco centers. The name of Disco (9am-1pm) center in the basement of the Novotel Hotel in Siam Square close to Siam BTS Station is worth mentioning.

**The Beaches of Bangkok:** To go to beach areas it requires few hours journey from Bangkok either by taxi bus or to some distance by train. Some beaches also have the facility to go by flight. Although it is relatively cheap to fly to beaches and islands, some people prefer to go by taxi with the intention of passing few days in the resorts of beach area. There are plenty of beaches with wondrous of natural beauty, some are quite and some are not.

# [52]

## My Journey to Bali, a 'Paradise' on Earth.

Bali is an Indonesian Island, lying in between Java on the West and Lombok on the East although it is small in size with a Hindu majority of about 93% in the area in a Muslim country, which is beautiful due to its surrounding natural beauty of land and sea and above all the beauty of the customary rituals of residents living there. All these made it so beautiful that it is as good as a 'Paradise' to all tourists. The Island earned a significant amount of foreign exchange from Tourists that has made a change in the life style of the residents living in the Island leading to a dramatic increase in Balinese standard of living. A bombing in 2002 by militant Islamists in tourist area of Kuta killed 202 people mostly foreigners and another attack in 2005 had severely affected tourism, that has brought a severe economic hardship to the Island. Indonesia is a country of South East Asia comprising of 17,508 Islands and having with inhabitants of 237 million people has made it the largest Muslim populated country in the world and the world's 4th populous country. In regards to its political history, the record said it was a Dutch colony once but later the Land was occupied by Japan. During the period of 2nd World war, at the time of deteriorating power of Japan by the fall of Atom bomb, the nationalist leader Sukarna declared independence 2 days after the surrender of Japan in August 1945. : In regards to its position in Geography Bali is lying 8 degree south of equator in a tropical Island of Indonesian archipelago and it is a part of the Lesser Sunda Islands, bounded by an area of 145 Km long and 80 Km wide and situated 3. 2 Km east of Java.

The highest peak of the island is Mount Agung, 3,142m high, an active volcano that was erupted in March 1963. Denpaser is the capital of Bali. Java and Bali both are two Indonesia's pleasant Island, decorated with temples and mega-hotels. Beaches are there along with volcano. People are terribly cuisine but friendly. Particularly Kuta and Legian are the island's most famous beaches. Best time for visit is April to September. But to enjoy adverse climate tourists can choose other months to experience rains, wind, rough seas, and sea weedy sand and oppressive humidity. Few about ten important sights of Bali are named by the authority for tourist's attraction such as (1) Ubud-Center of Balinese painting, (2) Kuta-a popular tourist resort, (3) Nusa Dua-a tourist resort in Southern Bali, (4) Tanahlot-a Sea temple on a huge rock which is surrounded by the Sea, (5) Batubulan-Stone figures on the road side of the village Batubulan, (6) Gianyar-Capital of Bali's old Kingdom, (7) Pura Besakih-Mother of Temple of Bali, (8) Terraced rice of paddies-a Scenic beauty in between Candidasa and Amlapura, (9) Pura Kehen-Heart of Bangli's temples. A huge banyan tree shades the courtyard—a beauty to see, (10) Gunung Batur-a volcano, which is revered by the Balinese as the sacred mountain on the island. Alaska Glaciers is wonderful to see. The highest peak of the island is Mount Agung, 3,142m high, an active volcano that was erupted in March 1963.

## Million dollar Villas are springing up along the cliff sides of South Bali:

The Island is gifted by the fall out of sea, the sea of sand carrying different colour. It is surrounded by coral sand dust of reefs because in the south it is faced with white sand while in the north and west it generates black sand. The generation of white and black sand is rare in nature and that has made the place wonder of rare. The place such as Kuta and Ubud is wonderful beach resort and center of Island's culture. Other centers are the districts of Legian, Seminyak and Oberoi. Million dollar Villas are springing up along the cliff sides of South Bali. Its population is counted as 31, 51 000 in 2005.

Denpasar International Air Port is Indonesia's third busiest airport: The flow of international tourist has necessitated the improvement of air-facilities. Bali Ngurah Rai International Airport also known as Denpasar International Airport is located in South Bali, 13 Km South of Denpasar, that has been improved as it stands now as the third busiest international airport. Thus much of development in the international standard has already been completed but the recent attack of terrorist has dampened the situation of improvement. The control of terrorist attack either by negotiation or by the force of iron hand is a big questions to the World now, how to maintain peace and allowing the people, the children of God to enjoy the beauty of the Earth by the exchange of love and brotherhood. Let us be happy by the illumination of disparity and making the mankind a family of the World without boundary. The journey to **Death Valley**, a several hour drive, as Las Vegas trip, is a memorable trip to a world famous destination of Bali.

The love of Tourism for a particular place rests with "the people and the place". The people who have the interest to go to the place of the Beauty of Earth and the place of Beauty Spot should have the facility to well-come the people and nothing else is required here. But the attention of the patriotic politicians is unavoidable, as the politicians are the thinkers of the nation as well as the people. Thus involvement of the politicians is there to maintain the beauty of the Beauty spot as well as to maintain the political atmosphere of peace for welcoming the Tourists of the World.

To high light the significance of Bali it is to be started wth earlier political history. In 1963 there was an eruption in Mount Agung killing thousands and that had created an economic havoc and forced many displaced Balinese to be transmigrated to other parts of Indonesia. This has created social divisions across Indonesia since 1950 and early 1960. Bali witnessed conflict between supporters of the traditional caste system, and those rejecting these traditional values. This issue of new settlement became an important issue of politics between PKI (Indonesian Communist Party) and PNI (Indonesian Nationalist Party) to get the support of people for political gain. Tensions and ill-feeling further increased by the PKI's land reform programs. An attempted coup in Jakarta was put down by forces led by General Suharto. The army became the dominant power as it instigated a violent anti-communist revolt, in which the army blamed the PKI for the coup. The saddest part was that at least 500,000 people were killed across Indonesia, with an estimated 80,000 killed in Bali, equivalent to 5% of the island's population. Upper-caste PNI landlords led the extermination of PKI members. Thus the 1965-66 upheavals allowed Suharto to replace Sukarno from the place of Presidency and the new order of the government re-established the relation with the Western countries. The pre-War Bali as "paradise" was revived with modern sophistication giving a large scale increase in the growth of Tourism.

In 1999, about 30,000 hotel rooms were kept ready for tourists. The Western people turned towards Bali and the visitor's number fuelled year after year, as of 2004, the island achieves over 1,000,000 visitors. The result of excess visitors polluted the beach atmosphere and eroded beaches, people suffered by the shortage of water, and a deterioration of the quality of life of most Balinese continued. This state of affairs of island is further deteriorated, by the bombing in 2002 and 2005 by Islamist militant. But Tourism becomes a challenging question to the Bali-people. By the untiring effort of the government and the people, the chance of further terror activity was reduced by taking all kinds of safety measure. Tourism strongly picked up again, with a 28% increase in the first quarter of 2008 with 446,000 arrivals. It is further increased by 2 million visitors by the end of 2008. But the long term problem of suffering with plague and traffic jams, remains an issue, in no way nearer to solution. Bali is still a paradise in the eyes of Tourist but that paradise also is not free from all danger. Air-crash accident, a big plane overshoot the run way and saved lives by crashing into Sea as shown in the internet picture and reported in the news paper.

# [53]

**My journey to Port Louise:** The city Port Louise is a beautiful harbor. It raises a curiosity to know how it came into being. The record of history tells the mystery of earlier story. It was in that period the Untied Kingdom was growing stronger and stronger year after year in competition with the mighty French. During that period, the two most powerful country of the world French and United Kingdom both looked towards Africa and Asia for the extension of their territory to be ruled by them because it was the Century of territorial expansion. They were successful to certain extent in this respect to establish their command in the region and had extended their territory even to the South East of Asia. The harbor City Port Louise was founded by the French in around 1735 during the French King Louise XV and the city was built by the French for extending its ruling and controlling over Asia. This is what to-day the beautiful harbor City is. As soon as the beautiful land mass in the vast sea of Indian Ocean came to the notice of mighty French, the King Louise XV, who decided immediately to turn the place into a beautiful harbor. The French King had brought number of architects from different places to give it a design to the best to make it a beautiful architectonic model of harbor. But, at last the Indian Tamilian craftsmen were finally chosen in real work to give it a final shape in 1728. Port Louise, capital City of Mauritius is a symbol art and architecture of Indian people as it is built by the Craftsmen of Tamil people of India.

To increase the attraction in many other fronts, the harbor City is solidly pulled upward by its beautiful mountain range. The race course is now become a place of attraction as the race course in the name of

Champ de Mars has built up there. Other attraction includes Candan Waterfront, Port Louise Bazzar, the Maruritian Chinatown, and the Port Louise Theatre.

**Port Louise in the last fifteen years** becomes a land of Sky-Scraper. It is a land of diverse culture and religion where Hindus, Creole, Chinese, Muslims and Europeans are living together. In the span of last fifteen years period the architectural beauty of Port Louise had changed to a great extent in the event of rise of population demanding the construction of high-rise buildings and tallest buildings. With the development of air routes the place has got the international importance as it is directly connected with the important cities of different continents. It is directly linked with New-Delhi in front, Melborn of Australia on the right and Rie de of South America on the left and also London on North-west. The best way to reach Mauritius is by air. Many international airlines provide air access to Mauritius from major international airports. The international air port of Mauritius is Sirseewoosagar Ramgoolan Air Terminal, 48 kms away from Port Louise. Tourists never face difficulty in the transaction of money as the credits cards are normally accepted by banks and most hotels, restaurants and shops. It is rightly said a **Sea of Paradise.**

Mauritius is a center for deep sea fishing species including the blue or black Marlin-the highly prized large size fish, all types of sharks, yellow tuna, and other varieties. Blue Marlin roam the sea and hunt around the island from Nov' to April, all these made it a Sea of Paradise. Fish boats can be hired from almost all hotels. The most prestigious deep sea fishing competition is the Martin World Cup which is hoisted in December by Pirogue Hotel. The sea temperature varies in between 22 to 27 degree centigrade. Foreign Tourists are always seen in the beach as they are found to be relaxing in the beach under sun ray.

**The beauty of Bay:** In the beaches visitors can get a treat for eyes while sands and blue water make a striking contrast. The beaches are well nourished and offer a host of water sports and activities such as water skiing, boating, swimming, sailing and fishing. The beaches are also the places to go for a sunbath and relax with near and rear ones. The beauty and happiness of marine life is enjoyed in the beaches. The famous beaches of Maruitius are—Grand Bay, Blue Bay, Pereybere, Belle Mare, Flic en Flac, Le Mome and Tamarin. Grand Bay: It is a place for shopping and leisure paradise. Its night is full of amusement having no dearth of restaurant, bars and disco. La Cuvette beach is well worth visit that is being recently renovated. **Pereybere:** It is a public beach which is popular because of its shopping facilities, restaurants and pubs. Sugar-beach of Mauritius is a beach to be counted in its beauty as well as in avenues of facilities.

Balaclava Ruins: Visitors will be able to see the sea walls, whose initial foundations were laid down by Mahe'de Labor donnais.

The TRiolet Shivla: It is the largest village in the island. Visitors can see the biggest Hindu Temples Maheswarnat

# [54]

**My Journey to the City of Macau:**

The territory attracted tens of billions of dollars in foreign investments, transforming Macau into the world's largest gaming center and attracting foreign tourists. It is in a location suited for both tourism and living as it is a beautiful city with clean street, gardens and picturesque of hilly landscapes along with the pleasure of sunshine, clean air, green lands and above all the delicious food of Chinese, Indians and mostly of European countries. The connection of two outlying Island of Taipa and Coloane by two bridges to Macau peninsula had increased the beauty of nature and beach sceneries. It is built on seven hills making it a beauty of nature and art and thus the nature is allowing many to enjoy the scenic views of the South China Sea.

**Travel to Macau is Easy:** There is air service of Helicopter between the helipads on the Macau and Hong Kong Ferry terminals. It takes about 15 minutes to reach Macau from Hong Kong. Tourists can use the service of Macau's international Air-Port which is located on Taipa Island. Air-conditioning Taxis are available at the Taxi stand outside the Air-Port which is not very expensive. The Air-port Bus is also available out of the terminal. Hong Kong has many facilities for Macau-bound travelers by sea. The Macau-Ferry Terminal and heliport is located a little away from Harbor. The booking offices are also here for sailing to Hong Kong. Turbo-JET, Cotal strip Cotai-jet like number of jet foils ferries is available here. It is an hour of enjoyable journey from Macau to Hong Kong open for almost 24 hours. Of course utmost care is there that all visitors must hold a passport or a valid travel document.

**Macau was a Portuguese Colony till 1999:** Portuguese ruled over the city for a long period of time making the place an international city. It is a small city with comfortable climate which makes it a European colony in China. Even at extent of highest population density and highest in the world in Macau, the city maintains a Chinese and Portuguese culture of high standard. Macau had been granted freedom of administration by the Portuguese and handed over the city to China on December 20, 1999 keeping a high degree of autonomy for Macau for 50 years till 2049 whereby Macau was administered by its own rules. Macau is especially administrative region like Hong Kong and situated 60 Km away from Hong Kong facing the South China Sea in the East and South. The territory has tremendous inflow of industries such as textiles, electronics and toys and notable tourist industry. The principle of inflow of money through commercial thrust of industry had made it one of the richest cities of the world. The popular industry that had made Macau rich is known as "Oriental Las Vegas" the gambling center. The gambling industry under discipline is growing in Macau day by day. It is booming and its economy rising to sky making Macau as one of the richest cities of the World. The City Macau on the land of Sea is something different from the Land of City. Macau is connected to China's Zhongshan Island by bridges:

Macau Port is a rocky, hilly peninsula. It is connected to China's Zhongshan Island by 700 ft wide bridge. It is also connected to two other small islands-Taipa and Cologue by bridges and a causeway. The City Coloane is the most popular city. Macau is a place of 'Paradise' for **gourmands** with wide range of delicious cuisines from all over the world including unparallel Macau-style Portuguese cuisine, and exotic food from Italy, French, Brazil, India, Japan and Korea. Its population is 90% Chinese and 10% others including Portuguese but the prevailing culture is western. It is a wonderful city of luxury.

# [55]

## My visit to Taiwan & Taipei:

The progress of the city is known by its Progress in computer science as because in the 21st century, the most progressive and useful science technology is nothing but computer science and as such the holding of Computer expo in every year in the city of Taipei at the Taipei World Trade Centre of Taipei, is a spectacular achievement in the City of world, exposing the world that a small far east City Taipei is no way lagging behind from the big Cities of big countries.

It is an Island in the East Asia between the South China Sea and East China Sea. It is Southeaster coast of mainland China. Taiwan is mostly mountainous in the east and gently sloping plains in the west. In the first Sino-Japan war, the Island was occupied by Japan in 1895. After the fall of Japan in 2$^{nd}$ World War, the People's Republic of China took control of Island in 1945. Later Chiang Kai-shek, democratic leader shifted to Taiwan and made Taipei as the capital of Republic of China in 1949. Since 1895 Taiwan was under Japan, who made Taipei a world class city making it topper in all front, the topper in Tallest Skyscraper, world's fifth topper in the construction of Museum, the topper in the new science of computer technology making it as one of the largest Computer expo centers of the world, the topper in making the High Speed Rail System, and the topper in the construction of Underground shopping molls. The record of Taipei in all fronts is a testimony of the Supreme technology of Japan.

**The Tallest Skyscraper:** The visit of the Tallest Skyscraper of the World was the attraction all over. Taipei 101 is a 101-floor (1474ft) landmark skyscraper that claimed the title of the World's tallest building opened at Taipei in 2004. The most striking feature is to get the access to tower's upper floor leading to observation deck, which is very expensive. But the vision from the top is superb and incomparable. This has made Taipei a center of attraction for global tourists. Besides, many shopping avenues that have built up by the time can easily win the hearts of tourists.

**The Museum** of Taiwan is ranked as world's top fifth making it a pride of Taiwan. The Museum was opened to public in December 24, 1983. However it was made by Taiwanese artists in a period of about 50 year's hard labour, where it had displayed the artistic supremacy. The beautiful garden in front of the Museum is worth seeing. Computex Taipei is a computer expo held annually at the Taipei World Trade Centre in Taipei and now it is one of the largest computer and Technology fairing center of the world. Taipei became a special administrative area in December 1967. Because of the production of high technology and its components, it became a global city. Its economic growth was increased to such an extent that it holds one of the world's largest foreign exchange reserves of over US$321 billion in 2009. The occupation of Japan for 1895-1945 periods was instrumental in the industrialization of the Island. **The High Speed Rail** System has reduced the transit time by 60%: Taipei's Public Transport system is unique in nature. Besides motor cars and Bus, it maintained Metro and light Rail system. The Rail system is based on advance **VAL** and **Bombardier** technology. VAL is a type of automatic rubber-tired people mover technology, discovered in French and used only in French, Chicago and Taipei. South Korea in 2010 has taken up the project to implement at the earliest. Bombardier is a company of Berlin in Germany giving technology solution for rail control. Taiwan high speed Rail system was opened in 2007 in Taipei. The bullet Train connects Taipei with all the big cities of west coast. The system had reduced the transit time by 60% or more what they normally are on a bus or conventional train. For convenience the Government has introduced a system of pass called Easy-Card. It is nothing but credits that are deducted each time a ride is taken. The Easy-Card is read via proximity Sensory panels on buses and in MRT (Metro) stations and it does not need to be removed from one's Wallet or purse. There is easy metro system for moving around the city. Taipei City at Night, towards Xinsheng South road is known as the road to heaven because of its high concentration of temples as well as shrines. The ancient history of a country is known by the treasures preserved in the Museum of the city. Keeping the importance of Museum in mind, the Taipei government has newly constructed and expanded the Museum. The new National Palace Museum of Taiwan was opened to public in December 24, 1983. It will work as an incentive for local young and an attraction for tourists.

**The City is arranged around a grid structure:** Taipei is the Capital city of Taiwan. It is a big city lying in a valley in the north of the Taiwan Island. The City is arranged around a grid structure, with wide roads running from north to south and east to west. Taipei maintains an extensive system of parks, green places and natural preserves. Xinsheng South road is known as the road to heaven because of its high concentration of temples as well as shrines. The night stroll is safe in Taipei and roaming at night in the night market around the city is a pleasure to enjoy. The visit of Downtown Taipei is enjoyable for its delicious meal in any restaurant. The population of Taipei is 70% ethnic HOKLO group who speaks both standard Mandarin and Taiwanese Minnan language. But English is learnt as compulsory second language. Maokong Gondola of Taipei is developing underground shopping molls, parks and public squares. Maokong Gondola is a gondola lift transportation system in Taipei opened in July 4, 2007. It is a crowning achievement of the Mayor of Taipei during his 8 years in office.

# [56]

**My Journey to Singapore:** Our first day journey started from Raffles MRT (Mass Rapid Transit) by car. There are different places to park the car on the Orchard Road but the parking charge differs place to place very much. It is desirable to look the cheapest car parking place for the whole day shopping. The Meridien center at one extreme end of Orchard Road is the one of the cheapest Car parking centers. The other end of Orchard Road is glamorous where parking charge is exorbitantly high. There lies the Orchard Central Coz. At night the area turned into a super gorgeous site of vision by the lightening of skyscrapers. The gorgeous building of the area displayed the best art of architecture. The next day our journey started on foot from Raffle MRT to Boat Quay along the Singapore river side. The icon of Singapore 'Merlion' decorated with the beautiful design of Lion and Fish is kept standing at the entrance of Singapore River, well coming the visitors day and night. Apart from shopping at Orchard Road one should go to see the nice place Boat Quay, the river side of the Singapore to enjoy the beauty of land and sea. We walked down to Boat Quay through the financial district. A woman will be satisfied getting the opportunity of marketing all kinds of girly things of her choice. Any body or every body will be tired off by the strain of marketing, when one will be looking for something to eat to be relieved off. Lots of restaurants had grown up all along the river side to get delicious Chinese food at Boat Quay.

**Downtown Core is the commercial center of Singapore:** It is in the South of the City-State of Singapore and the busiest center where Skyscrapers being grown up because of the presence of intense population. It is the center place of economic core, including key district such as Raffle place, and the administrative buildings such as Parliament house, the Supreme Court and City Hall. It is the centre of commercial buildings and cultural landmarks. The right policy in right time in the house of parliament was the secret of economic success of Singapore. Since independence, Singapore's standard of living has been increasing year after year with the increase of its economy. It is the 17$^{th}$ wealthiest country in the world now in terms of GDP per capita. Singapore is the smallest country in Southeast Asia. It is an island nation located at the Southern tip of Malay Peninsula. The great British were the pioneer of many beautifies spot and Singapore is one of them. A fishing village is transformed into a trading post on the island by the British in 1819. It was one of the most important commercial and military centers of the British Empire. Japan occupied Singapore during World War II, but the British regained it in 1945. It splited from the Malaysia federation and became an independent republic on 9 August 1965. The population strength of Singapore is approximately 4. 68 million. The majority people are Chinese but even then English is the administrative language of the country. A small island Singapore consists of 581. 5, KM but today the area of island has increased to 704, KM by land reclamation since its independence. The spectacular skyline and road outlines have increased the beauty of the island and attracted the tourists of the world. MRT Station is the most prominent and busiest station located in the Down town core area. It is a Mass Rapid Transit (MRT) interchange station connecting North-South and East-West of Singapore.

**Thomas Stamford Raffles was the founder of modern Singapore.** Initially Thomas spotted the importance of its location in 1819 and started its development as a British trading post on behalf of British East India Company. The British India office governed the island since 1858 and Singapore was made a British crown colony in 1867. Singapore became a self-governing state within the British Empire in 1959, and became independent in 1963 along with Malaya and others and gained absolute sovereignty on 9 August 1965. Raffles Place is a commercial place decorated with tall building and displaying the beauty of architecture of unbelievable infrastructure. The famous Esplanade theatre is here. Another day passed off visiting Sentosa. We also went through the Scotts Road, Orchard Road and finally to Suntec City Mall. **Gadget shopping:** If some one is interested with gadget shopping, all he needs to do is to get on the train at Orchard Station and get off at City Hall. Go to Funan Digital Mall, for costly sophisticated electronic goods or go to Sim Lim Square for cheap electronics. This is the place which may be rightly described as the heaven of electronic gadgets.

**Tourist Information Centre:** Besides shopping one must visit the Tourist Information Centre, situated at the middle of Orchard Road where the executives provided information about tourist spots, how to get there, what to see and do, maps and lots more. The visitors are also provided with tourists incentives. **Sentos Island**—It is a place of attraction. The Musical Mountain after 6 PM at night is superfine. The beaches of Island are the good entertaining site.

**Singapore is an Asian City:** Ethnic quarters like little India, Chinatown or Arab street can be found in the streets of Singapore, where each community is living with their distinct culture. Singapore is an Asian City where Chinese, Malayan and Indian are living in cherish together with the tradition of their own culture. The memorable things are: (i) Fountain and pools at Sentose, (ii) The fountain of wealth at Suntec City, (iii) Marine Bay at night, (iv) The lightening of Skyscrapers at night, (v) The site of buildings at the harbor.

People living in a place good or bad does not matter, gets fatigue and bored by the constant vision of a particular place and the constant routine works. Travelling brings freshness in mind and new vigor in the regular activity. Modern Singapore is a place of beauty; if some one is lost in the beauty by taking pictures after pictures, the person will definitely lose the real taste of leisure trip. It is here the opportunity of going to different places to see how the people are enjoying their life under different culture. This is what a life is in existence in the different parts of the globe.

[My visit to Singapore at Santosa with Director. Mr. K. N. Sharma]

# [57]

**My Journey to Vietnam:**-It is the easternmost country of Indo-China peninsula in South East Asia being surrounded by China in the North, Laos in the North West, Cambodia in the South West, and China Sea in the East. Its population is rises to 86 million. South East was a lucrative region for the western power to utilize the region for the benefit of business. A constant competition among the European powers had continued to capture the small island nation. It was neither the British nor the Portuguese but the French who made Vietnam as its colony in the middle of 19<sup>th</sup> century. To spread the business, the cooperation of the locals is essentially required. To bring the locals along with the French, the government took the advantage of the religion of Christianity. The love and generosity would win the heart of trivial locals. Keeping in mind the long term policy the French Government introduced western education in the country and encouraged to spread Christianity and simultaneously encouraged plantation in tobacco, indigo, tea and coffee to boost of economy. But by the turn of the century, the political situation had changed and the French had left the country in the 20<sup>th</sup> century after making a political division in between North and South and initiating the object of Vietnam War. However, Ho Chi Minh achieved Independence for Vietnam by Liberation Movement carrying for 35 years. Vietnam War began soon after the Geneva conference provisionally divided Vietnam into the Democratic Republic of Vietnam (North) and the Republic of Vietnam (South) in 1954. The War was in South Vietnam between the Government Forces aided by United States and the Guerrilla Forces aided by North Vietnam. It was escalated from a Vietnamese Civil war into a limited international conflict in which the United State was being deeply involved. The war did not end, despite the peace agreement of 1973, until North Vietnam's successful offensive had resulted in South Vietnam's collapse and unification of the South with the North in 1975.

**South Vietnam President Ngo Dinh Diem was against the nation wide election:** To end the colonial administration in Vietnam, French and Viet Minh agreed to a ceasefire in 1954. But in July 1955, after a through study of the ground situation, South Vietnam President Ngo Dinh Diem rejected the nation wide election agreed upon by French and North Vietnam at the Geneva Conference of 1954. Pro-Hanoi Vietcong began a guerrilla campaign against the President of South Vietnam initially but later under the name of Vietnam's People Army (VPA) under making an understanding with China and Russia. They had continued the guerrilla fight which was supported by China and Russia to overthrow Diem's Govt. The World WarII was ended but a under current war was going on in disguise between the two super powers. America was suspicious of the expansion of communism. To prevent communist expansion America supported South Vietnam's Diem Govt. Initially America supported the Army of Republic of South Vietnam (ARVN) by Air Force as America had superiority over air strike. The strategy was to finish the last force of guerrilla by air strike. Keeping this in mind in 1975, at one time, 150 Air-Fighter had been launched from US Seventh Fleet carriers, to bomb Vietnam to crush the guerrilla campaign. American Air strike, taking 150 Fighter in large number being launched from US Seventh Fleet carriers, bombed in discriminate to burn Vietnam and to finish the guerrillas to the last but the Americans had mistaken in calculation in the number. The number killed by bomb, the double the number remained in disguise. The heavy killing could not help to win the war and in the long run America retreated under humiliation.

**Ho Chi Minh:** In 1941, a communist and nationalist liberation movement had emerged under Ho Chi Minh in the name of **Viet Minh Force** to seek independence for Vietnam from French and to oppose Japanese occupation. The Japanese occupation had been collapsed after being dropping of Atom Bomb in 1945, when the lakhs of Japanese force had been killed and again thousands and thousands of Japanese force were fighting for survival of life. It was 2nd September 1945 Ho Chi Minh declared independence for Vietnam. People's Republic of China immediately recognized the Viet Minh's Democratic Republic of Vietnam and prepared the Chinese force to help and support the Viet Minh force. The former presidential palace of South Vietnam, is now Ho Chi Minh City of Vietnam, where the mighty America crumble down to little Vietnam's People Army (VPA).

## Hanoi, the New Capital of Vietnam (1976):

The dream of Ho Chi Minh was fulfilled. Vietnam should never have two capitals in North & South. Vietnam was one and it would survive with one capital. Hanoi was the Capital city of North Vietnam and the second largest city of Vietnam has now turned into the capital of Vietnam, the city is being suited on the right bank of Red River. The occupation of the City by Japan in 1940 and the occupation of the City by French in 1946 is now nothing but forgotten history. In July 2, 1976 the City became the Capital of North and South Vietnam and the City was rebuilt as such that it could function as the transportation hub of the country. The destruction of the City caused by Vietnam War was discarded and the City was newly constructed with the aid of China and Russia to make it a modern city of 21st century, befitting for Capital. After the devastation of war, the city had developed its two air ports, its rail connection to Kuming of China and to Beijing via China's Main Rail system and also linked to commercial port Haiphong and South Saigon (or Ho Chi Minh City) in the south. Since 1990, the economic growth of the city had been tremendously increased to sustain the annual average growth rate at about 20% till 2003. The economic growth had flourished the city to develop in different sectors such as in the creation of large-scale industrial park. The abundances of lakes and the inter-linking of lakes have changed the communication character of the city and hence it was also called the City of lakes. The lakes were designed in the beautification of the city with the growth of the economy. Today a devastated city has turned into a beautiful city of harbor, a pride of Vietnam.

**Virgin Mary going south:** Vietnam was under foreign rule for a considerable long time. There was conversion to Christianity and as such there was a lot of Christian was living in Vietnam. As soon as the change of government occurred, the people get afraid of and the people began to move to safer place. War subsided but killing and counter killing continued till the normalcy restored.

Diem Govt. executed Pro-Communist Forces in large numbers. Exodus of people from South to North and North to South took place. It was in the press "Fearing communist victory Virgin Mary is heading south". All Christian people migrated to South. Millions died in the street. The communist forces of China and Russia favoured VPA by supplying weapons to VPA along the Truong Son Road passed through Laos and Cambodia. By the time, there had occurred a change in the administration of the government of United States. After the death of Kennedy, Lyndon B. Johnson became the President of America. To sustain United States' credibility and reputation with its allies, US escalated the War to defeat the communist Force of North Vietnam. 3500 US Marines were dispatched to South Vietnam by March 1965 which was increased to 200,000 by December. Not only that an amphibious task group lands along the coast of South Vietnam, in July 20th, 1967 to defeat the North Vietnam Forces. United States has already entered in the battle ground and started to take active part in air strike, as well as in ground attack, or sea attack from the 7th Fleet. The strength of the Forces were increased and again increased after an interval and at a time the commando force raised to 500,000. The SEATO members supported the escalation by sending troops. The undeclared war continued with the loss of lives of Americans and SEATO members. The military plan to defeat North Vietnam faced with the tragedy of failure with heave loss of US force, despite the presence of a peak of 500,000 US troops in the country. The loss of American army life has brought unrest in the United States. Under public pressure in 1973 the US was compelled to halt all offensive operations in Vietnam and later in the year compelled to withdrawn all the combat-troops, ending the longest war in its history. The might of super power was defeated and might of humanity wined.

**Haiphong Port is one of the largest Ports in South East Asia:**
Haiphong Port is a large part of Red River Delta. It is connected to sea by a narrow access channel. It is one of the largest Ports in South East Asia. It was destroyed due to War but it had been reconstructed by Russian aid after the end of War.

**Saigon (Ho Chi Minh City) is the largest city of Vietnam:** Ho Chi Minh City, the new official name of Saigon since 1975, is by far the largest city in Vietnam. It accommodated 7 million people and it is the economic engine of the country. The city is known for its European style public squares.

**The mighty America crumble down to little Vietnam's People Army (VPA):** The mighty America was defeated to little force of Vietnam; the reason was more than one. Killing of Vietnamese army or common people by commando strike was inhuman, which was not morally supported by NATO force in spite of existing war agreement. However, the commando strike was a strike against the humanity that hurts every soul of human beings ordinary or army and in the war field the forces of major NATO countries of UK and Canada did not supported the US Force. There were voices of indignation in USA and condemnation abroad around all civilized countries. The protest against war was not only widespread in the US and but in everywhere. Under all humiliation America was compelled to recognize the sovereignty of Vietnam as recognized by Geneva agreement in 1954. The Parish Peace Accord was signed a fresh on January 27, 1973 culminating the war in humanity withdrawing all American combat Forces at home by March 29, 1973. But Ho Chi Minh continued the fight against the local guerillas till the fall of Saigon by April 30, 1975. North and South Vietnam were merged to form a Socialist Republic of Vietnam bringing the joy of unity under all bitterness.

# [58]

**My Journey to Dubai:**

Dubai is one of the seven Emirates of United Arab Emirate (UAE) and is located along the southern coast of the Persian Gulf Region. Dubai is known for its pearl exports until 1930. The geographical location of Dubai is as such that any traders and merchandise will get attracted easily seeing the ample opportunity of doing business. In order to save guard the region, Dubai made an agreement with the United Kingdom for its protection from external force in 1892 as it was a center of pearl exports until 1930. Dubai as well as Abu Dhabi both are in good location in the Persian gulf region and both have some common interest and that made them friendly hostile to each other. Boarder dispute arose in 1947 between the two gulf units which had been escalated into war. But ultimately arbitration of British led to cession of hostilities. The Dubai federal unit has extended its business in tourism, real estate and in the act of financial service to generate revenue which had attracted a largest population in the region increasing the density of population to a great extent. The real estate development projects have led to the construction of some of the tallest skyscrapers and largest projects in the world such as the Emirate's Towers, the Burj Dubai, the Palm Islands and the world's second tallest and most expensive hotel, the Burj Al Arab. The ten highest skyscrapers in serial can be named as (1) Burj Dubai, (2) Taipei 101, (3) Shanghais World Financial Center, Shanghai China, (4) Sears Towers, Chicago, Illinois, (5) Empire State Building, New York, (6) Chrysler Buildings New York, (7) Baiyoke Tower II, Bangkok, Thailand, (8) Transamerica Pyramid, San Francisco, (9) Moscow State

University, Moscow Russia, (10) Gherkin Building, London U. K. in the World.

In 1950, International air-port was established in Dubai and expanded to modernization later. In 1966, Dubai joined newly independent country Qatar to flourish business in the gulf region and set up a new monetary unit. In course of time, Dubai is emerged as one of global city because of its massive projects of real estate which has made it a business hub. Terminal 3 at Dubai International Air-Port, constructed in 1950, but the International air-port was expanded to modernization befitting to the demand of 21$^{st}$ century.

### The world events as well as business have increased the importance of Dubai:

In 1990 Persian Gulf War had a huge impact on the city. With the increase of economic growth of Dubai, the other Gulf units such as Kuwait, Bahrain move their business to Dubai. The city allowed refueling bases to allied forces during Persian Gulf War in 1990 and again in 2003 during invasion of Iraq. The subsequent world events have increased the importance of the place, the demand for army head quarter, business head quarter, company head quarter, and residential quarter increased which led to the expansion of real estate business in unimaginative scale. Dubai development clusters of new free zones, including Dubai internet city, Dubai Medic city, and Dubai Maritime city. The internet city is a part of TECOM (Dubai Technology). Dubai is also a city of pleasure. Dubai beach is a place to enjoy life's secret pleasure.

### Private real estate investment had started in Dubai after 2002:

Since 2002 the city had seen an increase in private real estate investment in recreating Dubai's skyline projects such as the projects of Palm islands, the world island, Burj Dubai and the Dynamic Tower. The robust economic growth in recent years have been accompanied by rising inflation rate as is 11. 2% in 2007 and simultaneously increasing the cost of living. The population is being increased to 14 lakhs in the area of 1287 Sq Km. The immigrants are mainly Asian 85%, out of which Indian 51%, Pakistanis 15%, Bangladeshis 10% and others 10%.

**Dubai waterfront is going to be the largest man-made offshore structure in the world.** Dubai's land reclamation projects the three Palm islands of Jumeria, Jebel Ali and Deira. Dubai waterfront will be the largest man-made offshore structure in the world, having villas, malls and holiday resorts in recent future. Dubai's Jebel Ali Port, constructed in 1970 has the largest man-made harbor in the world.

**Dubai adopted a uniform currency, UAE dirham for better financing.** Oil was discovered in 1966 in Dubai. The discovery of oil led Dubai to massive influx of foreign workers, mainly Indians and Pakistanis. Population density had increased by 300% in the period of 1968-1975. In the mean time, Dubai joined the Emirates to make a bigger business in oil in the united efforts and adopted a uniform currency, UAE dirham. The boarder dispute with Abu Dhabi that was continued even after the formation of UAE in 1971 came to an end in 1979 for the sake of unity in the search of better economy. There are innumerable achievements of Dubai is now visible which had made a world history in the field of development.

(i) **Dubai Marina, a residential district is the world's second largest man-made marina.**

(ii) **Sheik Zayed Road at Dobai.**

(iii) **The Deira Clock Tower is an important Land mark in the city.**

(iv) **The Burj Dubai, the tallest man made structure in the world—at Sheik Zayed Road.**

**(v) Burj al Arab Hotel, 305 meter tall luxury Hotel in Dubai, claimed to be the only seven stars hotel in the world.**

**(vi) Terminal 3 at Dubai International Air-Port is one of the busiest centers of the world.**

## Where is the Dubai City?

The answer is difficult to speak out. The whole of Dubai is a city. It is now one of the most or the best city of the world. There is no specific place called 'Dubai City'. Dubai beach is a place for wonderful beauty and pleasure. However, Deira in Dubai is known as the Business District and Bur Dubai is the main residential area. Jumeirah is a popular area closed to the beach and a bit expensive suburb. Dubai is a safe place. Here Dubai law is tough and there is no place for robbers. The people here are so kind and warm that appears their smiles are genuine. Unlike many Arabic countries, Dubai people have a different approach to their visitors. Dubai is creating something which is not available anywhere in the world. Burj al Arab Hotel, 305 meter tall luxury Hotel in Dubai, claimed to be the only seven stars hotel in the world. Dubai is one of the seven Emirates of United Arab Emirate (UAE). It is located along the southern coast of the Persian Gulf. The Dubai federal unit has the largest population. Dubai's Air-Port, is wonderful in all respect and probably the best in the world. Dubai is a new developing City, but the most modern city that is growing up in the world to the finest extent.

## Tallest Tower of Dubai: Burj Dubai:

The World's tallest Tower 'Burj Dubai' is opened to public on 4th January, 2010 amidst fireworks and dazzling lights in spite of acute financial crisis. The tallest tower stands at 2717 feet high and was inaugurated by Dubai Ruler Sheikh Mohammad who made a surprise by renaming the tower as 'Burj Khailfa' after the United Arab Emirates President Sheikh Khalifa. The Tallest Skyscraper, the Burj Dubai, of Dubai, the tallest man made structure of the world is constructed at the very popular site at the center of Sheik Zayed Road. The height of the tower had surpassed all the skyscrapers of the world including the 101-storey high Taipei Tower in Taiwan. The Gulf Emirates hopes the opening of tallest tower will lift up its global image and that will help in subduing Dubai's financial woes. The inaugural festivities were marked unveiling a plaque at the tower's base by the Dubai's hereditary Ruler that included traditional Gulf Arab dance performance and skydivers landing parachutes emblazoned with colors of the United Arab Emirates flag near the tower's base.

## The Unique Construction of Dubai-Tower:

## ['Burj Khailfa']

The construction of the Tower started in 2004 met an unprecedented engineering marvel involving 14,000 labourers mostly Indians and costing about $1. 5 billion. It is said that the tower will have 200 floors out of which 160 floors will be useable with 1,044 apartments and 49 floors of office space served by 57 high-speed lifts. While announcing the tower open, Sheikh Mohammad, the Dubai's Ruler said "Emirates has made a mark on the world and Dubai has built something for the world that is built by human beings," The inauguration got an international recognition as the US Secretary of State Hillary Clinton sent a special message to Sheikh Mohammad. The message read as "Your efforts to create international cooperation in our global economy are an important endeavour. I applaud your commitment to sustainable development".

## The Unique Character of the Dubai-Tower:

## [Burj Dubai]

It is unique in the sense that the Director of the project claim as he said "A plane won't be able to slice through the Burj like it did through the steel columns of the World Trade Center." It is unique for its observation deck on its 124th floor with 360-degree views of the entire city. The tower is designed to be the home of World's first Armani Hotel, luxury offices, and the place of residence, work and leisure for a community of net working class up to 12,000 people. It is marked by a swimming pool on the 76th floor and a mosque at 158th floor. So to say it is a vertical city of luxury apartments and offices. The question may arise "Do you really need to build a high tower in a desert region?" It can not be answered in positive from financial point of view but definitely it is being done for status, a landmark on the horizon.

The Empire State Building of NY, the World Trade Center's twin towers of NY (Tallest Skyscrapers of US) were listed at second and third place till the attack of 11th September. However, the new building 'Freedom Tower' is going to be constructed on the location of twin tower and will become the tallest building in the United States in near future. The history tell us the story that it was NY where the construction of tallest skyscraper was initiated in the early stage of 1930. The Empire State Building was the first building to be constructed with over 100 floors covering a height of 1,230 feet at the intersection of Fifth Avenue and West 34th Street in New York City. It was the tallest building in NY and was called one of the Seven Wonders of the Modern World by the American Society of Civil Engineers. It was also considered as the number one tallest building because of its design and architecture. But it lost its title of the tallest building after the construction of twin towers of the World Trade Center.

The City Chicago was not remained behind. The Sears Tower, at 233 South Wackier Drive has been the tallest building in the US since 1974 at 1,451 feet. It was one of the tallest building in the world with sixteen double Decker elevators. Once it was the vision of Sears & Roebuck Company in consideration of future growth to bring many of their Chicago employees into one location and hence commissioned the building. Now the Chicago Spire is scheduled to be built to a height of 2011 feet. The Sears Tower of Chicago is one of the tallest buildings in the world to be counted.

Just before '**Burj Khailfa',** 'Taipei 101, built in 2004, was the tallest building in the world with a height of 1,671 feet and the construction of world's fastest passenger elevator to the tallest building was in progress. A country feels to be proud of being subscribed to a tallest building. Taipei will lose its grandeur hence froth. It was once known as Taipei-101 Tower of Taiwan.

The Tallest Tower along with few of the floors was enlightened at the inaugural festival. Sheikh Mohammed, the Dubais Ruler has opened the Tallest Tower to public after performing the inaugural festivity. Sheik Zayed Road of Dubai was very much developed but after the construction of the world's tallest Tower, the road becomes a road of international importance.

Sheik Zayed Road at dusk is the beauty of the city, the activity of the lightening of the Tallest Tower, a vision for public during inauguration and at other occasion where the Tallest Tower of Dubai dazzle with light had made the road gorgeous and an unforgettable memory.